Also by Elizabeth Jolley

NOVELS
The Newspaper of Claremont Street
Mr. Scobie's Riddle
Miss Peabody's Inheritance
Foxybaby
Milk and Honey
The Well

STORIES
Five Acre Virgin and Other Stories
The Travelling Entertainer and Other Stories
Woman in a Lampshade

PALOMINO

PALOMINO

Elizabeth Jolley

A Stanley Moss Book

PERSEA BOOKS

New York

First published in Australia by Outback Press in 1980;
republished by University of Queensland Press in 1984.
First published in the United States by Persea Books in 1987.
Printed by BookCrafters, Chelsea, Michigan
First printing

For information, contact the publisher:
Persea Books
225 Lafayette Street
New York, New York 10012

Library of Congress Cataloging-in-Publication Data
Jolley, Elizabeth, 1923–
Palomino.
I. Title.
PR9619.3.J68P3   1987   823   87-2418
ISBN 0-89255-116-X

PALOMINO

AN UNWRITTEN LETTER

Dearest, It's midnight. It's Sunday, another Sunday is just coming. As usual I'm thinking of you. It's quite strange that the simple action of washing and drying your face, remembering it, can take up so many hours of thought. It isn't just the action of wiping the towel over your face, it's the feeling I allowed myself at that moment.

Remember I told you to wash the blood off your face? I was stern and cold when I told you to wash and then all at once an overwhelming tenderness blotted out all my stupid intentions.

It seems a long time since you went away. The house is still bald and empty as it was the night you left. My Dearest! I can only hope the best for you and I do hope so very much for that best.

Your Dove, I shall always think of her as yours, was safely delivered of a son so this time, d'you see, the farmer had some good fortune. What about you?

When you were here whatever I was doing was for you. Everything became part of a tender worship, the noise of the stream in flood rushing between the clay banks, the quiet green paddocks, the blossom and the fruit, all the harvest, when it came, even the constant changing of the season was yours.

Once you asked me if I treated all my patients as I treated you and I laughed at you as you lay there on the sheets looking up at me. When I examined you how could my hands and fingers avoid caressing you when every time we touched each other, gently and slowly, we always touched each other more.

1

Sometimes when I'm working down in the orchard I pretend you are up there in the house waiting for me, perhaps waiting for the little ceremony of unfastening the buckle of my belt. I used to look forward to coming in to you so much that I left things, now I go on working but, all the same, I can't help pretending.

I'm working at present just beyond the top paddock, you know, the little clearing for the olive trees. It's the time of the year for the cuckoo and the acacias will soon be in flower. Do you remember the fragrance of the acacias on the soft wind just when you came? Sometimes I think I hear the noise of an approaching car and I hope it is you coming back. And then I remember what we said and how we meant what we said and I know you will not be coming.

If it is a car it's only Murphy coming down the track to get water. He is camping up the back sleeping on the ground with his four girls; his pigs live in the old car. The welfare people have taken his baby and every day he drives into Queens Meadow to try to get the little boy back.

Dearest, it's not the immediate thing one misses but something from before . . .

PART 1

THE GENTLE LARK

I can't think of a name for these feelings or sensations, this reawakening of something not just in the
body but in the whole being, feelings which make me
wonder quietly and think I am alive after all. Perhaps
they are brought about by the gentle vibration and
throbbing of the engines. It is most noticeable at the
very top of the ship on the sun deck. It is pleasant to fall
into the pattern of life on board. I have just been lying on
a long chair lazily on the top deck and became so warm
and stimulated that I had to walk restlessly about the
ship hoping to catch a glimpse of a certain person with
whom I hope to make an acquaintance. That is an old-
fashioned phrase, but a true one. I suppose I am old-
fashioned and that's why I sit hidden behind the glossy
pages of the *British Medical Journal*, which I have now
no real right to read, watching her secretly as she lies at
the edge of the swimming pool trying to brown her thin
pale body. The skin of a sick person does not tan readily.

Between this person and the person I have become
since the very moment of sailing there exists an inde-

3

scribable delicate possibility of a friendship, something deeper than an ordinary friendship. It needs to be approached cautiously and with a tender gentleness. A clumsy movement on my part would result in the complete loss of what could be the most rewarding experience either of us could ever have.

It is clear we have the same feeling as if we are both on the edge of extreme happiness, with the knowledge of despair and unhappiness just beneath that same edge of happiness. It is as if tremulous expectancy is stretched between us; and the days have gone by, placidly punctuated by shy glances towards each other during chance meetings on the decks while walking for the pleasures of fresh air and exercise.

Though we have been so near each other, stepping aside for each other, even standing back at the heavy double doors to let one or the other pass through first, we have not exchanged a word. We have not really exchanged a look properly for our eyes never actually meet and neither of us can really know the questioning or answering there.

Though I am disturbed and restless over this young woman I am grateful to experience real feeling after so many years when all feeling seemed gone from me. There are certain events in my life which I have learned not to think about. Suppressing thoughts of painful events led to the suppression of all feeling. I was persuaded to make the voyage round the world by the fear of this lack of feeling. It was as though a part of me had died and, for most of the time, this partial death seemed still a part of my life, until I became aware that she was aware of me.

One symptom of this partial death, a physical symptom, there are others of a more subtle sort, is a cold patch on my back. Sometimes it is so cold I am obliged to wear a soft woollen shawl at all times of the day and nurse my shoulder with a hot water bottle at night even when the cabin is warm with the warm air of this part of the world. And another thing, my right hand when holding a glass, it doesn't matter what it contains, be-

4

comes icy cold and is unbearably painful and I have to put down the glass with the drink unfinished and hurry to the dining room for dinner where even on these warm evenings I have to choose soup simply to get my hand warm.

Hands must be warm for love especially my sort of love.

This time, coming down from the sundeck in the state I was in, heightened by the rich food and the unnaturalness of a life confined to a ship, I told myself that if I met her, I would speak to her. I would ask her a simple question. Something which would, with her reply, lead to a second question and then a third. I paced the decks full of the well-being of desire sustained, with the pleasure of desire having returned. At my age and with the kind of life I have been living lately, before I made my self-healing voyage, I am grateful for the return of feelings which I had thought gone from me for ever. Fortunately, and I say fortunately because in one sentence I could never have arrived at the meeting and conclusion I needed and so might have acted clumsily and lost her for ever. Fortunately she was nowhere on deck and not in either of the lounges and not in the library. We did not meet each other and I went to my cabin where, in the quietness, I gave myself up to wondering about her, what and who she was, what she liked, where had she been and where was she going and most of all what was she doing now. I thought she might be lying in her cabin resting and my thoughts about her became more gentle and tender and I said her name softly several times repeating it and, every time, loving her more.

On the far slopes of the valley which is my home there are horses. They are Palomino horses and they are lovely to watch. They do not belong to me but from my verandahs I can see them every day as they run together in their neat paddocks. They are the most golden of all creatures; they seem to move together with such grace and affection. It is their colouring, the honeyed colours of their shining coats and the creamy blonde

5

manes and tails. She is the same golden colour as these horses, or would be if she were well.

She is very pale, it is the pallor of illness, and her very fair hair has the lifeless quality which follows illness, perhaps malnutrition. Her hands are thin and white and her skin, especially round the mouth, is almost greenish at times. Her name is Miss Andrea Jackson and she sits at the next table. With her at the same table are two elderly vegetarian ladies, Viennese, who have taken possession of her at once. The tables are so close I am able to observe and overhear everything. I can't help looking at her. There is something about her which attracts me and I notice every detail about her, the way she clasps her thin fingers beneath her chin and how her quick eyes look from one old lady to the other as they tell her things. Her hair should be shining and honey coloured. Her light boyish step is a little too light. She walks nervously.

On the exposed part of her throat is the fragile glitter of a tiny jewel. I first saw this jewel at dusk as the ship was just leaving port. In the distance the decaying buildings and forgotten wharves were dun coloured in that cold mist which is the first and last caress as a ship approaches or leaves the coast of Britain.

Her throat was white in that half light. We stepped out at the same moment on to the deck leaving behind the airless cabins where there was always the smell of toast and scented groins. Both of us must have, at the same moment, wanted to anticipate the fresh breeze from the sea. She stood aside to let me pass and as she turned I saw the green stone sparkle and I saw the gold chain. I felt a kind of envy because possessing and wearing the jewel meant it had been given to her, someone cherished her in the giving, it was a kind of blessing she wore round her neck. Like a faint warm perfume it was with her all the time. I thought I had seen the jewel before, that I knew it but failed to remember, knowing of course that there are many such pendants.

I don't know why I did not speak then. Not only did we not speak, which in itself would have been natural, we

6

did not even exchange a glance. There was just a small pause and we went in opposite directions to pace about on the decks of this great ship which was to be, for the time being, our world.

By the next day we were quite accustomed to having water on all sides of us. The great ship with a knowledge not entirely her own made her way across the world of the sea. It was not possible to stand either at the back of the ship or at the front without admiring the strength of the structure, the massive construction and the complication of ropes and pulleys being transported and in themselves necessary for the transporting of the ship across these oceans. After a time it seemed always that the ship was steady in the great ring of blue water and did not rise to answer the sea. The monsoon had not broken the barrenness. Most of the passengers kept huddled out of the wind. They did not think of all this.

The young woman and I met and parted wordlessly, often, on the various decks and on the way to and from the dining room and at the entrances to the writing room and to the many lounges. And all the time the ship's rail moved above and below the horizon with that prolonged rise and fall which is at the same time the delight and the boredom of a long voyage.

Repeatedly we meet face to face though our eyes glance shyly away. The gold and green pendant compels me to take an interest. In spite of our withdrawn behaviour I am sure she is as much interested in me as I am in her though perhaps she is not aware of it as I am. We are drawn towards each other though neither of us acknowledges this by any action or word. Any feelings either of us has towards the other are deeply secret at present.

She comes late to breakfast. Later and later. I sit on at my table in the dining room watching the door through which she will come. It is pleasantly strange to feel the absence of one person, someone not even known to me, in this great number of people. With trembling hands I take another fresh roll and slowly breaking into its soft whiteness I slowly spread butter.

7

"Steward!" I call in my low shy voice. He comes.
"Madam?"
"I'll have more coffee please."
"Certainly madam."

And I sit longer and longer waiting for this fellow traveller who is so late every morning. I can't help wondering if she sleeps late because she sleeps badly. As I think about her sleeping I wonder what she looks like asleep; she is so lovely, walking about the ship. I know I am so much older and that it is partly her youth which attracts me. I admit everything painfully to myself, I have plenty of time for examining myself. It is the tiny jewel which attracts me too on the softness of her delicate yet strong throat. This jewel could make me speak, but every time I lower my eyes and turn and step away. In this way as in the times gone by I am stern. I am, as always, my own keeper.

Often during this long sea voyage I find myself thinking of home. Though the ship takes an even course, in my heart and mind, I am hurrying back home. I think about the empty house with its wide wooden verandahs. On three sides of the house the paddocks of tufted grass come right up to the verandahs, in front are the terraces of vines and fruit trees going down to a small pear orchard. Different pieces of furniture, bookshelves, flower-patterned dinner plates and the polished mellow corners of the rooms suddenly are very clear in my mind. And sometimes at unexpected moments during the day I actually hear my own clock in my study at home chiming in the cabin. More than once I have stretched out my hand to lift the corner of my bedroom curtain as if to peer out across the sunfilled paddock, but beyond the porthole is only the grey wide sea.

When I think of home I remember gratefully the large bare rooms and the quietness of the house where I live alone. I think of the comfortable iron and brass bed, it is painted dark red and the bars are decorated with little white flowers. Father bought the bed for a joke years ago and it was in the sitting room for months before he had it moved into his bedroom.

8

"My death bed" he called it, but in fact he died one night after dinner quietly still sitting in his chair. He died on my birthday, I was thirty-five. We ate our meal in silence, my father only commenting now and then on the good flavour of the roast meat and on the fresh vegetables. It was his habit to please Mrs. Platt. I sat opposite him as usual and towards the end of the meat course he said:

"It is your birthday today Laura, my gentle Laura, many happy returns of the day," and he raised his glass to me and finished his wine. I said:

"Thank you, Father."

After the meal we moved from the sombre room which was the dining room (later while I still lived in that house I never used the room) to sit together in Father's study. I sat there with Father and neither of us spoke any more. Father slept and died in his chair. Mrs. Platt had gone home when I discovered he was dead so I had to leave him in his chair till morning. Both of us, being doctors, were acquainted with death and the habit death has of being a long time coming. I was glad he died quickly.

I have the bed still, it is in every way suitable for the old house in the country where I live now. It has often crossed my mind that one day I might lie in it, ill, and die there. To this bed I am now hurrying, not to die of course, but more alive perhaps than I ever have been. Somehow the bed high and heaped up with soft white pillows in the seclusion of my house seems the place for me to take my new friend when she becomes my friend at last. That she will be my friend and will come with me to the comfortable bed to be loved tenderly and gratefully is without question. It is only a matter of being careful how I approach her, delicately, with her happiness in view, it is for me to give the invitation to come for I am the elder and so am in the strong position of being the one able to invite. And then after her surprise and happiness there will be mine.

The slow dying, which was my reason for the self-healing voyage, seemed to be worse while I was travelling on land. There was no music. On board a ship there is the music of the wind and waves and the voices of people and music for dancing is played every night but there is no real music, just as in Europe there was no real music; concerts and recitals of course, but not music to listen to alone where for example it is possible to give oneself up completely to the cello. I longed at times for the Beethoven Triple Concerto and for Brahms. I forgot that I had the Beethoven Quartets on records and now on this ship I remember them and try to recall phrases of the music, the reasoning and the pain in the quartets, the cradle songs and the dances, and I am unable to hear in my memory one cascade of music so that all the more I am wishing to be home quickly; or was wishing to be home quickly. I am not quite so impatient now as time is needed to achieve what has become my dearest wish.

Music is like mountains covered with snow and valleys of deep meadows sprinkled with spring flowers. If I can't be part of the land then I am tired quickly with just looking at it. It is the same with music, I tire quickly of sitting and watching people perform it.

I saw an elderly violinist. He played the Kreutzer Sonata and then something by Strauss. He played the more commonplace music best so that it seemed better music than it was.

For the Kreutzer Sonata the two players should have an emotional and spiritual closeness which is apparent in their playing. At one time in my life, before everything changed, I was studying carefully this possible closeness which human beings could explore and experience, something more than the perfect sexual relationship. The playing of the Kreutzer Sonata when I could not see the players made me aware of the depths of possibilities, but the elderly violinist and his pale pianist had no relationship of this kind, this was evident. The Kreutzer Sonata rattled on in a kind of frenzy of failure. A desperation which held all the disappointment of being sleepless and having to understand that sensation is not always enough, even when there is response, to bring about the desired relief and satisfaction.

It was clear they liked to play Strauss best; no relationship was needed. My colleague Dr. Esmé Gollanberg, now dead, would have known the deep significance of all this. They played the commonplace best. There is no one with whom I can discuss now; sometimes I write a little, but the knowledge that I can never publish again with any authority on a subject makes me half-hearted.

Snow-covered mountains patterned with magic light and blue shade rise round Salzburg and the trees are frosted with snow. Everything the tourist sees charms. There are little churches with gilded steeples sparkling in the morning sun, quiet rivers with grassy banks and men waiting in the water patiently to grab a fish. The little houses are crooked with attic roofs and pink and yellow colour-washed walls. Roadside shrines are everywhere carved and cherished with leaves and branches and the people seem so happy and friendly. When I travelled there I wondered if I would feel the loss of it afterwards and suddenly I was tired of it.

When I get back home I want to walk along the dry creek bed and touch the dry hard earth and break it with my fingers. I want to smell the hot earth and I want to walk between the trees and smell them too.

There is a bird I want to hear again. It is like a lark. While I was travelling the bus stopped at the edge of a cornfield and we listened to the larks' rising song. And once when I was a child walking with my father I found a lark's nest and later that day, when the mist cleared, I heard the lark's song. My bird sings in the heat. It is not my bird really, it sings somewhere above my place; it is like a lark, the song rising in hope and in love, not to hurt anyone. A gentle song from a gentle lark. I want to look at my fruit trees, go round them all to cherish them. It will be the time for cherishing. All life seems withdrawn in the intense heat of the summer. I long for the silence. It seems a long time since I left.

I want to see my horses, Lucy and Charger. They are

11

always stabled and looked after on the adjoining Palomino property. The country across there looks like Tolstoy country, that's how I see it. It seems so long since I crossed the paddocks on horseback to inspect the fences. I love to ride. I would love to have her to ride with me; a companion for riding would be superb if it could be her.

After a time I stopped looking at the world. Somewhere between the terraced vineyards on the banks of the Rhine and a winding road between palm trees and tiny grass, thatched huts on the way to a wide gentle bay, pink and blue in the sunrise in Ceylon, I stopped looking at the world and I am disappointed with myself for not looking.

I went to all the concerts and theatres even the marionette theatre for a performance of *The Magic Flute*, the puppets moving with such ease it was not difficult to forget they were manipulated with strings, and all round me people sighed with the tenderness and longing and love Mozart has in his music, and I sat like a block of wood. All my attempts to restore myself failed. I stared with terrible blankness in picture galleries and yawned through museums, passed close to fountains without seeing them and, standing before great churches I failed to take in their history and to absorb their mystery and significance.

At the theatres I sat on the edge of every human predicament and took no part; grief and suffering, mystery and laughter fell at my feet and I did not stoop to pick any of it up. Nothing alarmed or shocked or amused me, not even the productions where underclothes and nakedness seemed a part of the play. As a doctor I have seen all kinds of underclothes and am acquainted with the naked body in all positions and, as a gynaecologist, I have an even deeper acquaintance with the nakedness of women. In spite of my detachment and trained knowledge I was surprised at a sudden scene of pink naked innocent bodies, the shy dainty fashioning of the young man in particular was touching. The lovers were graceful and restrained and entirely unselfconscious on the stage. They were together in love and in tenderness and they were alone in their love for they were brother and sister realising their love and the joy and the hopelessness of their situation. In the audience we seemed to feel no shock only sympathy, from the loneliness of my expensive seat, seeing the young graceful bodies so close and I couldn't help thinking sadly that I was getting old. There was no hint while they loved so deeply of all that follows such a loving.

Again this evening I come face to face with the gold chain and and green jewel. I want to love her, I want to tell her that I love her and while I am feeling this I do not for a minute think what the consequences will be. Tonight I shall sit behind her at the film. It is *Death in Venice* from the story by Thomas Mann. It is an extremely suitable theme and I can continue the delicacy of the film, I have seen it before, and work on the impact it will have on someone like her. If only it was the evening now.

I am glad to be obsessed. All the time I was in Europe I handled all the famous places as if with forceps. And even on the ship I go through the daily conventional movements of the day's eating and washing and walking but now I feel I am once more alive. I am even catching snatches of conversation when before I never paid much attention even when people were speaking to me.

The two vegetarian ladies are called Irma and Hilde. They seem to be all over the ship all the time.

"Wait Irma! I have just to put on my shoes," I hear Hilde's shrill voice, sometimes they speak in German and sometimes in English. They have been lying down for a rest under rugs after lunch and now will walk on the deck for their health. Fortunately I have a cabin to myself, although at first this was not so. By some mistake I was in a cabin with three other women, one of whom even had all her things hanging in my cupboard. I thought I would be suffocated in there and went at once to the Purser to object and to get what I wanted. My cabin now is really very pleasant with two portholes

13

and a writing table and an armchair and I have an attentive steward. All the same I am impatient to be back home and especially if I can take her with me. This is my great wish and I have the idea to invite her and really show her the country, find out what she likes doing, indulge her in every way and deepen the friendship so much that it will not seem out of place to give her a handsome present when the times comes. She will find it impossible to resist anything, she will be so grateful and happy and will want my love; this is what I want. I want to love her and I want her to love me.

Yesterday Irma sent for the chef to commend him on his dried fruits. Irma's shoes are called Physical Culture, she tells everyone with delight. She wants everyone to have these shoes. She is concerned tremendously with the body. I suppose every ship has a passenger like Irma. Everyone calls her Irma. If you listen to her you can find out everything you need to know. I suppose every ship too has the passenger like me, the withdrawn quiet person hiding behind a *British Medical Journal*, reading articles which are so specialised I no longer understand them; they are intended for the research student, for the doctor in practice and for the specialist. They are not meant for someone like me. I subscribe still because it comforts me to have something to fetch regularly from the little post office at Queens Meadow, and I suppose I like to feel I am keeping in touch with a life which was once mine though it is all so much changed and, in any case, I no longer have any right there.

Irma speaks to everyone she meets. She is so interested, "The Suez Cenell was soch an interestink part of the voyage! I remember the little tradink boots wiz woven slippers, inled plates, brass trays ent coloured beads unt carved elephanten, all was so delightful! Now we do not pass srue zee Suez Cenell!" It seems Irma talks all the time. She is seventy-three and her skin is perfect and her blue eyes are clear. She is full of vitality. I wonder if she has ever suffered as I suffer. I think she has and has overcome it.

Experience is all stored up in me. I tell myself. Knowledge and training. I have written several worthwhile contributions on obstetrics and gynaecology. These were my subject, my life really, before the events which caused me to leave my work and my home and caused me to change my whole way of living. In the old days I studied the needs of women from ectopic gestation to the normal menstrual cycle and the gravid uterus. I knew everything about women, changes in their hair and their skin and the more subtle things too interested me deeply. Everything I wrote about was written clearly and intelligently. I loved my work and the thoughtful correspondence with my colleague Dr. Esmé Gollanberg; from her I learned a great deal, and from her was to come the great change in my life. My father and my uncle were surgeons, both professors of obstetrics. From them I learned too, but it was Dr. Gollanberg, even though she was thousands of miles away, who really gave me inspiration.

"Let the orgasm come quickly whichever way it will." She wrote this and I made it the text of one of my more important chapters. I believed it and the chapter is about the needs of women in love and women who are not in love and are not loved. All this interest and knowledge are quietly a part of me.

And now my interest is the experience of trying to understand the sky and knowing which clouds will bring rain. It is the harvest which concerns me now, my land and my trees and what can be produced from them. Because of what happened, years ago, I am no longer a doctor. From my orchard I am learning about the secret flesh of sweet fruit whitening beneath the glow of fragrant ripening and I know too the strange harsh voice of the heron as it flies alone searching for food.

"For ze body, for your body und for mine body!" Irma's voice is all over the ship. She talks easily with everyone. The emaciation of my green jewel has touched Irma's heart and at every meal time I can hear Irma, "Miss Jeckson you mosst hev a spoonful of honey in hot wasser before goink to bed," and, "Miss Jeckson take five deep

15

breathinks every mornink like so!" and Irma breathes "So healsy!" and Hilde breathes too. I hear them telling Miss Jackson what diet to follow, every meal time I am close to them and I hear their voices and listen to everything about her. I discover she has been ill in Ceylon where she was teaching.

Years ago I knew a Jake Jackson, a building contractor, and his wife Eva. Eva was at school with me. I knew Eva for years. I loved her. There must be lots of Jacksons. Eva is almost the same age as I am; we are old enough to be this Miss jewel Jackson's mother.

Again this evening Irma sends for dried fruits and the chef comes himself to bring them and to watch her arrange a pattern of prunes on the salad.

"So gut for ze bowls!" Irma says, "Good healse is beginnink in ze bowls as vell as hope und joy. Hope und joy sprink from within the body so the body must be soroughly cleanink inside und out."

I excuse myself quietly from the table and leave the dining room to walk in the fresh air.

Tonight is the last evening on the ship. I shall see *Death in Venice* again to carry out my plan.

After dinner this evening she seemed to be looking at me intently and she walked twice along the ship's rising rail in front of where I was sitting. As she passed she seemed to look at me, really to look as if inviting me to speak. I refused for my usual reason of discipline to lift my eyes to hers. As usual neither of us spoke. Tonight after the film I must speak or else it will be too late.

* * *

On this last evening I am sitting between Irma and Hilde in the dark. This is something which can happen on board ship especially on a long voyage. We are in the place where the films are shown. The ship shudders. As on the top deck one feels this shuddering more in here than anywhere else on the ship. Irma prevailed upon me to sit between her and her friend. "Dear Frau Doctor," (the *British Medical Journal* earns me this title) she

16

says, "Pliss you mosst sit wiz us for zee film. Hilde would like!" So I am here and Miss Jackson is just in front and a little to one side so that I can see the delicate shape of her neck and the way in which her head is bent forward very slightly.

Irma and Hilde are talking about her. "She makes the voyage to visit her peoples. Her brozzer especially she is fond of," Irma says. "Ziss brozzer is married unt his wife is havink first baby and Fraülein Jeckson is goink to stay wiz them and help wiz zee housekeepink."

"Ja!" Hilde says. "She look too thin to help anyone. She look like she needs big rest for a long time."

I can't help wondering what has been wrong with Miss Jackson; gradually I piece information together about her. I wonder why they talk of her across me as if they want to tell me indirectly about her; but they talk all the time across all kinds of people about all kinds of things. They are bored with *Death in Venice*. The yearning of the older man to feel seems to mean nothing to them, nor does the slow return of feeling over youth and the pattern of movement and colour and the music of Mahler, though both exclaim with real pleasure every now and then.

"Vot a beautiful hett Irma!"

"Ach Ja! Und such dresses!"

I wonder why I sit between two bored and restless women to watch this film which moves me so strongly. When Irma and Hilde start to discuss their nutmeat and boiled onions I whisper an excuse and slide out of my seat and quietly sit alone at the back and think about the conversation at the end of the film which will be the beginning of the new life for me.

* * *

And now on the last morning of the voyage we are already in Gage Roads since half past five and the untidy flat country both beckons and repels from the other side of the wharves and sheds and the familiar buildings of the customs and the railway station. We are side by side at the rail. We have spent the voyage in an isolation of our own, we chose not to join in the life of forced fun at parties, we refused the tavern society and the fancy-dress balls and we did not join in the long drawn out quiet exchanging of family history from one reclining chair to the next. We are side by side at the ship's rail watching the wharf and we could speak now and, though the small space between us seems to vibrate with longing, neither of us says one word to the other.

I have two houses and I have land; for me it is a homecoming. My voyage for the healing of my spirit is over. "My house in town," I could explain, "is let on a long term lease to some very good people, they pay their rent and look after the place which used to be my home when my Father was alive and later while I was still a doctor. I live in the country now and I live alone." I could say all this, I could explain to her. "Here is my address." I have the advantage of being a lot older than she is. I could invite her to come with me. But I do not speak the necessary phrases, they seem self-conscious and formal, and I don't say anything.

We are dressed like strangers in clothes ready for the other world away from the ship. The green jewel shines on her throat. Though we are both looking across to a familiar coast and it is for both of us a homecoming I feel an excitement as if the landing is to be the beginning of something I don't know anything about yet. She is quite still at the rail looking across, I suppose she is going either to her mother or her brother. Irma and Hilde were talking about her at breakfast. Do they do this, I wonder, for my benefit? Can they have guessed? Is the privacy of my love and my longing invaded by these two elderly health-infested women? Perhaps they know this love. But of course not! All the same I have to consider that they too might love and think about this loving.

I tremble as I stand at the rail. I tremble with a wish to speak to her, the jewel. She is smiling and leaning over the rail. She is even more handsome when she leans and smiles. There is someone out there on the

18

crowded wharf for her. I would like to be the one out there for her.

Supposing I ask her now to come with me, just for a short time, a week or ten days just to rest and to see the country before she buries herself in the kitchens of small suburban life, that sterile existence of supermarkets and Sunday walks passing other people's meaningless gardens. She could come with me before going to help her sister-in-law. I want to ask her but am afraid she will refuse or not be able to come. I don't think I could bear a refusal from her, better not to ask her at all.

All the years I am my own wardress. Years ago with Eva the experience was too painful and then later there was the unforgettable disaster of Esmé Gollanberg; these things have left a warning for me. There are sinister qualities about the memories and the knowledge I have and there are the reasons why I am no longer the doctor and the competent gynaecologist I was once. I live hidden away in the secret folds of a narrow valley where the land is mine and no-one else can come there without my asking them to come. In the country I have become used to a solitude which is at the same time voluptuous and frugal and has about it a severe orderliness so that these two qualities alternate with a kind of regularity.

There is a silence in my life in the country which wraps round and somehow calms and comforts. It is as if I am taken up into something which consoles even if it is indifferent. I think of Wordsworth's Margaret in the deserted cottage, and at the end of what is really a very bleak and sad story he looks at the ruined cottage and says that it has often given him "so still an image of tranquillity" and a sense that "consolation springs from sources deeper far than deepest suffering". This is how I feel about the place I am going home to though I am very glad it is neither ruined nor deserted. I would like to take Miss Jackson there. When I go through the gate and am actually on the land I feel no harm can ever come to me; this is what I want to share with her. I want to teach her, to show her everything, I want to be with

19

her and stare with her at the trees which change with every change of the sky and the sun. The trees change too with the seasons. Most people do not know this and think that eucalypts are the same all the year round. When I have taught her eyes to see and herself to feel she will know this is not so. The sap rises and retreats. It is like the scenery in the Bible and the Song of Solomon. There are two winters. The winter of the damp and cold and the winter of the stillness. It will be the winter of the stillness now, of the great heat when all life seems withdrawn. In between the winters are two springs but no autumn. Miss Jackson is tense but she is sensitive. I can imagine her trembling. Living and working in Ceylon she has developed ways of sitting and standing and of holding her head and her hands. She conducts all her movements in the ways of the people she has been with. She has taken the best from those people and their country and made this best part of herself. How I long to have real conversation with her, all to myself. I have had the chance, I still have it but do not take it. I restrain myself with the habitual restraint of years. This restraint has become a power against which I am powerless.

This parting at the ship's rail when there has been no real meeting makes me even more excited. There is still time.

* * *

We are driving the long way, by the back roads. "Take the back roads," I said to Murphy. Murphy is my hired man, the tenant or whatever one calls him, on my property. It is a curious arrangement. He lives there, I provide a house and he pays rent and I pay him a wage and supply him with meat. It is Murphy's way however not to pay the rent. He paid once, the first time, and then Mrs. Murphy borrowed it back from me. As well as meat I often supply them with milk and bread and potatoes.

Murphy came with my car to meet the ship. I wrote and asked him to. I have not told anyone that I am coming home a month earlier than arranged. Rodney Glass and his wife and the Forts, one-time colleagues of mine, would have been at the ship, but on purpose I let them think my arrival was later.

Murphy is not pleased to drive the long way as he has been driving most of the night, and because of the delay which accompanies the docking of a great ship, he had to wait some hours for me. I expect he feels it is selfish of me to want to be on these bad roads where there is only a thin strip of bitumen down the middle of the rough red gravel. Some of these roads are really only tracks. Murphy says nothing however as he knows that if he complains I will drive and he hates to be driven by a woman especially through the townships of Mount Margaret and Roseville.

When I see Murphy after all this time of not seeing him I suddenly remember the disadvantages of my tenants. My car hasn't been cleaned and it smells of urine as though his children have been sleeping in it. I suppose he has neglected everything while I have been away, hopelessly, for that is the kind of man he is. When I bought the place it seems I bought the tenants too. It seems impossible to get rid of the Murphys. They live in a flat asbestos house just across the paddock from my own house; a wire fence separates us and encloses a small grassed area which is their yard. For most of the year, and it will be at present, this patch is all dust, the grass being trampled to death by Murphy's children and two insane dogs which tear up and down inside the wires all the time when they aren't eating or asleep. Several times I have tried to turn the Murphys out. The crazy barking of the dogs has been enough reason besides all the other troubles with such tenants. But even when legally possible there were always personal reasons; sometimes Mrs. Murphy declared herself sick and pregnant and even gave birth to a wizened baby on more than one occasion when I confronted them with the idea that they must leave. Murphy himself either has a back or a leg or both, and is never able to do his share on my land, let alone keep his job at the foundry. If there have been times when he has had his health then he has lacked transport. Something always went wrong with his car and, in the end, it gave up altogether right in the middle of the serene view from my window and I had to pay to have it removed. For a time, before I went away, I drove him the five miles to where the foundry, like an open wound, black and suppurating, fills the valley with ugly granulations. I could feel the Murphys despising me for my kindness and, after he was sacked from the foundry, I left them alone for a time. But I was forced to take pity on them as the children appeared at my kitchen door every morning, really hungry, begging for food and firewood. And I felt them despise me even more, the older Murphys, when I gave them groceries and a sheep and cut wood for them myself. They despised me for being soft.

"Mam she's putting more wood 'side the gate!" I heard the horrified childish voice shrill into the dusk. "Mam look ya, more wood! She's puttin' more wood!" Indignant, as though I was trespassing in order to keep them warm. Scornful, as though I was a fool when there was wood lying around in the bush beyond the paddocks and there were four Murphy children big enough to go and collect it. Laughing at me for being so easily taken in. "Soft heart never gets anyone anywhere." The Murphys go cold rather than burden themselves getting wood.

Mrs. Murphy is scrawny like a sick hen. She did her utmost when I first bought the property to take away all my pleasure in it, as if she guessed how much I needed it to please and comfort me, as if she really knew why I had given up everything to live there. On the first day she came over to the wire fence and, draping herself over it, she hailed me in a dreary persistent voice. When I did nothing more than just nod in her direction she came slithering snakelike through the rusty wires.

"Don't let little old me hold you up." She edged in at the kitchen door. She looked me up and down, curiosity coming in spikes from her cold little eyes. Her gaze greedily taking stock of my boxes and cartons.

"You bought the place?" She did not wait for a reply.

"There's not much here 'cept trouble," she said. "Terrible hot in the summer. Your kitchen's like mine," she put us together; an unwanted equality, "faces the wrong way. Terrible cold in winter real frost up here you know. Clouds come up," she continued "but no rain never falls when you want it. Your creek's salt so is your soil. And, if you sink a bore that's salt too even if you go down a hundred and sixty feet it's salt all the way. Your soil's clay down there on the flats and up the slope nothing'll grow — it's all eroded, washed away, only them dead trees up there and granite outcrops. In any case if you plant you goin' to plant anything? — if you do plant the bandicoots and crows will take what the rabbits don't have an' then there's the whirligigs. Mr. Murphy tried cabbages oncet but the whirligigs ruined the lot." She drew dreath with her mouth in a line.

At the time I felt I ought to be friendly. "Thank you," I said to her, "I'm just unloading the car, if you don't mind . . ."

"Aw don't you mind me!" she took up the space between the table and the cupboard so I was caught between the stove and the sink. "Aw jus' you get on!" But of course I couldn't get on, I wished she would go away. She stayed. I should have been firm. She eyed the provisions on the table.

"That reminds me," (sitting beside Murphy in the car brings it all back to me), "that reminds me," she said, her eye resting on the butter. I don't forget how she looked at the butter, especially now that I know how much she wanted some.

"I'm right out o' butter. That's the worst of the country if you're out of somepin then you're right out for longer than you like to be."

Of course I gave her a packet of butter.

"Aw! I see you've quite a store there, half a pound won't go far with my lot," she put her thin fingers into the box and it reminded me of a rat the way she scrabbled at another packet. She was triumphant with her second half pound. "Of course," she never stopped talking, "there was a snake around last year. Mr. Murphy

23

was agoin' to shoot it but it got away over this way." And all the time she was talking I could see her looking, peering about trying to see as many of my possessions, which were already in the rooms and visible through half open doors, as possible. "I dessay it's still here," she said.

That first visit from Mrs. Murphy was too long. She stayed for over an hour and she left clutching butter and sugar and tea to her thin chest. It was quite hard for her to scramble through the fence, she had so much to carry. As she scurried into her own place I was left with a disagreeable picture taking the place of something idyllic and delightful, something I had been looking forward to. I looked forward to this place with the kind of shy pleasure lonely people experience quietly when they are about to achieve something they have wished for. I looked forward to living in this serene valley. I imagined beforehand what it would be like to walk and work on the warm slopes. I knew the sun would come first down from the top in the early morning and then, as the light faded from the northern hills, the last caressing rays would come across from the west and redden the white trunks of the wandoo trees as deeper shades of the approaching evening raced each other through the surrounding bush which was first to be dark. After seeing the place a few times I wanted to be there all day and every day to know all the hours of the sun and to see the changing light and shade with the passing of the sun. The paddocks on the other side of the valley are hay fields and fenced off areas where the cream-coloured horses run. It reminds me, when I look across there, of the Russian countryside and I wanted to look across there to this Tolstoy country, but Mrs. Murphy took away all that I was looking forward to. My first night there I went to bed uneasily and slept hardly at all and then overslept so that I did not wake up early to the spider-webbed morning in time to see the sun fraying the mist into ribbons and I missed the harsh cry of the heron as it flew alone searching the stagnant pools of the creek bed.

While Murphy drives he smokes stale cigarettes. I feel better now that we are out of town. I thought a short time ago I would have to leave the car; I suddenly suffered a terrible attack of claustrophobia. Murphy chose the road through the markets and by the railway station and at this time of the morning the road is thronged in both directions. People with the blankness of washed-away sleep in their faces crowded the footpaths waiting and watching in bunches to cross the road or to catch buses. Shopkeepers were opening the mean shops along the street. Fruit and vegetable trucks, leaving the markets, tried to edge into the solid line of traffic. It was then that I had this fit of wanting to escape from the car. I tried to open the door but something was wrong with the catch. When I looked at Murphy he was sitting with his eyes half closed in a cloud of foul smoke. I tried the door again and my fingers became claws which ran over the glass. It seemed as if all the people in the cars and on the street had ugly or diseased faces or the heads of nightmare animals. I wanted to scream and bang on the car door, to beg Murphy to let me out.

The solid street is long. I knew its length and I knew I must sit there till we came to the end. I tried to look at the verandah boards and at the posts. I read the names of the shops and as we went by the station I read the names of the trains "Australind", "The Prospector", "Albany Progress" to try to get over this attack.

"I am home," I keep telling myself in the car during this long ride. I stepped back into my dream of the green jewel before we were through the heavy traffic.

The parting at the ship's rail was abrupt. We were separated suddenly by the crowds and the complication of getting ashore.

There is something unfulfilled about the way she walks. Perhaps it is a style of walking copied from the people in Ceylon. While I was waiting for my luggage, after disembarkation, I saw her again. I thought I had seen her for the last time at the ship's rail and now seeing her again it was like a renewal of acquaintance after a time which seemed like years, except that it was only about thirty minutes and of course we were not acquainted. She was in the crowd and as the people parted I saw her hasten towards her brother. There was no doubt about her brother, he had the same eyes; these eyes have a deep golden light in them and a direct steady look. I have never seen eyes which are so brightly lit up from within. I think her eyes have seen a great deal. I can't help wishing now that I had allowed myself to find out all that she had seen and known.

Why am I sitting here in the car all alone with Murphy! I could so easily have had it otherwise. She is now somewhere beyond my reach, I do not even know where she is. She might even be unhappy with her unknown sister-in-law, I do feel this might be so after what I saw. I watched the brother and sister meet, I knew nothing about them, but I feel now I know everything there is to know. They met, in the crowd, as if a very deep and close relationship drew and held them together. The brother and the sister, the man and the woman, they clasped each other closely in a long embrace as if shutting out longing and loneliness forever and they walked off together as if they were not only made of the same flesh and blood but as if made and shaped for each other.

It was at that moment I realised that all the time I had intended to speak, every day I had had the chance, but kept putting it off with the secret delicious knowledge that I could speak, could and would introduce myself and step off into friendship which would go deeper into discovery every time we were together. This putting off is part of my nature.

When I was at boarding school often, at night, I had times of make believe when on the borders of sleep I was at the opening of a tent in a quiet clearing in a deep forest and I put out my hand to open the folds in almost a caressing way, slowly, holding back from the moment of going in to my beloved. This pausing on the threshold of happiness became my way. This secret of putting off the delight of getting to know this woman had carried me from one day to the next and now quite suddenly the chance had gone. And I am left without the secret.

The place where they met soon filled with other people. A group of Italian migrants talking fast, their delight in each other was so great that they looked greedy and coarse and selfish and I wondered why people were so often completely under the spell of Italians and the glamour of their culture as if they possessed some magic qualities.

So much did these people fill her space I began to hate them and began remembering Italian patients: women who behaved crudely in childbirth and relatives who screamed and shouted through hospital doors, greedy people who collected lotions and tablets and dozens of prescriptions and who trampled over an exhausted doctor in an emergency.

This emptiness which lies before me now on the long repetitive stretches of the road gathered about me then as I stood there in the middle of my luggage waiting till I should see Murphy.

I am returning home to my valley. I am returning too to the Murphys. Sometimes I wish for Dora; it would be comforting to come home to Dora. Now there is no Dora to come out to meet me, at all hours, pulling her thin blouse across her round breasts.

After Mrs. Platt died Dora, Mrs. Platt's niece, came to cook and clean for me, that was in the other house, but instead of leaving every night as Mrs. Platt did she stayed as she had no home.

"Sweet Dora" was my name for her. I never said it to her face. She was so good natured, red cheeked always like a child; she still was a child in so many ways. She slept the deep sleep children sleep, and when she roused herself in the night as my car came down the drive, often I was out operating or delivering a baby, she seemed completely refreshed by her sleep as children are. She was always ready to look after me whatever time it was, day or night. She would come, her plump arms folded round her breasts, to lean on the car door to ask, "How was everything?" and "Will I make your coffee or your bath first?" and so on till I was quite

27

soothed and cared for and rested. I could never have endured the loneliness after the ridiculous and horrible affair which ended the friendship I had with Eva if Dora had not come soon after. She seemed to fill that empty dark house with cheerfulness and safety and I missed her intolerably when she left to be married. Missing her I worked harder than ever and began the research into the Gollanberg theories of response. I corresponded with Esmé Gollanberg with an intensity which matches everything I do.

Now there is no Dora and I live alone with only the Murphys across the paddock. Mrs. Murphy is supposed to clean my house but I am relieved that this part of the agreement fell into forgetfulness.

Of course I do not need Dora, I know this. I have no night calls, no long hours operating and no patients sitting and waiting for me outside my consulting room. I am not writing on surgical technique and I don't spend hours studying and writing letters and reports about patients. When I write now it is for myself, and if I spend time on that it is my own time. I don't need Dora. I am glad Dora is married happily to that bullet-shaped little monkey of a man and keeping house for him in Port Hedland. Sometimes letters in long sloping handwriting come to me, "Dear Doctor", from her. She tells me about her children and her curtains and her furniture and what she is knitting and I can't help longing over her. It was something more than the comfort of being greeted by her whenever I came home and the cheerful order in which my house was kept while she was the keeper of it. In her own way I suppose Dora was cherishing me. It is nice to be cherished. It is rare to be loved. I suppose what I felt from Dora was love, and perhaps she felt my need without understanding it, and perhaps might not have been safe. Once I was looking for the key to an outhouse and thinking Dora was out I opened the door of her room, perhaps the key was on the shelf there where she kept other important things. She was not there but, because of the weather being wet, she had hung all her foolish and ragged little bits of under-

28

clothing all round the room, some of these, though cheap and pretty, had the sophistication of keeping up with the women's magazines and others were washed out and so childish that I was moved by the sight of them and wanted at once to take her in my arms and really love her and buy her some lovely things. That night I prowled about restlessly, a monster really, thinking of her and appalled at what I was. I went to bed about four in the morning and wept because of what I was. I'll never forget the gratitude I felt when she brought in the coffee for my breakfast, her face was still rosy from the good sleep she had had and a bit of a line was still on one cheek where she must have been lying on a crease in the pillow. The gratitude was for her rosy face and her happy smile; if I had gone in to her in the night her eyes would never have met mine in the morning, and, sleepless, she would have been pale and haggard, she might even have wept and hated me. I was grateful things were not changed. I was forced to understand my loneliness more.

When we leave the crowded streets of the town Murphy is able to drive faster and on both sides are the familiar squat concrete warehouses and small houses with neat gardens and a bit further on the market gardens which are green and filled with rows of beans and tomatoes; peaceful, in spite of the noise from the main road and the smoke and smell of industry, and in spite of the harsh climate.

From the window of the Paris Express when I was looking out sleepily across the flat sodden fields I saw a woman with a small rotary hoe trying to plough, a bit too early, I thought, changing the seasons, but ploughing all the same. And in the quick glimpse I wished I was doing the same thing. But at that time I had quite a lot more of my tour to get through. The woman alone under the grey sky on the outskirts of the small town on the way to Paris is quite unknown to me as is the market gardener here who has chalked a notice by the roadside "melons cheap". Big pale green melons are piled in bulging triangles on the withered grass. All over the world there are unknown people working at the soil to grow food. Perhaps it comforts me in some way to belong, by what I am doing, to these people now.

A kind of comfort comes now too as we go further on and reach the place where the road turns and goes through the vineyards. There are grapes heaped on trestle tables set back under enormous fig trees. The early morning sun drops a golden dust through the leaves and branches. The sun enhances the tranquillity, the place is still the same as it has always been. Time seems to make little difference, only the seasons change but they return in their turn.

In the cool intimate shadows of the vines there are white and blue bunches of grapes hanging in secret modesty — my own vines will not be like these. I am afraid for them and anxious to be home. The claustrophobia is gone and I rest here at last beside Murphy.

Again we turn to the east, the sun is blinding. The sun touches the folds of jarrah forest and lights up the tops of the trees and patches of the scrub under the trees and between the trees. The forest is on both sides of us sparse and thick at the same time. The great marri trees left standing in places along the edge of the road are covered in balls of creamy white flowers.

"Oh! the red gums!" I can't help exclaiming aloud. It really is as if the country is alight with these big old trees. In all the years I have known the country I can't remember such a flowering.

"Means an early cold wet winter so they say," Murphy, who has not uttered a word all the way, suddenly speaks.

"Oh! does it," I am thinking of Miss Jackson. "Stop the car please," I ask Murphy. "Just along there under that superb group of trees." Obediently Murphy slows and pulls off on to the red gravel and I wait while he fiddles with the broken door catch.

When I step on the ground I feel lifted up in the light air and I hear the silence and the noise of the country and smell the warmth in the gentle wind. It is quite personal this little wind. The marri trees are full of bees, their noise is like an organ playing in the branches. Flowers fall from the trees into the flowerless bushes of the scrub making them look as if flowers are growing there.

"Honey trees," Murphy says. "There's a heat in that sun even though it is not properly up yet," he grumbles.

I have forgotten this warm dry air, I have forgotten this fragrance of the eucalyptus and dust. I would like to sit here on the warm earth and enjoy the quietness. I do so wish I had spoken to her, the green jewel, I wish I knew her real self, I wish she could be here with me. I could show her the marri tree flowers, tell her to listen to the bees, tell her to sit on the warm earth to touch the earth and breathe in the fragrance. So many things there are to tell a friend if there is a friend. I wish I had spoken to her, now I know I have such a lot to tell her.

"Come on!" I say with irritation to Murphy. "We better go on."

In my kitchen I have opened a tin of camembert. After the cheese in France it seems tasteless. For some reason when we arrived Murphy had to drive the car round the long track to his own door.

"So you're back," Mrs. Murphy appeared at once, dishevelled as always, her shabby clothes washed beyond all hope of endurance. In one hand she had a chipped beaker.

"Cawfee?" she asked her husband.

"What about the Doctor? You'd like a cawfee? eh?" Murphy followed his words with a terrible yawn and disappeared into his dreary little house. Several children, girls, fell out of the door as soon as he was inside. They gathered round to stare.

"Yers I'll fetch youse a cup," Mrs. Murphy said but to my relief, she forgot this indiscretion into hospitality immediately. Mrs. Murphy is thinner than she was before I went away, she has even more little spikes of curiosity coming from her steel-coloured eyes.

While she spoke to me she leaned on the door post.

"Just our luck!" she turned up her eyes so that only the whites showed. "They was all sent home from

31

school, school sores and impetigo, school nurse sent 'em home. Terrible havin' them under me feet all day and Willie's got 'em too." She seized a kitchen fork from Willie's ruthless hand and, setting down her cup on the window sill, she attempted to untangle the child's knotted hair with the fork. I tried to ask Mrs. Murphy how she was and a few things about the farm but Willie's voice was so raised in howls I had to give up.

As a doctor I was accustomed to a position of authority but in Mrs. Murphy's presence everything I once possessed, authority, dignity, integrity, personality, everything fades; everything I have is destroyed. This destruction starts immediately I am with her and I have to give up trying to be myself or even to say anything with sincerity.

Mrs. Murphy shook her little boy, slapped him and set him down hard on the dust where the grass should have been.

"Come orf er that dirt," she shouted at him. "It's a filthy place, the country. Just look at him!" The child crawled back into the house which from the outside gives the impression of being dark and empty and very uncomfortable. Through the door, which is always stuck partly open, the ripped, burst upholstery of an old couch is visible; it seems the ultimate in feckless poverty. The dirty flock stuffing is always on the floor and the doorstep and seems like the symptoms of a disease which refuses to be hidden.

I had forgotten so many things. Now I remembered them all because in all the time I have been away nothing has changed. It is as though Mrs. Murphy has been leaning on her door post in all weathers, night and day, all the months I have been away.

"Now how'd youse like Murphy to drive the car for you whiles youse gets used to bein' back 'ome," Mrs. Murphy offered. "We've to go to Queens Meadows this arvo on account of the children gettin' to the clinic for their treatment." I could see there was no question as to who would have the car. I did not even try to say I wanted my car myself.

"Well you better have yor bags, eh?" Mrs. Murphy put her small head into the doorway.

"Patrick!" she screeched. "Pat! the doctor wants her bags you great gormless oaf what did ya bring her bags round here for?" After a time Murphy appeared, and going to the car, reluctantly took out my cases. They are so expensive and new these cases, they looked entirely out of place there.

"Take too long to drive back along the track," Mrs. Murphy explained as if I didn't know quite well how long the track is and how it curves round. I know the tracks on my own property but did not try to say so.

"I think I'd like my car," I tried to tell Murphy.

"Aw! Youse take a rest today!" Mrs. Murphy pushed me to the wire fence, the dogs began their frantic barking, the fence was theirs. Mrs. Murphy held up the slack wire for me to squeeze through. Murphy, groaning aloud, put the cases over the fence one after the other and staggered back into the house.

"Ain't youse goin' to carry them acrorst?" Mrs. Murphy screamed at his back. "Don't you go layin' down!" she bawled. "I tell 'im," she said to me, "if he lay down on the ground the white ants would make straight for his 'ead," she tapped her own. "Wooden head! The ants 'll get him," she said "straight up the leg of his bed and into his head. He's laying down too much. He's got a shoulder as well as a knee. Whatever next! He'll think up sumpin. And Lily's done her block and flounced off! What a family! Nowhere much to flounce to 'cept the back of the barn, and I'll tell you this if Murphy don't sleep at night, no-one else can."

Murphy reappeared and crossed the yard and shut himself in the lavatory.

"Well that's that!" Mrs. Murphy said. "Shan't see him till dinner time."

This is how Mrs. Murphy stops me from seeing and feeling things. She stopped me from looking at my valley, she stopped me from breathing the air of it, all I felt was the burden of the neglect the Murphys were guilty of. More than anything, at that moment I wanted to be alone, back in my house, to enjoy my return to my place.

"I'll halp you acrorst," Mrs. Murphy began to pour her thin body through the wires. The sun was hot. I was still dressed as I had been for the early morning disembarkation. I was too hot and wanted to take off the woollen suit and the Italian leather boots, have a bath and change all my clothes quickly.

"Thanks but I'll manage," I said. "Thanks all the same." I was afraid if Mrs. Murphy came over I would never be rid of her.

A great roar came from the Murphy house.

"Mom!"

"Aw!" Mrs. Murphy was sorry. "I'm sorry I'll have to go, they're yellin'. Always wantin' somepin." She tried to squeeze back through the fence.

"Take a holt of the wires will ya?" she said and then it was as if her thin body gave way and she slipped between the wires tearing the worn out material of her frock and tearing the worn out paper skin of her shin and thigh, wrist and elbow.

"Aw my Gawd! Give us a hand will ya!" she was gasping. I watched horrified to see how unexpectedly and easily the human body is damaged. At times the body can take such twistings and poundings and suffer no ill effect and now from this tiny fall in the wire fence was all this blood.

The children raised a cry and rushed back into the house. With difficulty I disentangled Mrs. Murphy and helped her up. One of the dogs at once flew at me and leapt at me barking and then without barking and with open jaws it jumped at me and bit my clothes, holding on, growling deep in the throat through teeth clenched on my skirt and only the whites of the eyes showing.

"It's becos you've got yer hands on me," Mrs. Murphy said proudly. "That dog'll go for anyone 'as has a hand on me!" It did not seem to concern her that I only had my hands on her in order to lift her up.

"I'll have to get inside. Silly old me!" Mrs. Murphy held on to me and began to make for the door. Murphy came out from the lavatory; he kicked the dog off my skirt.

"Git!"

"There's some flavine and wool in the wash house cupboard," Mrs. Murphy said. I helped her to a chair in the dirty kitchen. The children gathered round the far side of the table as if waiting for a puppet show.

I couldn't see the flavine or the wool as there were so many things in the cupboard. I imagined they would think I was peering at their possessions and I felt uncomfortable. Even though they were poor things they were private. Vaseline in a battered tin is very personal.

The cotton wool was the coarse sort and when I tried to dab the flavine on the thin white bleeding legs the wool did not absorb. Everything I did was ineffectual. Mrs. Murphy sat and screamed orders at her girls.

"Lily there's some rag down by the bed," the eldest girl hurried off, in some importance, and came back with a piece of old, soft, washed-out sheet.

"Tear a bit offer here," Mrs. Murphy offered the grey stuff.

"Silly Bitch!" Murphy grumbled in the doorway either at his wife for falling or because she was bleeding or because I was so clumsy. "Silly Bitch!" the low growl filled the kitchen.

My hands have always been able to handle the human body in any kind of predicament and now, with this woman for whom I know I can never be right I was awkward, out of place, fumbling hopelessly.

When at last I open my door and step inside my house after being away for all these weeks of travelling the rooms seem thin and transparent as if they have been starved.

Everything is in order. It is only the hot dry light of summer cleaning all the surfaces and corners. Everything is as I left it. If Mrs. Murphy has been in she has left no trace of herself.

Mrs. Murphy has certainly managed to detain me for a long time and she has stopped me from having the pleasure of coming home to my house and to my land. I want to walk out alone in the quiet fragrance. I want to stand and look along the narrow paddocks where they lie sleeping between the fringes of the jarrah forest. I want to walk down to the paperbarks and the sheoaks and listen to the small whispering of the wind beside the dry creek bed, I want to examine my fruit trees; and I want to do all these things in peace.

As I am hungry I have opened the cheese and am eating it straight from the foil; it is tasteless. The water from the tap is warm and milky. I'll have to look for the kerosene for the lamps and the refrigerator.

The Murphys want to use my car. They can have it and bring groceries for me too from Queens Meadow. After today I will have my car for myself. I will be firm with the Murphys and if they are unmanageable then they will have to go.

As I eat my cheese I look up the sun-filled slope to the great old trees which border the top paddock. The sun is wrapping colour round their bark and the trees remind me that time passes while it seems to stand still. It suits me to be here alone today without a car.

On the ship I heard someone say to Irma:

"I am intent Dear Irma on opening up another aspect of my personality."

"Zat is Gut! Very Healsy!" Irma approved. I heard her, "Ja! Und when I get back home to the U.S.A. which will not be for a while you understand . . ."

Irma understood perfectly.

"I intend to consolidate my files!"

"Oh mine Freund! My shipboard Freundin. How very excellent!"

Though I did not join in this conversation on the ship or in any other conversations I too want to open up another aspect of my personality and consolidate my files though I have no friend like Irma and no American accent and would never have put my feelings into words like these.

When I was a child I thought if I could only burrow through the leaves and the grasses and the undergrowth I would emerge in some magic place where I would make some sort of fresh discovery. I suppose it is the same now when I feel on the threshhold of discovery, as if I am about to come upon the reason or the truth. I have never stepped over this threshold and for some years have not even approached it and now as I think of that American voice and Irma's replying I feel again on the edge of some enchantment, a magic truth and a very real reason.

Alone in my empty kitchen I agree with myself. I will get rid of the Murphys and I laugh.

"I agree! I agree!" I say and laugh aloud in my empty house.

All my life I have been with older people, older colleagues, senior doctors and senior sisters and matrons, my father, Uncle Tod, Miss Beverly and Mrs. Platt, all of them dead now and I am no longer the younger one relying on the wisdom of the older people. I am not young any more. Dora was so young, only a child when she came to me, fifteen years, but ready in herself quite soon to be a young mother and I, with all my years and my meaningless body, relied on her. I let her cherish me, advise me even.

Eva was younger than me. I loved Eva. Both Dora and Eva had qualities on which I rested.

I must forget them both. I have forgotten them, especially Eva. I must clear my mind and heart of all that hurts. I have been quite alone for some years. I really have no-one, and except for a few arranged visits between the Forts and Rodney Glass and his family I see no-one. During the last years I have received kindness and advice of a conventional kind from these people who were colleagues of mine. Michael Fort took my post, reluctantly yet with a kind of gratitude, when I was forced to leave and give up my work at the hospital.

I am alone here in my place in the country and I must make a decision about the Murphys. They have to take their children eight miles to the clinic at Queens Meadow. I am fortunate, I suppose, that they don't want the car to drive the two hundred miles to town. They have to have the car today; they need food and shelter; these things have been provided and I will not think of them now.

Today I will go back on to my land. Today I want to step out, untroubled, into the warmth and to the steady reassuring noise of the cicadas. I want to breathe in the warm fragrance. I have forgotten the fragrance of my land and I want to know it again.

* * *

For these first few days I seem in a kind of daze while I reacquaint myself with my house. The rooms, which are large, seem empty because most of my furniture is being used by the tenants in my other house in town. This emptiness fills the house and lies over the land in a hot still quietness which I feel all the more after the thronged life on board ship, and after the excitement of continental railway stations where there is a feeling of great distances being brought together, in the times of arrivals and departures, the names of great cities being put up and taken down, exchanged for other names as famous trains come in and go out. People and languages and habits from all over the world pass close together for a short time and then are separated. Thousands of miles of land and sea seem to gather with the noise of all the people and there is never a time when there is no gathering.

White clouds have begun to come up passing two ways at once and I stand or walk on my high verandahs watching the clouds and waiting for rain. The house overlooks a shallow ravine of trees, a lonely heron flies there searching for food and sometimes I see a wedge-tailed eagle. The long hot summer brings these wild creatures closer because their search does not yield what they need.

I keep walking down the summer-warmed slopes between the young fruit trees to the creek bed. Seepage water has made little pools of stagnant water. It is a question of simply waiting for the rain to clear the creek and fill it with noisy running water.

I have not asked the Murphys to leave. They are quiet. The car, partly cleaned, has been returned. Murphy himself seems to have disappeared somewhere inside the house. It is as if they know of my intention and are keeping out of the way on purpose. Even the dogs are quiet and the children have not come to the door to ask to borrow anything. It is as if they are not there, except that the rubbish heap in front of their door grows steadily bigger. One night it was suddenly doubled. The terrible sofa with the sinister holes in the seat now lies on top of the heap, the escaping flock crawling in lumps all over the battered cans and cartons and all round are the indescribable remains of one of Mrs. Murphy's rubbish-burning fires.

At first as I walk over the land I just pick up wood in a leisurely way, stack it and slowly rake bark into heaps. Later I will burn this and feed the ash to the fruit trees. After a few days I am able to look more closely, I am more accustomed to the change of climate and scene. In the peacefulness I hardly think of the Murphys; there is no intrusion from them and I feel suddenly so at peace that I realise people must be themselves at all costs and that the Murphys have the right to be themselves. It is simple of course to allow people to be themselves if they are not being seen.

A little later on, as I go on looking at everything, the neglect I have been afraid of is more evident. The treachery of neglect. Some fruit trees have not been watered, the pear trees are quite blackened by the heat; they are like ghosts of trees with black burned buds. Magpies are attacking the mornings with their voices tumbling above the twisted brittle vines. Nearly all my vines are dead. I snap off the dry twigs and rub the leaves, scorched and curled in death, between my fingers. A sharp fragrance comes from the dusty earth when I pour water round the vines. The water runs in snakes over the dust. It can't do any good. The sheds are in disorder, the fences are down in places and the machinery is uncherished. I can't find the sheep, a few are huddled under Murphy's house at the other side, fly-blown and sick looking. Most of the poultry, hens and ducks have gone. There has been no explanation about this.

In a fury I start to work to try to overcome Murphy's neglect and, raging, I work too hard in the heat and have to go to bed exhausted and with all the things I know should be done turning over and over in my mind. I can't control my thoughts at all, all the work which needs to be done piles up in my head and my legs and arms can't rest, I feel as if I'm falling instead of going to sleep. I get up and write out a list of fruit trees to order to replace the dead ones and when this is done I walk about the house and I think how different it would have been if I had asked her to come for a visit. If I had spoken on the ship and invited her the short visit might have turned into a long one. I might have made her so happy she might have wanted to stay on, never wanting to leave. If I had asked her to come I would not feel so alone. The house could be filled with our talk and our laughter and our music. I wish she was with me, I'd stroke her little palomino-coloured head all night. It's no use trying not to think about her. I have been trying. This kind of thinking only makes me feel more alone.

It's a hot and restless night, the east wind is uneasy and restless and the house creaks as I walk and murmurs in the wind. Across the dark valley little blue flashes of lightning dart wickedly and I start nervously and stop and listen pausing in my prowling through the unlit rooms.

I am so overtired it is no use to try to sleep. I look carelessly through manuscripts of an unfinished textbook on gynaecology. Better to think of other things.

I think of the miles of jarrah forest, of the green tree tops cradled in the wind and of the roots deep in the safety of the earth, close to me along the boundaries of my own pastures.

I search for the address of the place for the new fruit trees and I try to work out on a scrap of paper how many sheep I should buy for the number of acres available.

40

And all the time I know it's the middle of the night and I am sleepless and lonely and uneasy and must force myself to make a reason for doing things.

It depends on the season how many sheep I shall have. Murphy said once you could get seven years for stealing and killing a sheep. I don't know what happens if you starve a sheep through ignorance and misfortune. I wonder, if you know of someone who has stolen and killed a sheep, what you can do about it, perhaps several sheep. What does all this matter . . .

I must have been dreaming: I went to a house where there were tubs of green jade and I knocked on the door and I thought someone was coming but no-one came, it was only the beating of my own heart which sounded like footsteps. In the dream there was a familiar green light. I knew the house.

But when I wake up I can't remember the house at all, I only remember something vaguely familiar. In the dream there was a little child with cold little hands and I tried to warm her in my lap. She seemed to caress me and I felt I should not let her because she belonged to someone. I can't think whose little girl she is now. The tubs of jade are mine. The jade must be years old; it was here when I came. No-one knows how old jade is; it survives in the most difficult conditions of drought or flood and goes on living. Fleshy green in tubs on my verandah. The dream was so vivid but really the confusion can have no meaning other than I am overtired. Caresses though, in a dream, disturb.

Outside the cocks are crowing and the east wind is cold. I am cold too and, for some reason, thinking about Eva when I wake up again. Her little girls will be grown up and the baby boy too. I should have delivered Eva when her son was born twenty-four years ago; I promised I would look after her but broke the promise and never saw her again. I thought about her often and in my mind kept the children's ages in order. I could even imagine, so well did I know Eva, at what times she would be talking about dresses, swimming classes and examination marks with her friends. All this however

41

belongs to another time, and since then I have stopped thinking about her. She belongs to some other time.

Every day the sun wraps colour round the rough dark bark of the red gums and warms the earth. I am struggling with the fierce heat and the drought. I am wishing the season away. It is hard to imagine a time will come when I will need my boots and waterproof clothes and I cannot think that I will ever feel cold. I have tried making tents from sacks for some of the vines and trees but I think it is too late. Every few days I fetch groceries and I long for the drought to break. When I fill the troughs for the sheep I see how dirty they are. Murphy should never have let them get so crusted. Two more sheep need to be shot; probably it would be best to shoot the lot.

The cicadas keep up their endless concert and the nights seem long and oppressive. Clouds come and just at the beginning of the shallow ravine they divide and go separate ways leaving the valley hot and dry.

I have to go over to the Murphys. Mrs. Murphy greets me at the door by looking me up and down so that I feel over-fed and over-dressed. She turns up her eyes so that only the whites show.

"One thing after another," she says. "They've all got the squitters now. I'm afeared for the septic. They're in an' out of the toilet all the time. I sed to them jes' stop pullin' that chain there's a water shortage. Could you get a mixture for us?" Mrs. Murphy adds the last sentence in the all too familiar whine.

"Yes of course," I say to her. "But I'd like to see Mr. Murphy please."

There is a silence between us, Mrs. Murphy has no intention of moving from the door post.

"We-ell he's layin' down, havin' a lay down."

"I'll come back later," I tell her; "I must see Mr. Murphy. There are things that must be done and if Mr. Murphy can't do them I'll have to get other tenants." She just looks at me and I turn on my heel and walk stiffly up the dirt slope.

"Yu'll not forget the mixture" Mrs. Murphy shrills,

"An can you get" she is suddenly at my side, detaining me, her thin dirty fingers holding on to my blouse. "Can youse git me a bag of pertatoes," she says. "I give 'em nothing but pumpkin for a long time now, boiled pumpkin and jam. A pertato an' some salt, I'll give you some money later, a few lemons, a lemon or two. There's none here the fowls have done for the tree look at it jes' a skellington. I could do with a lemon." Her lips are cracked and dry and I tell her of course I'll get the potatoes and the lemons and some butter too and tea and sugar.

When I drive through the wide countryside all lit up with the white marri tree flowers I think how can I enjoy any of this with such impoverished people on my step. They are quite without prospects, they are ill and without food; if I turn them away they will have no home, there is no place in the world for them. Whatever could they do, wherever could they go. The bush looks so lovely in the long slanting light of the sun but it would look very different in the blackness of the night if there was no home and no shelter to be going to.

In the night there is a real storm with lightning and thunder so loud till it seems that the valley holds all the noise of the storm within its narrow boundary. Of course I can't sleep but lie in the comfortable bed listening quietly, with my hands crossed over on my breasts. I think of the jewel. I wish she was here with me.

And then I hear the rain. The house responds to the thunder. The earth answers the rain. The sharp scent of summer is caught and released as the heavy rain washes the earth. I forget everything now except this smell of the first real rain. I am so comfortable in bed.

Somehow drawing her close I feel she is here and the sharp fragrance, almost like an anaesthetic, is her fragrance. Perhaps this is the closest I can ever get to anyone.

And then I remember the doors of the barn open all the long hot dry summer, big double doors and now, because of Murphy's feckless ways, still open and this tremendous rain sweeping straight in there. All the

43

seed is stored there and other things in calico sacks; dry foods, oats and wheat. There is nothing to do but to get up and go out there. It is so dark and wet. Old water courses, down the slope, are suddenly reopened, water rushes down in a thousand streams bringing leaves and twigs and branches. In the morning the slope will look different, the rain has a way of altering the appearance of the land overnight. Slowly with the torch I make my way to the barn; the huge doors are wide open. I have continued in Murphy's way to leave them open; water is pouring in. As far as I can see with my torch the roof seems sound, though this is not because of Murphy. I have to admit in my soaked state that all summer I have not thought about the roof of the barn. That surely is the tenant's job. I try to close one of the doors but cannot move it and when I try the other that is stuck too. Straining all my muscles I try to bring the doors together. The seed sacks are wet and other things and I am wet through. I can't help crying aloud with anger and helplessness and I stagger off across the sodden paddock to the Murphy's house. In the dark and the wet, the smell of rotting rubbish seems more intense and a terrible stink comes from the sheep huddled under the verandah at the other side of the house. I must do something about these neglected sheep even if it does mean getting rid of them all.

The door side of Murphy's house is level with the ground. There is already a small lake across the dirt yard. It takes time for water to go through very dusty earth; but it is probably seeping under the house steadily. That is another thing which must be seen to, for though one half of the house is built high, this side of it is on the ground and probably rotting.

I have to bang and rattle on the door for a long time and then it opens letting out the stale air from inside.

"What is it?" Mrs. Murphy calls from the other side of the door. "Wha' d'ya want? An' wha' dy'a want at this time an' in the rain too!" The dogs, chained, move and growl.

"The barn doors are open," I shout into the blackness.

44

"She says the barn doors are open," I hear Mrs. Murphy relay the news to some, though there is hardly room for it, obscure part of the house.

"It's raining hard!" I am shivering. "The barn doors won't close. Tell Mr. Murphy please to come at once!"

"He's seck," Mrs. Murphy's voice comes back closer. "He's too seck to come out."

"He's to come out at once!" I raise my voice and try to push open their door but it sticks hard on the floor. "If he doesn't come . . ."

"Orright then, orright then!" I can hear Murphy getting up and knocking things over. A child begins to cry, and after a few moments he appears pushing his shirt into his trousers.

"It's a wild night!" he seems thin and very gaunt in the wet darkness. I am afraid he will be too frail to close up the barn. But in spite of being sick and half starved and nearly asleep Murphy has strength in his stick-like arms and thin body and he shifts the doors from where they seem to be growing on the floor and closes them. We are both of us wet through.

"It's a wild night!" he says again and we go back down the slope, Murphy comes down with me instead of going across the paddock to his own place. It is so uneven with the water rushing. I slip and I think I feel Murphy's hard fingers clutch my arm to hold me. As I steady myself, my shoes full of water, I wonder whether he has tried to help me or not.

At my kitchen door he stops and says, "Goo' night," in the light from the house I see his tired thin face. He starts off hunched against the wild weather. His wet clothes hang on him.

"Will you stop and have a drink," I call after him. I do this in spite of myself. He turns and hesitates. "I'm going to have one," I say, "must get warm somehow."

"Are you sure now?" he seems shy, unlike the Murphy who blots my valley every day. He follows me into my clean kitchen, water is running from us dirtying the floor, he pulls some newspapers from a chair and makes a place for us to stand. I reach for towels and we both rub ourselves.

"Funny thing," Murphy remarks, "How ye have to towel yer 'ead dry first." Our clothes clinging to us make us look ridiculous, that is what I think and then that it is strange to be alone in the kitchen in the night with Murphy and after thinking these two things nothing seems ridiculous or strange any more.

"What'll you have?" Murphy asks me, shyly assuming the position of provider. "Whisky?" He reaches into the dresser for the bottle.

"That will do very well," I say. Quickly he opens up the stove which has not been used all summer and he screws up some more newspaper into tight balls and pushes them in and lights them. He tears up my cardboard grocery box. The blaze is wonderful.

"I'll just hot up a tiny drop of water," he says. I am amazed at his familiarity but warm myself gratefully. I watch him make tea in my silver teapot and pour it into two mugs, he adds sugar and a squeeze of lemon, he seems to know where everything is, and then the whisky and then he hands me one of the mugs and we sip together breathing hard into the steam. Murphy's ears are bright red. The drink is very pleasant. We have a second one. Murphy has to hunt in the lean-to for another box to burn and we warm our cold backs. In the buttonless opening of Murphy's cream flannel shirt I can see his chest covered with tightly curled yellowish white hair, it is an intimate thing to see. Murphy is hideously thin, he looks ill; I feel sorry for him. Really his eyes are kind. In his eyes too, which I never have really noticed before, is the expression of someone who is perplexed. If he is lazy it is chiefly because of the lack of possession and the feeling of being entirely without importance and without any particular place in the world. He has no real interest in the work he is supposed to do; even if I gave him sheep of his own there would be little return from them, and if he neglects them as he does my sheep, there would be nothing from them. I find myself looking at him through the steam of the drink he

46

made so quickly; he can have no idea what I am thinking. The Murphys must have some meat. I am supposed to supply meat, but then he is supposed to work for me.

"Take a sheep tomorrow Murphy," I say. "For yourselves I mean. A good one I mean, for meat."

"Thank you," he says and drains his mug. "That's better!" I have always wanted to grow potatoes; two years I have tried, both times with Murphy helping me and Mrs. Murphy, thin, like a poor quality fencing post, stuck on the fencing wires watching,

"You trying potatoes?" Mrs. Murphy always sucks in her cheeks when watching what I am doing. "We already tried 'em. Frost always got 'em. Frost will get 'em when they're so high," she indicated with her yellow hands how high the haulms would be when the frost took them. "You'll do no good."

"I'd get somepin in the abbetoyers if there was somepin going there," Murphy breaks into my memory of the potato failure. "Them payin' people off there so there's nothin' to go there for."

"Yes of course," I agree with him and I am trying to think what there could be to do on my land. I haven't enough cleared land to make a living. That is not my concern, but I keep trying to think of something which would open prospects for Murphy, and of course encourage my own reasons for being here.

"Now that the rains are coming," I say, "we have our seed and I'll get some calves."

"Yes o' course," Murphy agrees. "Well must be getting back home," Murphy rinses his cup. "Thanks for the drink, it was very nice," he smiles at me. "That fire'll die down orright if you close up the stove tight."

"Yes, yes I know." I watch him disappear into the wet lonely night. I know Murphy's house is damp; it is too low on the ground at this side. Better get him to work on it tomorrow first thing, though I know that nothing will make the water-soaked and streaked asbestos look better or be better in any way. Really the Murphys should be sent away and the house and its horrible outbuilding pulled down, but that is impossible to consider just now. Perhaps it would be an idea to get several calves and give some to Murphy as his to fatten.

Alone in the kitchen with Murphy's little fire I am full of great and noble thoughts. I like his little fire, it is something I would never have thought of doing myself. He has picked up his pieces of wet newspaper. When he went he had them screwed into a tidy ball under his arm. The night is so wild and Murphy's care so unexpected that I almost miss him, and yet I would not have wanted him to suggest he sleep in my house.

I spread a piece of bread and butter and cut a thick slice of ham. I should have told Murphy to take some; he is sure to be hungry. I take the food and a book to bed and forget about Murphy.

All the time I was away travelling I really wanted to come back to my land. I was glad I wanted to come back because when I set off I seemed to have no wishes at all for anything. I had no wish to leave yet I left because I had come to be afraid of this lack of wishing.

Everything seemed to change when I saw Andrea Jackson in that unnatural world on the ship, when I knew I wanted to see her and it seemed as if she wanted to see me. While I have been waiting for the rain I have thought of her less and less. She only comes to me at times like now when I am in bed again listening to the rain pouring all over the grateful land. Just now I think of her very intensely.

All the time I was away I thought of the boundaries of my land. Just before the place where I cross the boundary there is a wide shining dam with dead trees standing in the unrippled water. When I reach this dam I see the first fencing posts which are mine, and when I am once inside the first gate, on my own land, I am safe. The ugly dam is not mine but it pleases me to see it. I always feel that when I am on this land which is mine nothing can happen to me, nothing can harm me. I feel safe in bed now after Murphy's drink. Murphy has a way of making me feel all right and yet most of the time he does nothing and does not even appear.

As well as the noise of the rain I can hear the water

rising and swelling along the creek bed. Very quickly the brook runs full and deep, the bridge can be covered in a quarter of an hour with rain like this. The water fills and floods quickly and it flows away quickly. I am pleased to hear the water running at last.

I have a cold patch in my back and my right wrist is cold and aching. I turn over to try to warm my back and then I turn again. I am comfortable and close my eyes. And all at once I realise my eyes are wide open staring into the blackness. The second hour passes, and the third, and the slow quiet terrible desperation of knowing I will not be able to sleep comes over me, and I know I don't want the night and the day after the night and the next day and the week and the next weeks following. Sleeplessness is like this.

I try to think of ways in which I can help the Murphys. If I give Murphy a calf I am afraid it will get ill and infect my calves. It is Murphy's way to let things take their chance and with him they have no chance. I could buy some clothes for the children, but this may not be so easy. When Dora first came to live in as my housekeeper she had few things, and nothing warm for that cold house. I discovered quite soon though that she folded all my presents, the jumpers and singlets and stockings carefully and kept them neatly in clean plastic bags in her cupboard and just went on wearing the thin blouses which she pulled tight across her round breasts while she shivered.

If Dora were here in this house and I could not sleep she would get up at once and make a fire in the stove and make tea. She would do these things half asleep, for Dora could always sleep. She would wait on me and see that I had everything I wanted. When she brought me tea she used to put the sugar in the cup and bring it carefully stirring to make sure it would be just right.

I tell myself I do not need Dora now. If I need these things I can get them for myself. Just as I unpacked my cases myself and put away the expensive travelling clothes. I probably will never need them again; they are all put hanging and folded away in the cupboards. I am ashamed of all the pairs of shoes I have and would rather not have them. I do not need Dora or anyone to look after me. Dora's red cheeks and her habit of pulling her blouse tight across her breasts might even annoy me out here. To overcome my sleeplessness it is best to think of the things I will do. One thing is that I will buy some new dresses for the Murphy girls . . .

* * *

When I collect my letters from the post office, which is like a little shed in the main street of Queens Meadow, there is a postcard from Irma. I had forgotten her. On a ship there are people one sees every day and they become so familiar it is difficult to imagine a life where they will not be. So quickly I had forgotten Irma!

The card makes me remember her for a time but of course I'll never see her again or hear her voice and so I'll forget her. This is the way of shipboard acquaintances. I don't suppose I'll ever see the little jewel again. I don't forget her. I don't think I want to forget the reawakening of feeling.

Irma has written in her careful blue handwriting:

> *"The eagle is flying alone*
> *The raven in flocks*
> *Society needs the fool*
> *Solitude the wise man*

Dear Friend from the Ship this is from a poem by our poet Rückert; it comes to you with all good wishes.   Irma."

The red gravel outside the post office and the triangle-shaped paddock opposite, crowded with sheep, seem so far away from the world of ships and ports and capital cities and crowds of people. The postcard with a surface mail stamp has taken a long time to arrive. Perhaps Irma is with her daughter in the apartment overlooking the Danube, or, most probably she is back at work in the vegetarian guest house in the mountains not far from Vienna.

There is too an invitation to dinner from my old colleague Rodney Glass. Rodney and his wife have always invited me to dinner and I always go to their parties,

50

though I find them and their guests trivial and commonplace. When I go I have to stay with them for the night as it is such a long way to drive. They always make me comfortable.

Rodney has scrawled on the end of his note, ". . . *have asked the Forts to come. Fort's daughter Margaret has married a young pathologist who is now following our primrose path. Margaret wants to keep the old profession in the family, she will get him through his exams! I believe he is the son of an old friend of yours. They will be at dinner too. I think we should have an agreeable evening. Cheryl and I really hope you will be able to come.*"

When inviting me Rodney is always careful to tell me who will be there, it is one of his ways of being kind to me. Really I don't want to go anywhere to dinners but I will accept the invitation. As years go by it becomes clear that people, friends and acquaintances, are necessary so invitations must be given and must be accepted. In any case the date for the party is some weeks from now. Rodney always gives me good notice.

Which party was it, Rodney's stupid wife, Cheryl, arranged. She is like a china doll, blonde and hygienic with vulgar movements and ugly clothes. She wears harsh blues and greens and covers herself with sequins for the evenings. It was my fiftieth birthday. I was just out of prison then and recovering from an illness; how can I forget that year! Cheryl Glass and Yvonne Fort made a surprise party for me. Comforted with the wine and the food and the warmth I was deeply touched by the efforts of my colleagues to make this pleasant evening with carefully chosen company and unexpected presents. I felt pleased and talked and laughed and was delighted in turn with every present. I did not have to act. I really was able to be relaxed and pleased, the first time for some years. Ten years later I still remember it vividly because for me it was such a terribly hard time. Rodney pretends. He disregards that time or refuses to remember. Sometimes he asks what I think about some detail in surgery or the use of certain equipment as if I had not lost my qualification and was not all these years

51

out of touch. He knows I have several half-written manuscripts which I cannot go on writing. Sometimes I am afraid he will ask me for them. What would be the point of such a request!

The thing about that party which was so dreadful was that quite suddenly Cheryl Glass, with her usual lack of tact, called across the room.

"Laura Dear! do tell me who your friends are!" There was a pause in the talking and laughing and then she said, "Most of the people I tried to ask had excuses, previous engagements, you know the usual things, and couldn't come. It was really hard to rake up a few guests for this party wasn't it, Edith." Sister Dobson from the Wentworth Nursing Home (now retired and on gin for the rest of her life) nodded lazily. "Too Right!" she agreed, "It was bloody hard to find a few bloody people to fill a bloody room," and she indicated with her podgy white hand she'd have four fingers of Scotch.

"Oh," I laughed. "I've got some friends," I began to reply. I was still laughing and then I stopped because they had all gone quiet and my voice sounded so silly.

"Oh Laura Dahling! do tell us who they are so that we can ask them on another occasion ..." everyone was laughing, everyone of us drank too much. Companionship was a hard labour. We had all reached an age when we drank either whisky or brandy and we drank hard and ate a lot and breathed heavily as we got through our evenings.

I almost said a name aloud and I saw all the guests waiting for my list of friends.

"I have no friends," I said. My voice hardly came. The pain of it was suddenly too much.

"What about bed Laura?" Rodney's voice was gentle, very close to me and private. I couldn't stand this either but I knew he was trying to help me.

"We could all do with an early night," he said. And I suppose the party for me ten years ago ended then. Outside my bedroom door I took the two white capsules Rodney held out to me on the palm of his hand.

I don't really need capsules any longer. I have plenty

if I should need them. If I can't sleep I give myself up to sleeplessness, sometimes I walk about the dark house in the long night. I have become familiar with the unfamiliar appearance of my land when the trees and the slope and the terraces of vines are splashed and shadowed in the moonlight. When there are long nights without sleep I try to keep off the desperation of knowing I am not asleep. At that time, ten years ago I was entirely unable to do this. Now with difficulties known only to myself I am managing.

It seems that Murphy is right about the flowers of the marri trees. The opening rains are heavy and are continuing. Suddenly it is cold enough to light fires every evening. The season changes, and my life changes with the work of the season.

PART 2

PALOMINO

Andrea

I wonder if it's true what they say about Laura. Mother always hinted about things but never came out straight with anything. Mother said she, Laura, was very intense when she was young. I suppose intense means hung up. I never listen to Mother, she's hung up in her own way; she thinks a black suspender belt and black pants are a sign of being not quite nice. She doesn't even realise that no-one wears suspender belts now. Mother and Laura were close friends once though. The thought of anyone being close to Mother is so appalling I never think of it. Never.

All through dinner I am watching Laura. She has a shy graciousness, I suppose people would say she is well bred. I find her beautiful when I see her looking at me which she can't help doing. We are opposite each other at the table. The expression in her eyes is so kind. I never saw eyes with so much tenderness in them. All the time we were on the ship she looked at me like that and I pretended not to see.

And then when I was with Christopher I didn't think about her till we met here at this dinner party. Christopher married Margaret Fort, she was at school with me. That dull lump Margaret Fort is the same age as me, six years older than my brother! She was determined to marry him and determined he should be a doctor. He wants to get on in the world. I can't bear the word marriage for my brother let alone the sight and knowledge of their marriage and I've been in the same pokey little house with it some weeks now. I left because I couldn't bear it and then I came back to stay with them not because I was over the thing but because I've been ill and had to come home and I can't stand being at Mother's. Oh Christ!

They are married! Marriage. Oh Christopher! Oh God! Awful in that little house! God Awful! I have to stick it. No wonder I don't look into his eyes. I never look into Christopher's eyes, never looked into anyone's eyes until just now I look at Laura. I could look forever into hers.

It's all lace place mats and table napkins and glass and silver on polished wood and tuna mornay, mushrooms and sweet corn. Surgeons Glass and Fort exchanging words quickly neither of them finishing a sentence. They don't need to, their wives take up the ends of the phrases and do what they like with them. They have all known each other for years. "Close friends."

I think Laura sees there is something the matter with me, she questions me with her look but how can I reply. I do so long to talk to you Laura. Oh my God!

Rodney Glass tells his joke and everyone laughs. Laura laughs and turns her glass round and round with a gentle movement of her hand.

"Oh," says Rodney Glass, "medical jokes nowadays are so sophisticated. When we were young it was all farts and buckets of pus." He pours more wine for Michael Fort, my brother's father-in-law. Mr. Fort can open the right doors and knows the right people for the successful advancement of dear Christopher. He fills

56

Laura's glass too. Like them she can drink well at dinner.

My little school among the coconut palms, Ceylon, my pupils, my illness all seem so far away, yet during this dinner I disappear down these little paths which go between the tiny huts and the places where men and women squat in the mud under water gushing from municipal taps to wash themselves. They are so clean, shining and clean in their white or bright coloured clothes even though it is so dirty where they live. The people in London afterwards seemed drab and un-washed.

The road through the jungle goes on to the wide pink bay. In the pink light of the mornings I walked at the edge of the sea. Every day I felt so light and fresh and the snake charmer sat with his flute and basket of snakes in a warm patch of gravel below the stone verandah of the tea house. He waited there for the tourists to come.

"Yes I know the place," Laura says across the table. Her voice is soft and tender like her eyes. I heard her gentle voice sometimes on the ship, and now she is speaking to me. I must have spoken aloud about the jungle road coming suddenly out to the pink and blue morning hovering over the tranquil sea. I didn't know I had said anything, it is so noisy at this table, my head aches and throbs. It is the anaemia following the illness. Either I said something just loud enough for her to hear or she knows what I am thinking about.

Just five words and we are looking into each other. It is as if the dinner table does not exist, just the candles and Laura's eyes looking straight into mine.

When she lets me go from that look they are talking about a boating disaster in which seven people, three of them children, lost their lives. Glass and Fort condemn. Their wives show curiosity and Margaret has no opinion. Her baby is asleep in the next room. I say hers because I don't allow it to be Christopher's too though I know I have to. He is only my brother after all. Oh Brother! I can't live without him. I can't live there with him and with her. Oh God! These long weeks have been pure hell.

A carpenter knows where to make a hole for a screw, Surgeons Glass and Fort, ordinary men, clever with their stubby hands, holding lives in their hands, safely like screws with carpenters. I never look at Christopher now. Soon he will be exactly like Mr. Glass and Mr. Fort; he will be Mr. Jackson and mother will boast about him. I never looked at Christopher only felt him, perhaps I should have looked. I only want to feel him that's all but it's everything till it's over and then I want him again. All that time in Ceylon I managed and now it's just as it was. Laura if only I could ask you to help me. I can't ask out loud. Laura please. Can I call you Laura? If only I could tell her what I'm thinking.

Is it true what they say about you Laura? Cheryl Glass and Yvonne Fort, what ugly dresses you have on, turquoise blue and shocking pink, Margaret will be like you soon, ordinary and safe! Why did Christopher marry her. She's like Mother, that's why. Thank God Mother's not here. Mother's as bad as all of them.

I wonder how it was between Eva and Laura. Now Christopher is speaking, everyone is quiet for him, "My sister," he says, "needs a good rest. She has worked so hard since coming back from Ceylon. Our house with Junior" Oh God! Christopher Junior! "is no place for a rest." That's me he's talking about and Junior's his bloody son. "She wasn't well when she came to us."

So that's it. Christopher wants a rest from me. Is that it? The last time we were together he was uneasy, not himself; how can a man make love to two women, under the same roof. Taking turns in the bed! I suppose she is ready for him now to put it crudely. The post-natal six weeks is over; she has had her check-up at the clinic and they can start again. They don't even need to wait till I am in the bathroom. How could I sink so low! God Awful! We tried while she was in the bathroom but didn't make it of course. I suppose her shaved off hair will have grown. I'm so sick of their plucked chicken joke. It's terrible being on the edge of married people's private little jokes.

Everyone is quiet, waiting. Michael Fort (Christopher calls his father-in-law Sir) is telling his very own funny story.

"To stop this fellow snoring, you see he was disturbing all the other patients, well to stop him snoring we thought we'd give him a fright. One of the fellows managed to get a whole pile of pig's intestines. If you snore so much, we told this man, all your insides will come out. Well that night we put all the intestines on his pillow. Next morning he says, 'You were quite right, you know. I did snore my insides out, but I managed to get 'em back down with my tooth brush."

"Desert everyone?" Cheryl Glass is handing round little glass dishes, while the laughter subsides. The suburban joke about deserts in little glass bowls. More laughter.

I can't eat this pudding; nuts on top of cream and marshmallow and meringue. I can't stop my hand from shaking. Once I could hold my hands in one position not moving for hours if necessary. My hands shake and I feel I can't look at the pudding. I should never have come out to dinner, and yet how could I stop in the desperate unhappiness of that house, alone for the long evening.

"I have a quiet place," five more words in that soft deep voice.

Oh Laura they say you loved my mother. I don't suppose she ever loved you she wouldn't know how.

How was it?

In the change rooms at school?

In a corner of the playing fields?

But you were boarding, it was a boarding school wasn't it? You would have had all night together. Perhaps you had all night?

So you have a quiet place have you Laura.

"I think Laura's valley would be a gorgeous spot to go to for a rest," Cheryl Glass is pouring coffee into tiny cups. I'd like a big mug of coffee. "Horses to ride, long walks in the bush, fresh eggs and cream, and long quiet mornings to sleep in!" Cheryl Glass sighs. "You could sit and read or sew or paint and no-one would disturb you. Laura doesn't even have a telephone! The peace must be heavenly. And all the time in the world just to do as you want to do!"

"I'd like to come," I say to Laura at the quiet table.

"Come then," she says just like that, "Come."

Christopher thanks Laura. He thanks her too much. Just think of it: Laura was to have delivered him. Sometimes Mother hinted about the tragedy of Laura's life. She always dropped her voice and never really said anything. Christopher, little baby, Big Man! I sat on Laura's lap when I was a little girl. Now I'll go to Laura's place and let her nurse me better from all the things that have gone wrong in my life. Perhaps it's only a rest I need, but I'm afraid it might be more than that.

During dinner this evening I see for the first time that Laura has quite a large mouth. There is something very honest in her expression especially when she smiles. She was already here when we arrived. I heard her laugh and I wondered who was here. She was warming herself by the fire. Rodney was with her. I noticed her long plain dress, some dark soft stuff leaving her shoulders bare. She always looks well dressed, it is partly the way she holds herself, but of course, good quality clothes too. As we came in she straightened up and turned round and I saw who it was. At the moment of meeting she seemed startled and then looked pleased. I saw her glance quickly at the pendant I wear; she looked at it all the time on the ship.

These people are like hundreds of others all the same as each other. They have hundreds of friends and acquaintances but hardly mean anything to one another. Their friends are all clean too like these people are clean. Very clean. Clean clothes, clean hair, clean houses, clean swimming pools, clean cars and clean minds with nothing in them. There must be a dirty side so that bowels can be included like the sewage works on the desolate side of town, bowels and drains and shameful infections and muddled thoughts and muddled sex. Sex isn't dirty but it's a bit of a mess for very clean people.

Laura is not like these people. She is like herself. I want to know her and I want her to know me. Just for once I want something real.

Laura speaks to me below the noise of the dinner table, just for me to hear. I lean forward and listen to her.

"Down the slope of my land there is a winding path made by people who lived there years ago. Perhaps I feel nearer to them than to anyone on earth when I follow this old path. It's nearly hidden now from lack of use; it goes down to a narrow gate and crosses the stream on a crazy bridge made of railway sleepers," she says.

She speaks to me in the poetry of herself, quietly her words reach me in spite of Michael Fort's rasping platitudes and Margaret's whipped cream presence. I want to take in the meaning and the music of what Laura is saying. She is telling me, I hear her words between the noises of the dinner table.

"It's tranquil there. Come and feel the tranquility of my place," she tells me.

I don't need any persuading. I would have gone with her from the ship if she had spoken and asked me before I saw Christopher. I was ill on the ship, I had to go somewhere. Christopher came to fetch me. I had to go to him when I saw him.

Christopher is explaining about Dad's death; he, Jake, died recently, it was a coronary. I didn't come home for his death. How can you come home for your father's coronary? Even though Dad died Mother still has her own mother, Christopher is explaining to Laura about Eva. "Eva and her mother live together," he says. "Yes," he explains to Laura. "Gran's still alive, she's a wonder! She's still first to answer the door or the 'phone. Mother says she's always been first to answer everything."

God! What a bore you are Christopher, I'd like to tell

61

you that to your face in front of all these people. He's telling now about Eva's flowers and how she and her mother take it in turns to rush out and put back the beach umbrellas every time they blow off the infestation of hydrangeas they have like a mould clinging to the brickwork. Oh the arguments about the hydrangeas! Jake couldn't stand anything near the house; he tore up the place. Coloured concrete slabs, clean new clothes, remedial reading and dental floss; the boundaries of a childhood.

"Eva is busy sewing for the little man." Christopher I never noticed what an incredibly dull voice you have. Has it just happened since you married that Meringue Pie? "Sewing for the little man"! Let me always remember you stuffed up and suburban like this, it will help me. Don't let me ever again see your bare throat and the gold hairs on your strong arms and your teeth white in the half light in those moments of passion which should never have been ours. I am never coming back to you, Christopher, Never ever! Let me think of you calling your baby "the little man." Let me remember the closing of the bedroom door with you and her together on the other side of it. Stop with that cream filled pudding of yours and that fat product of your smug union. God! I've had too much to drink! Oh God! I'm tight! What shall I do! I had to leave Eva and Jake, their lives stifled mine. I had to leave you Christopher, we were killing each other; and now I have to leave you and your wife. I must, it's up to me. I must go!

"I'd like to come back with you tonight," I say to Laura.

She looks as if she has two lamps alight in her eyes. She is looking at me with these eyes.

"Oh Laura always stays overnight when she comes to dinner," Cheryl Glass is motherly all at once. "We wouldn't hear of her making that long drive home through the night, would we Rodney. She only drove here today, it's too far for the double drive, and in the pitch dark too! Laura needs a good sleep before going home."

"Certainly not Laura!" Rodney Glass says quickly, "Not with all that alcohol in your blood, and you've not had your brandy yet." He, smiling, offers her the brandy which she does not take.

"Oh come Laura! You never take coffee without brandy!"

"Yes Laura," Cheryl Glass is anxious. "Your room's all ready for you. Bed made, electric blanket on, Laura I won't let you drive tonight. Miss Jackson can start her holiday tomorrow," Cheryl Glass smiles at me. "I'm sure you'll agree tomorrow at noon would be a good time to go."

"Biscuits and books on the bedside table," Rodney is listing all the preparations made for Laura's comfort. They are taking possession of her, they are taking her away from me. I look at her steadily.

"I want to go tonight!" I speak angrily like a tired child.

"Be reasonable Andrea!" my brother says sharply.

"It was you Chistopher, who kept on about my needing a holiday and a rest," I smile at him without looking at him. "I want to go tonight. Tomorrow it might be too late," I say in a low voice to Laura looking at her, "I want to go tonight, please," my voice is almost a whisper. She is sitting very still and I don't take my eyes off her. I want her to take me tonight. If not tonight then it will be never. I know this. If I go back with Christopher and his piece of pastry something awful will happen. I can't be sure of my own actions. I can't be responsible. I've lost my calm. I must go tonight or else give way to something desperate and violent and horrible in me and in Christopher. He must know. That's why he's urging me to go away. He is good at urging people, like urging Margaret to go and wash her hair to give him ten minutes with me. He is afraid too. If he weren't afraid he wouldn't have asked Laura to have me. That's what he has done really; pushed me on to her. I should never have come back to him. I should have stayed in Ceylon and died there.

Christopher looks so big and honest and so full of

promise, the young pathologist who is going to study medicine. Good on you brother! Doctor C. Jackson and your empty headed pavlova bummed wife; doctors often marry stupid women. By the time he qualifies he will have five or six children without any of the passion he had with me. He will work hard and be admired by all who know him. He'll have his yacht and his hobby farm and I'll just be a plain old aunt for his children to expect presents from.

Rodney Glass and Michael Fort have boats; they are always talking river and boating. Jake had boats too. People with boats are always talking boats and river accidents. I hate little men in little boats. They spoil the river.

"More coffee anyone?" Mrs. Glass is filling the awkward quietness while I am looking at Laura. I am really pleading, though no-one can know this. "More coffee? Laura dear? Yes? Good!"

"I must tell you about this chap I took on as crew," Michael Fort is laughing down his nose at his reminiscences. "He begged to come. Newcomer y'know. Never been in a boat but was dead keen," Fort looks round the table to claim attention, his story relieves the silence.

"The long and the short was that rough weather came up suddenly; we capsized and instead of helping me to right the old girl, he treads water and bawls at a passing vessel to give him a lift. 'I CAN'T SWIM!' he's bawling, 'I'M AFRAID I'LL CATCH COLD!' Chap couldn't swim a stroke and afraid of a cold, so there I was in gale force winds and really choppy waters alone! hanging on trying to pull her over! Afraid of catching cold I ask you!"

I am looking at Laura steadily. Her eyes look into mine with a tenderness I can hardly understand. Well Laura, what's it to be! You didn't speak on the ship. You have spoken now. You have said to me to come and I want to come tonight.

The candles spread their soft light in polished circles and Laura and I look steadily at one another. We have never sat opposite each other before. If we had, everything might have been so different.

"Do you remember the beef tea we had on the ship?" I ask her. "Squat old ladies lining up for their broth at eleven."

"Do they still have beef tea? How quaint!" Yvonne Fort remembers her own voyage out.

These people know we were on the same ship. They know a lot about Laura, or think they do. They think they know everything about me, especially Christopher, he thinks he knows, but there's one thing he doesn't know. It's all too serious. Oh too serious! Oh Christopher if I come back tonight to your neat and pretty home it will become a terrible place for us all if I am there. I am not responsible. I am not responsible.

With blinkered knowledge Rodney Glass writes books on surgery, big thick books, Christopher admires and wants to emulate. You do this Christopher, I am leaving you in peace to do what you want to do. Emulate!

Well Laura! I'm waiting while you drink your coffee. I want to say out loud: Laura, I am waiting.

That mattress on the floor in Christopher's study. We trembled all the way back from the ship, touching each other. The more we tried to steady ourselves the closer we held each other, he with his strong arm guiding me and I leading him. Together. The mattress was the only thing I saw when we entered the house, dishevelled and urgent. The house was dishevelled too, for the creamy one here was already away in the hospital at that very time panting in the labour theatre trying not to cry out. We panted too. Briefly, and shamelessly cried out, calling each other by name in those few moments of passion, frightening in their intensity. We had not even undressed properly and our voices, with our feelings, shocked and relieved simultaneously.

Well Laura?

"Yes I remember the beef tea," she says softly. "But I don't think I had any. You know," she adds in a very low voice, "I think they will soon replace it with ice cream." She laughs gently and then moves her chair softly back from the table and gets up singing in her surprising voice, from the opening of one of the closing passages of the St. Matthew Passion.

"In quiet grief dear Lord we leave thee." No-one in the room can stop Laura from doing what she has made up her mind to do. And with Laura singing and laughing, we leave the party.

* * *

Laura

The land is dark and penitent after the heavy prolonged rain. The land is relieved and promised.

I have not slept yet. Everywhere there is a strange profusion of colour, of almond blossom, pink and white, and dark grey cloud chalked white at the edges. Planted on the clouds the eucalypts are motionless, their leaves sharp and glittering, tremulous in the sudden sunlight. The frogs on their mud bank pillows are croaking down there under the willows. Suddenly the fine bending branches are bursting with new leaves, fresh and bright green.

Water is pouring over rocks, rushing down washing away the clay banks. Such a lot of water. Streams are running where usually water never runs and the little birds, wagtails, robins and wrens dart back and come closer in apparent freedom. The startling blue tails of the wrens are upright and so small. Little birds, busy and shy and bold.

She has not slept yet either. I am taking her round my place to show her what it's like here. It's the early morning, we have really only just arrived. The suffering has gone from her eyes. She begged me with those golden eyes during the dinner.

Now of course I remember the green pendant. It was mine once. I gave it to Angela. Andrea is Eva's daughter, "the jewel" is the little one, the younger sister, the little one who sat cool and naked in my lap years ago in Eva's clean suburban kitchen.

Eva had every electrical thing in her kitchen, the whole house was clean and modern. The bath water was always running steaming and scented for Eva's two daughters, Angela and Andrea. The time I am thinking about is just before Christopher was born.

All round that house were Jake's coloured concrete paths, but on the window sills Eva, who seemed to take with her something of the long summer of childhood, had little blue jugs of grasses, summer pink, and flowers.

It was another life over twenty years ago.

Andrea and I are walking gently together in the fragrance after the rain. All round us are the wet leaves and wet green spikes, and glittering dripping rain drops fall in bright showers as we disturb branches when we pass. The valley is quiet and the clear air is filled with the voices of the magpies as they swoop and fly in the morning sun across the paddocks of my land. The early morning is sparkling.

I can't believe she is really here with me. I glance at her shyly as we walk side by side. Now that she is with me, the jewel becomes less important, I can look at her instead of at the pendant. I suppose I ought to feel tired but I don't. She must be tired. During the long drive she slept, sometimes she leaned, as she slept, lightly against me. I wanted to protect her. I felt so much fondness for her. It seemed like a foretaste of even greater happiness when I had her asleep beside me in the car. Perhaps there really is no greater happiness than that secret joy of being beside someone you love while she is asleep. Perhaps this is really "the secret bliss the lover knows".

She is very thin still as she was on the ship and very white faced. Especially round the mouth she is pale. Her skin is drawn and grey, that greenish pallor I have seen in very sick people. Mostly I think it is unhappiness of some sort. Her fingers are white and thin, and during dinner she twisted her fingers together nervously. At the table it looked as if she never really rested. She needs to be cherished. How can I let her know how much I cherish her in my heart. How can I tell her that I am longing to really know her, for her to know me, that I want to take her in my arms and keep her safe. I want to kiss her and love her with all the tenderness I have stored up.

I want her to like my place. I wonder if she likes it here. Certainly it looks best this morning, everything is so fresh and pretty because she wanted to come with me. I am thinking of things to do for her to make her feel better.

"We'll walk a little further into the forest," I say to her. "If you're not too tired? There may be a few flowers, early ones." We are very shy together. I tell her about the different flowers, that will come later, the intense blue, the tiny white and yellow petals, exquisite as if they are enamelled, and the ones with fringed mauve edges and the pink tipped pale green sundews like little plates pressed into the gravel.

There is so much to show her and to talk about. But she must rest.

"What's this lovely smell?" she asks me. We stand still, close together, alone at the edge of the forest. There is a warm sweetness in the air.

"I think it's the promise of the acacias," I explain to her. "They'll be in full flower soon; it's the fragrance which comes before you really see the flowers. They're such fine trees on a property across the valley, quite massive, dark dark green and then masses of yellow flower. I suppose someone planted them years ago. The fragrance is very sweet isn't it."

She smiles at me, she has a quick shy smile.

"Every year," I say to her, "I forget about them and then they surprise me!" She laughs then. Oh she is sweet when she laughs!

We both laugh. She says the white gums, the thin ones, remind her of silver birches and I agree they give the same impression.

"We're like natural history teachers," she says laughing.

"Yes, I suppose we are." Because I can't talk of the things I want to talk about I tell her about the trees.

We walk back to the house. She must rest, I tell her.

It is strange that she is Eva's daughter. I can't understand how and why things happen as they do. It is a strange pattern of destiny. I am afraid to think back to other times to let unhappiness and disaster from what seems now another life come into the present time. I won't be afraid. I have taken leave of the past. It's gone forever.

* * *

Andrea

I am not sure what Laura will demand.

"We must look at the sun shining through the wet leaves," she said to me this morning. "We may never see the jarrah forest like this again." Does she mean that because of some experience we shall have together, or is it the rain she's so crazy about. I'll have to wait and see.

She took me round the weather-beaten sheds. It's all in a dilapidated state with little patches where she's tried to fix things. There are rotting tins and tubs of plants, rosemary and mint and other herbs, she has them on planks of wood resting on oil drums in tiers like an outdoor theatre only it's little bushes sitting there and not people. She took me up into the scrub where she has cleared the undergrowth, queer little intrusions into the wild growth, they hardly seem to be clearings, firebreaks she calls them. Then we walked down the slope.

"My vineyard," she said. "Tokay, Shiraz, Muscat, Grenache, Pedro and Frontignac, I'm afraid some of them are dead," she said. And then further down the slope, "My orchard," she said. "Cherry Plum, Satsuma, Plums President and Golden Drop. Star Crimson apple, blue lupin ryegrass and strawberry clover. Peach Elberta, Peach Hale Haven, apricots and nectarines. Just a small cultivation in a lot of land!" And she smiled at me. "These are the small changes a person on her own can make on the land!" We walked between the little fruit trees, Laura bent down to clear wet grass from some of them and, very neatly with her knife, she cut out bits. "Suckers," she explained, "should have cut them out before this!" Further down she paused. "More orchard down there. Packham Pears, Quince Champion, Winter Nelis and Josephine. All crops if they come," she said, "are certain crops! Some of these died, too much salt and clay. It's all very wet after so much rain. Let's go back to the house."

I have a big bare room in Laura's house.

"This is your room Andrea," she said as she took me indoors.

She seemed very pleased that I liked it. I sat down on the floor. She smiled down at me.

"Since I have so few chairs here," she said, "it's useful you are used to sitting as the Asians do." She went to the kitchen. I could hear her dropping things and moving things about. I suppose she is tired after so much driving. She made us coffee and burnt toast. Everything smells and tastes of kerosene.

"Sorry about the toast," she said. "I'm not used to having anyone to stay, perhaps I am nervous," and she laughed.

The house is not big but it seems spacious because it is so empty. Laura says she relies on the light and colour from outside to furnish her rooms.

"There's really nothing to see in the house," she says with a small shrug. But I do see all sorts of things. On the window sills are jugs and books, there is something made of copper by the fireplace, a big black kettle on the wood stove, books, more books and papers, some in handwriting, are everywhere. A good many of the books are medical, others are poetry and in several languages. There are brandy and claret bottles and books and gramophone records all over the floor of the room she calls her study. On the walls of this room are sketches in soft black pencil, anatomical, arms and legs and hands and repeatedly there is a horse's head, the head tossed high and the head down submissively. I can't help looking at all these interesting things, "Angry stallions and reluctant mares," Laura says as I examine the drawings. "I really must tidy up!" she says with her smile. "These are not just one week's bottles you understand, I was not expecting a guest. The thing about having a visitor is that I'll have to clean the house!"

Over her desk is a portrait. I asked her this morning who it was. "You don't mind my asking?" I said.

"Oh!" she said. "That's the poet Schiller. I liked his poetry when I was young. Of course I don't mind what you ask!"

"And these two photographs?"

"They are of my father and his brother, my uncle," she said. "They have been dead for some years."

This place is so different from Christopher's. I feel wonderfully high up in clear light air. Laura's verandahs are wide and from every window I can see grass and trees and sky. Christopher's house was such a prison to me. There was no air in it, only his carpet covered with fawn chrysanthemums in all the rooms and all the windows were low and flat. Already I feel so much better.

Laura sang in the car, in German and then, "Joy fairest spark divine" in English. "Daughter of Elysium. We approach with hearts aflame, O Goddess your sanctuary. It's Schiller, 'Ode to Joy'," she explained. "I don't realise I'm singing sometimes, I suppose it's a habit." She laughed. "One doesn't realise habits till someone else is there! And then they seem all too evident!"

The rain really came down but she drives very well; it seems as if she enjoys driving. "Sometimes it's tedious," she said, "But not tonight! I feel I could drive forever."

One of the things which she has always noticed, she said, was the repetitive stretches of the road, long curves in the road one after another. One exactly like another one; gentle rises in the road and then a bend and a steeper hill, one after the other exactly as it was some miles back and as it would be some miles further.

"Often," she said, "when I get to a place on this road I think I've already been through it." I couldn't really see what she meant.

"I don't really understand," I said.

"Oh it doesn't matter," she said softly. "The road is

lovely in places, especially when the late afternoon sun is shining through the trees and long shadows lie across the paddocks." And then she said it was a pity there was no moon. "Banks of cloud make it a very black night," she said. "Long stretches of the road go through the jarrah forest, you can feel it colder now we are in the forest." Because there was no moon we couldn't see the trees, only feel the cool dark presence of them on both sides of the road.

"You'll know the road one day," she said.

Most of her furniture is in her house in town but her other possessions are here. She showed me her record player. She loves music. I said I did too.

"I've two horses over at the stud farm," she explained. "We'll go riding when we've rested." I told her I'd like that. She smiled.

I suppose Laura must be about sixty. She doesn't look it. She has cupboards in the hall full of clothes which she does not wear at all here. I suppose Mother would call Laura elegant. I don't want to say the same things as Mother.

Laura looks lovely in her clothes. I wonder what her body is like without them. I suppose a person who has lived alone all her life would be very reserved; she would not be used to anyone being in her bathroom, and no one will ever have looked at her naked body. She will have a reserve which it might not be possible to break down. She is so many years older than I am. She may be shy about having me in the house and shy of being seen. I must not push in on her shyness.

I must not think, of the friendship between Mother and Laura and wonder why it went wrong. I can't even begin to imagine such a friendship ever existing. They must have been so very different.

I'm not going to think about Christopher either.

I will think about Laura, only about Laura. Laura says I must go to bed early as we haven't had any sleep. I suppose she is right, but I don't know if I'll be able to sleep. It's all so strange.

We have come a long way. We seemed to drive into

another world. All through the night Laura brought me to this place which is quite by itself. On the way, as we went through the townships, she told me "They are very small places, just a few houses and a shop, sometimes a school and a church on the main road. The people will be all asleep," she said. She has explained that, because of the way the road curves round, we actually passed the end of this long paddock some miles before we got here.

"From the road my long paddock looks lovely," she said. But, because it was dark, we couldn't see anything. She doesn't have a track through to the road because it would spoil the way the field lies between the edges of the forest. "It's so serene through there," she said. "You'll see it in the sunlight and you'll see for yourself what I mean. It's a long paddock, it flows back from the road curving back like a slow winding river bordered on both sides by the trees. When I come to it on the road, I know I am nearly home. It's always called the long paddock."

I want to ask Laura to help me. I don't know how to ask her.

Laura is outside again. It's still raining.

In my room is a big old-fashioned bed piled up with pillows. There is a cupboard and a table. There are a few painted chairs on the verandah. Laura threw an orange rug on the floorboards.

"I'm sorry it's all so plain," she said.

"I like it Laura, really I do."

Just now, as I said, she is outside by the fence talking to a woman in a green coat. The woman walks like a drake. She must be the woman from the terrible little house across the back-yard. I suppose they are the only other people here and they work for Laura.

I must be careful with myself, and I must be careful with Laura. This is the only place I've got at present and I need to be somewhere. I'd like to say goodbye to my life, to the part that I've already had. I'd like to think it had gone forever.

* * *

Laura

"The fruit when it comes is yellow, shaped like plums with four brown seeds, shining like beads inside." I am trying to tell Andrea what loquats are like. "They are fragrant and sharp and warm and sweet and the birds love them. Outside your window is one of the trees so you'll have all the birds there to disturb you later on!"

We have been listening to Beethoven. The Ninth Symphony, by the fire. I love to listen to music with her. I knew I would like this very much. When I listen to Beethoven I am included in a kind of harmony which is comforting and sustaining, and to share this harmony with her is something I could have wished for, even hoped for, but never expected.

She seems to really share the music with me. She is not in the least like Eva. I don't want to be reminded of Eva, I won't think of Eva. I have not thought about her in the way I once did for years.

We are very tranquil together. Her palomino colouring and her quiet way of sitting is part of this tranquility. We are both very tired but seem elated with being together. We are waiting to know each other. I think we are both waiting for the same thing. I hope she will not mind that I love her. I talk of other things because I must be sure of her before I talk to her of love. I must be quite sure that there will be no shock, no soothing to be done, I mustn't be clumsy with her. It must not be like that. I want our love together to be perfect.

When the right time comes I want to buy her a Palomino horse. She loves horses, she says so. She will love the Palomino, it will be her sort of horse, the same creamy gold colouring. When she is better her hair will brighten and her face will have the radiance she lacks now. I will look after her so that she will glow with health and with happiness.

Tonight I cooked and she helped me. We prepared the vegetables together. There were so many things to laugh about; things like looking round for old boxes to burn up so that we could get enough hot water. Both of us needed hot baths. We ate the meal, meat and vegetables, sitting on the floor by the fire here in my study.

Because of waiting to know each other, a kind of reserve exists between us. We talked at random, nonsense mostly.

"That portrait over your desk does look like you Laura," she said. "You know I wondered why you would sit looking at a drawing of yourself all day!"

"I assure you I don't sit here all day and I assure you Andrea," how I loved to say her name! "and I assure you, Andrea, it is the poet Schiller and not me. You can see it is a young man. If it was me it would have been years and years ago, in any case. I used to admire Schiller very much."

"How can I see it's a man, it's only a face!"

"Andrea!"

"The interesting thing is the face could be either a man's or a woman's."

"Yes," I agreed with her at once, "D'you see, even the shape of the head, the line of the brow, of the mouth and the gentle turn of the strong young neck . . ." I stopped quickly. I was afraid of being too serious in what was essentially an amusing conversation.

"Go on," she said.

"That's all," I said. And the shy reserve was between us again. How wonderful to have her here with me. Her presence alters the whole house. It is like the first cautious phrases of a Beethoven symphony, the Fourth perhaps, or the Ninth. I hope this cautious movement lasts and goes forward as it must surely do, nothing ever stays the same, with the same grace and harmony and pleasure as the symphony does. I hope she will always want to be here with me. There are so many things I want to say to her. They are things which cannot be said, so instead I have been telling her things about the country, about the waywardness of the stream and the islands in the creek bed and the birds, the doves and the magpies which are the only companions one can have at times. I don't suppose she really understands how lonely it is out here.

She is so pleased. She is like a child. She is a child and

yet is not one. I can't begin to understand. I can't understand how and why she is here with me. When I see the green jewel on her throat I feel it isn't true and I am just seeing the pendant worn on her neck as she walks by me. But I could reach out now and touch the jewel we are so close. But I don't do this.

Gradually I will let her know, very slowly. I will let her see how much I love her. It does not make any difference that I am so much older, that she is Eva's daughter.

Who was it who wrote, "the lover is nearer the divine than the beloved"? Once again I think of "the secret bliss the lover knows". I am the one who loves, deeply I love, and in secret.

At that dinner party I couldn't believe I was hearing properly when she said she wanted to come to me. I was afraid I was only hearing something I wanted to hear. If we had not left at once, in urgency, it might never have come about. Sometimes that is the only way things can happen.

I had to leave at once and take her and drive off into the night. We didn't even stop for clothes. She has on a gown of mine while her things, which she washed, are drying by the kitchen stove.

Really I ought to suggest she goes to bed but I am putting off leaving her for the night. Tomorrow, it is a wonderful thought, we have tomorrow, it is Sunday and after that another Sunday. We have all the tomorrows for each other and we can listen to Beethoven as often as we like. I am too elated to sleep, I ought to allow her to go to bed even if I can't sleep.

She sits on the floor in stillness. "You can sit so still," I say to her and she smiles without turning her head.

"Your hair looks wet, perhaps you shouldn't lie down while it's wet." It's as if I think of reasons for putting off the parting. Neither of us moves to go to bed but neither of us suggests we stay together. Her damp hair makes her head look small and round and very vulnerable.

Suddenly there is a knock on my study window.

"Who can it be!" She is frightened.

"Oh! It's Murphy. Whatever can he want at this time of night!" I push open the window, he's out there in the blackness.

"It's Mrs. Murphy she's very sick. Can you come? Can you come and look at her please. I'm sorry to trouble you, I'm really very sorry but I'm worried about her. She's crook."

So this is it. I must go with Murphy.

"You go to bed," I say to her. "The fire will be quite safe."

"Let me help you Laura," she says. "I'll come with you."

"No Andrea, you must go to sleep, it'll be all right. I really do insist you go to bed. Please do." Somehow it is characteristic of the Murphys that they need me just now, tonight. Now. I put the guard by the fire.

I go with Murphy. It's dark and cold and wet. He leads the way. His back is thin and bent, huddled forward. "I have pigs coming," I tell him. "For both of us," I want to make him feel better. I want him to think about the pigs. I don't want to be questioned about my guest. If I can make him feel better perhaps I can get back home quickly. Even when she is asleep I want to be back there, all the more so. But Murphy does not seem able to listen to me.

"I'm always good to the Abos, Laura," he says to me. He never calls me Laura. I realise he has been drinking and this is unusual too. "Always take me hat off and say G'day to an Abo, Laura, and Laura I always say it first." His voice is furry and thick, he doesn't sound like himself at all.

"Yes of course," I say to him gently because his behaviour is unpredictable and I am afraid. He is quiet for a few steps and then he says again

"I'm always good to the Abos, Laura," repeating himself.

"We don't have any Aboriginals round here Murphy so why explain all this to me, we don't ever see any here."

We are at the fence and he holds up the wire for me to

go through. He is not listening to anything I'm trying to say.

The house is badly lit and cold and filthy with dogs and kittens. The little girls are all there in the kitchen and the baby is crying. The place smells of urine.

Murphy swings a fist at the eldest girl. "See to yer brother," he growls at her. With a careworn look she picks him out of the cot and swaying her thin body to and fro she holds him against her chest.

Mrs. Murphy is on the big bed with all the covers from the rest of the house piled on her. She opens her eyes and the spikes of curiosity poke out even though she is so sick.

"Silly old me!" she whispers, her lips are cracked and swollen. "Silly old me when you've got a visitor? Fine thing me going sick when you got someone staying?" The remarks come out as questions. She is unable to quench her thirst, she keeps asking for water. I give her some and she drinks and drinks as if she is burning up inside, and while she burns she shivers. I try and listen to Murphy's account.

"The doctor says her kidneys is all shrivelled up into knots, doctor tells her today and then when we come home she gets down under the covers crook like this."

"It must be an infection," I say to Murphy. "She's got a virus or something like it," he seems unable to listen to me. "We must keep her warm," I say.

"It's her kidneys, can't you give her summat? Can't you give her summat to ease her?" he asks me.

I don't know what to do about her and I don't know how to tell him. It's intolerable in this house with the sick woman and the demented man and all these children. I must get back home. It's no use to tell Murphy I haven't had any sleep. I control my impatience.

"Help me get her into the utility," I say to Murphy. "We'll wrap her up and take her to Queens Meadows to the hospital. We'll have to get her there quickly, as quickly as we can."

"Can't you give her anything, Doctor?" he begs.

"No, I can't," I say. "I don't know what's wrong." It's

no use to try to explain to Murphy. Mrs. Murphy is complaining of terrible pain in her head and down the back of her neck.

I have never been afraid of illness however infectious or dangerous it might be. I simply never think about it. Yet here with Mrs. Murphy I feel contaminated and I feel afraid and I don't know why this should be. And then all at once I know it is because of something evil. Mrs. Murphy is wanting harm for me, she is hostile; it is her hostility I am afraid of, not the illness.

I want to go home. I think of Andrea and our evening and it seems to belong to another world. Whatever can I do here. Whatever I do will be unsatisfactory and wrong. I will do the least thing possible. It is midnight.

"Come along," I say to Murphy and together we half lift and half drag Mrs. Murphy out to the car. It's only eight miles to Queens Meadows. I don't want to go but I can see Murphy can't be responsible, he might run off the road in the state he's in.

I tell the children to go to bed and that everything will be all right and, with Murphy drunkenly supporting Mrs. Murphy, I start off slowly along the back track to get on to the road to Queens Meadows and the safety of the little hospital there.

* * *

Andrea

The roosters were crowing when Laura left my bed. It was already light. I felt her leave and I saw the pale ceiling and I let her go and I slept again. I didn't wake up till just now, it is the middle of the day.

Laura has gone off somewhere. I called all over the house but she isn't anywhere, only her watch on a leather strap is on the chair beside the bed. She has left her watch here with me.

Laura wept in the night. I could feel the tears on her face after it was over. I wanted to tell her not to cry but I was too tired to speak. Perhaps it's best that she cried. I think it was the first time for her. Perhaps it's best that she's not here just now as I must sort out the terrible muddled thoughts in my head. I couldn't tell her how I feel just now. It's so stupid! She's so kind and gentle and she loves me and here I am crying on this big comfortable bed because I have been unfaithful to my brother! How can a sister be unfaithful to her brother? No faithfulness of this sort exists. How can I get free from this and give myself up to loving Laura. What would Laura say if I asked her about it. She would say "Love the person you love and let that person love you".

I never thought it would happen like this. I never thought we should be so close so soon, and I mean really close, together in this bed, but it's like Laura taking me away from the dinner party so quickly and driving all through the rest of the night to this place just because I said I wanted to. "I want to go tonight," I said to her across the polished dinner table. I said it straight into her candlelight eyes.

I must try to straighten out my thoughts. I won't compare it with what I have with Christopher. There is no way of making comparisons. If I'm not yawning and relaxed this morning it's not Laura's fault, I wanted to experience her experience. I couldn't explain that to her just now, that I urged her to give herself up completely, which she did. Her perfume haunts me, it makes me want her again, I want us to lose ourselves again in that same urgency. This time I want it for me too. Oh Laura I do want it again!

I must have gone off to sleep as soon as Laura went to the Murphys. I was so tired. And then I heard her come home. I heard the dogs start up. And then the headlamps of the car swept like a searchlight round this bare room. It gave me a shock, I was startled out of a deep sleep but the next thing was Laura's voice saying, "Andrea! it's only me. Are you awake Andrea, it's only me, Laura, don't be afraid."

"I don't know where the lamp is," I called out to her. "What time is it? You must be frozen!" I started to get up.

"It's about half past two," she said coming into the bedroom. "Don't worry about the lamp. I know my way round the house. I expect you were asleep and I've disturbed you!" she came to the side of the bed. I felt her hands, they were so cold. She was shivering, really shaking with the cold.

"How is Mrs. Murphy?" I asked; a terrible yawn came with the question. "Oh I'm sorry!" We laughed.

"I've taken her to the hospital," Laura said. She sat on the edge of the bed. "She's very ill, it was the only thing to do."

"Oh Laura," I said, "you must be so cold and tired." I moved over in the bed. "Come into bed, it's lovely and warm, come on." She hesitated. "I'll make room for you," I said.

"Shall I really?" she asked. "Can I really come into the bed? Just for a minute then." She undressed herself quickly in the dark. "I'll just get my gown," she said and very quickly she got into bed. "You know Andrea," she said, "It's awful really it is, Murphy fell asleep in the utility on the way home and I can't rouse him. He's out there asleep in the car. I've covered him with sacks."

"Oh poor Laura," I said, "Come on quick under the covers, here, you'll soon be warm. I expect Murphy's all right, there's supposed to be a special providence that looks after drunks and little children," we laughed again.

"He isn't a drunk really," Laura said and then she said, "Oh God! My back! I'm really frozen stiff and my back aches!"

"Poor dear Laura!" I really felt sorry for her. "Let me rub your back, lie down and turn over. Don't be shy! Come on, I'll make you feel better." Her smooth back under her gown was cold to my warm hands.

"Oh Andrea," she sighed so deeply, "it is nice of you to make me comfortable. That is good. Thank you! Sometimes I get this cold aching back!" she sighed again. "You know," she said, "I feel awful disturbing you, you must be tired. You are making me so very comfortable!"

I liked massaging Laura's back and I let my hands wander up and down and around the sides of her body and I wanted to go on for ever just stroking her.

"It's all very upsetting, Mrs. Murphy's really ill," she said after a few minutes. "Murphy never drinks heavily and he's not himself. I always feel she hates me! And I've left him asleep out in the cold!" Her sigh was deep.

"Forget them," I said to her. "He'll be all right, he'll get up and go into his house when he wakes up, and no one could hate you Laura! Forget them! Just rest and feel warm. Are you warmer now?"

"Oh yes thank you Andrea! I'm not used to such care!" her voice was very low.

"You spoke so softly Laura I didn't hear what you said." I bent over her to speak to her. She turned her head towards me.

"Andrea, dearest!" she said. "I said I'm not used to such care. It's more than care, it's very sweet. I'm not used to caresses like these."

"Laura," I said, "I love stroking your back," and this time I gave her a tiny kiss on her brow and let my hands go gently all over her, gently I drew her towards me and she turned. "Shall I go on?" I asked her softly. She sighed again and then she said,

"Andrea I think I ought to go. I think I should go till this has passed. I really think I ought to."

"Stay," I whispered.

"I'm afraid to stay," she said. "Really I must go!"

"How can you go now Laura," I whispered teasing her. "We are so close." I held her. "Love me," I whispered to her, "like I'm loving you. You can't go! Love me!"

"Andrea," she said. "I want to more than anything I have ever wanted. Are you sure you want me? Are you sure?"

"Yes Laura," I said, "Put your hands on me, kiss me. Kiss me. Of course I want you. How can you talk of leaving," I held her closer.

"Are my hands warm enough now to touch you?" she asked.

"Of course they are," I said.

"I want you," she whispered. "All of you. Now."

Her face was wet with her tears and we laughed because our hearts were beating so close to one another.

"Oh Andrea," she said. "I might have dreamed of this but I never expected it. Andrea, you are so dear to me. Is it the same for you? Is it?"

"Of course it is," I said.

There was no need for words.

There is no way of making comparisons. It's all so very different.

I can't help wondering where Laura is. I am very lonely here without her. Perhaps she has gone off because she is afraid to see me, afraid the whole thing is ridiculous. It is rather! But then so much of life is ridiculous really.

In the night Laura's heart was beating so hard. She said she could feel my heart beating. I don't suppose she has been so close to another person's heart before. She said she was used to listening to hearts and feeling them but she was not used, she said, to being part of another person's heart beating.

"It's as if our two hearts are beating like one," she said softly in the night. "It's right for hearts to go on and on!"

Just now I would do anything in the world for her. I have never felt like this about anyone before except Christopher, and now I realise that what I felt for him is not the same. It is part of this strange unfaithfulness. If he came into this room I would be embarrassed to see him here; I never felt like this before about him. I don't need to feel this. Christopher never wept because he loved me, he never wept for me or for himself. Feeling unfaithful to Christopher is stupid and quite unnecessary.

Will I be able to ask Laura about it?

I hope she is all right this morning. Of course it is quite natural that she has gone off somewhere. This is her place, her work is here, she has things she must do. She is probably out there somewhere telling that Mr. Murphy what has to be done. Perhaps she has gone to the hospital to see about Mrs. Murphy.

The leather watch strap smells of Laura's spiced perfume. When I hold the watch its elegance attracts me and I breathe in that fragrance which is hers and I miss her. This is loneliness. I can't be alone just now. It is so quiet here. All round the house are the yards and paddocks and the empty paddocks reach far out towards the jarrah forest which goes on for miles beyond the edges I can see. It seems no-one is here at all except me. I'm not frightened, it's just that I'm alone.

I don't think I'm frightened of Laura. I suddenly know her so intimately and at the same time don't know her at all.

How will it be when we meet after what happened in the night? Will it happen again? Will she hold me again as she held me in the night? Will that tender passion be there again?

They say women bruise each other when they love. I am not bruised, she is gentle. She told me she loved me. How do I tell her I want to love her. In the night I was too sleepy, perhaps I should have said more to her.

This must really be her bed and her room as I can't find another bedroom properly furnished. She has made up a bed on the couch in her study but of course she did not sleep on it. She gave me the bedroom and the comfortable bed, that is the kind of person she is.

I will go out and look for her in all the wild places round this house.

* * *

Laura

It's such a private thing.

All night the moonlight lay along the leaves of the loquat just outside the window and, where the curtains hang, restless leaf shadows trembled as a small soft wind stirred among the vines. I'll never forget this night.

I have walked right across the valley. It is like the shared music, a perfection of harmony and rhythm. I keep feeling the perfection and I seem full of the music, the Beethoven, the harmony and movement fit so closely to this private cherishing. I am singing to myself and have walked quite a long way. The morning is cold and clear and I have come across to the Tolstoy country, right up to the paddocks fenced with round poles for the horses. This is the stud farm where I shall bring her to choose a palomino horse. We shall be able to ride together. I am looking forward to this. Riding fits the rhythm too. I never thought I should know such strange perfection. She is so young and so lovely. I do want to talk to her about it. It may be something we can't speak about. I'll have to wait and see.

I can't help wondering how she is this morning.

Somehow it's like this.

Years ago I walked with my Father in the mist on the hills in Scotland. Suddenly in a parting in the wet grass we came upon a lark's nest with four eggs. It was a secret perfection. I felt the joy of the discovery for a long time and now I have the same quiet joy of another sort of discovery. I can't really believe that it all really happened. I love her so much.

I loved the larks in Scotland. There are no larks here, there is a bird with a gentle tiny climbing song a bit like a lark, it sings during the hot weather. If I could hear a lark I know it would not really be the same as this bird. Till just now I had not remembered the lark's nest. Now all sorts of forgotten treasures come back into my mind, the low flight of cormorants over the sea, I used to like to see them, and dolphins diving in pairs and swimming over and through the waves, loving her reminds me of all these things I used to be pleased to see.

In this quiet place where my land borders on the stud property I can stop and think and dream in perfect seclusion. Everything happened last night as it did in my reading and studying but I have never read or studied anything about myself. My thoughts won't stay in any kind of order. I am not in the least calm, the calm following this love-making does not seem at all evident; rather I am excited and happy and a little sad at the same time. And I want it all over again.

I wonder if she is still asleep. When I left she was asleep like a child curled up under the covers. She is only a child compared with me. That makes me all the more grateful. I am quite overcome with the sweetness of all that took place. Sometimes I am not sure that we really did caress each other so intimately, it is as if she belongs to some secret night in some other place. And yet I have a small proof, on my left breast is a tiny bruise, it might even be a very small bite.

I am not far from the house though it takes quite a time to walk down through my vineyard and orchard and up this side of the valley.

The palomino horses are lovely to watch. They are running together in their paddock. They are slender legged, short coupled horses. They are light tan or cream-coloured creatures with cream or white tails and manes, and they shine, well-groomed, golden smooth and well-fed. I am impatient. I want to give her the present at once.

From here I can see the verandahs of my house. She is there leaning on the rail in her green Indian dress with the yellow pattern. She is looking for me and can't see me though I can see her quite plainly. We are not within calling distance. She has not the slightest idea where I am. If I start back down the slope, away from these trees, she will see me.

She has seen me and we are hurrying towards each other, I think she is hurrying as I am. I don't think I have ever felt so happy before. Suddenly there is so much meaning in everything. The magpies are swooping and pouring their voices into the morning and I can hear the sheep and cattle from far away along the valley, but mostly I hear the hard beating of my heart. How lightly she walks. It is not as it was on the ship, where we walked and went by each other. Now we shall meet and look into each other's eyes and speak. I can't believe it, it must be some strange unreal dream. I am afraid to meet her because all of it may never have happened.

* * *

Andrea

Laura works like a man on her land. There are certain things which she says have to be done before the summer comes. She rakes and clears by the swollen stream. If there is a dead sapling she snaps it off and hacks out the stump. She has a chain of fires and she spreads the hot sticks and ash over the grass to burn it off. She works with the whole of her body and I see her shirt wet on her back and afterwards she is white-faced and exhausted and cold. It's clear she can't bear to be interrupted when she's working. I have seen her listening to the Murphys, trying to hide her impatience, especially if their troubles interfere with her machinery. She is obsessed with the small plough and the chain saw and spends a lot of time attending to them. A kind of fury gets into her when something goes wrong and she can't get the engine of the plough to start. She cherishes the machinery. I suppose it is because she needs its strength and I think she knows this. She loves her land and working on it is really her life, she told me this.

When she comes in she takes off her great boots and socks and her feet are strangely slender and clean in spite of the work she has been doing. She burns up an old box and makes herself a bath full of hot water and afterwards she is so tired, sometimes she falls asleep by the fire.

I thought she would make demands but I was wrong. Since the first night we were here she has not come at all to the bed where I sleep. Once or twice I thought she was coming, but she stayed on the verandah leaning over the rail high up in the dark as if listening to rushing water and persistent noise of the frogs. I don't know what time she goes to bed herself but she is always dressed and out with Mr. Murphy early in the morning. They are busy fencing part of the long paddock with round poles. Laura says she wants to buy me a horse! When I said to her I couldn't let her do anything of the sort she said she had two horses of her own, they are at the stud on the other side of the valley. She keeps them there. We can see the horses running together in their neat paddocks over there, glimpses of them as they cross the open space beyond the trees on Laura's land. And when I said I hadn't clothes to wear for riding she said she would love to get them for me. She said we'd drive to town to get them.

"You would look so nice in them Andrea," she says to me. And then she said that she wanted to ride with me. Riding alone was one thing but the rhythm of riding when two riders were involved was a different thing. This is what she wants.

"It's like listening to music with someone, waiting with that other person for certain moments of harmony is exquisite," she says to me. I told her I knew what she meant. I think I know.

"Oh Andrea!" she says quite suddenly. "It is so strange and lovely that you are here with me. My whole life seems entirely different. Can you understand?" She talks to me by the fire after supper, she plays a record, something she loves.

"I find this wonderful," she says to me, "I must talk about it. I hope you don't mind if I talk!" She stretches herself on the couch and puts her arms up behind her head and when she does this, her breasts lift up and though they are not big she seems suddenly powerful and strong. "Don't move," she says to me. "I love to watch the way you sit, you sit so still, not a movement, it's restrained; there's something very powerful in restraint though I must say I haven't been very restrained since you came," she looks across at me.

"I was thinking of power too," I say. "Yours!" And we laugh. I sit still and she goes on talking.

"It's wonderful, do you see, quite often in a relationship, I'm afraid to use that word! you understand; one of the two people is a commonplace sort of person, but with us this is not so, we are both very special!"

We are drinking coffee. Laura always has brandy in her coffee which she has very strong and black, even in the mornings. She made me try it and really it is very good. She says the fragrance of the coffee and the brandy really go into her and she needs it; she has two heaped spoons of sugar and says she needs this too.

"I can't wait to see you in the riding clothes," she says after a little silence and she leans over and I think she is going to kiss me but she doesn't though we are close enough. She talks instead about what she calls erotic harmony in music. "It's the same on horseback, the rhythm I mean, I'll give you a little lecture on my theories one day," she says and we laugh again. It is very peaceful talking quietly and laughing together. I think Laura is a very clever woman. She is very good to me. I have never in my life ever been really loved by anyone, I can feel that Laura loves me.

This evening though when I know I should be really happy here being cherished and looked after I am not happy. Perhaps I want Laura to kiss me and to take me up in her arms and make love to me and make me forget the thing which worries me so much. She doesn't come to the bed. She sleeps on this couch in her study with the fire scattered on the hearth and all our cups and glasses and gramophone records just left around the room. Sometimes she tidies up, sometimes she writes, but mostly she rests and talks and we have the music.

All day I am alone because she is busy. I go outside but it is a wet winter and the work is not my sort of work. I ought to help her I suppose as there seems a lot she needs to get done.

This evening we say goodnight to each other. "Sleep well," she says to me and I linger picking up the cups. "Oh leave those till tomorrow," she yawns and stretches and I really want her. "I'm so terribly tired!" she says. So I go off to the big bed in the room which is mine.

Now in the night I feel lonely and I want to go and wake her and ask her to help me. I would like to tell her everything. I wonder if I should. There is something she doesn't know about me. The trouble is that if she doesn't understand she might be hurt and think I am just making use of her and her place, and if she is hurt she might change towards me and might not want me here and I need to be somewhere. I really have no place to go to. She is so good to me, always thinking of things to please me. I don't want to hurt her.

God! I must talk to her! I don't want to wake her, she is tired but if I can't stop crying she'll hear me! Oh God! Oh

Christopher! Why oh why has everything turned out the way it has! I'll go to her.

In Laura's study there is still some light from the dying fire. She is asleep on her couch. She must have been too tired to undress. I can make out her face from the doorway. The shadows from the firelight strengthen her features and as I see her sleeping it is as if she grows older; age fleetingly passes over her cheek and brow and seems to stay. Without her eyes looking at me this is what she would be like in death and she will die long before I do. I am afraid to be here alone as she lived here alone. I am afraid. I am afraid of being alone.

"Laura, I'm afraid!"

* * *

Laura

I ought to be working but I'm dreaming instead. It is an unbearable sweetness, agony almost, a mixture of these together with concern and respect. It is the ultimate in discipline and love. My heart and my body ache as if I were a young woman again. "Why do I care so much?" she asked me in the night. "Because," I replied; but I couldn't say why. There are so many reasons and there are no reasons. Why did I see her as someone apart on the ship? How did she know that I saw her in this way so that she responds? Who can answer this sort of question? I don't want any answer I told her when I held her cradled gently in my arms in that unspeakable tenderness which came just as the sky was beginning to lighten outside the window.

Last night I was so tired I must have fallen asleep quickly on top of my bedclothes, still dressed. I have done this often during the last few years. Then I heard her crying in the dark, I woke to hear her sobbing. She had come in to me.

"Andrea!" I called out to her. "What's wrong? Were you dreaming? It's me, Laura. Don't be afraid. Why are you crying?" My voice must have sounded rough, I was half asleep.

"Oh Laura!" she cried aloud and came over to the

90

couch sobbing like a child sobs alone in the night. "I didn't want to wake you up," she said, "but I couldn't help it and I'm sorry to disturb your sleep, your back will ache if you don't sleep."

I got up at once and took her in my arms. I was afraid I'd hurt her in some way, perhaps by something I'd said.

"What's wrong Andrea, come and tell me what's the matter. My back will be all right!" I took her close to me to warm her, and she spoke so fast.

"Oh Laura if only you knew how horribly mixed up I am. I can't sleep. What can I do! I can't bear it! How ever can I tell you. I'm so mixed up!"

I had to make an effort to wake up properly to talk to her. "Andrea stop crying," I said. "Listen to me! Being mixed up depends on what you're measuring yourself against." I tried to explain to her the things I had discovered years ago when I felt I had in some way to measure myself against the standards of the conventional married couples I knew.

"If you're trying to be like the kind of people you can't be like you're making a mistake, d'you see Andrea? The people you've just been with I don't think are really your sort, and if you compromise yourself in order to fit in it doesn't always work." I tried to calm her, I told her that I thought that the kind of lives some people had would not be enough for her. "D'you see Andrea there's something terribly depressing about some marriages. You know what I mean, the lives people have together year after year with nothing between them except money arrangements, the education of their children, lots of clean clothes and showers and big meals and conventional good behaviour with other married couples." She nodded and let me wipe away her tears. How could I tell her I loved her? It might seem like selfishness to talk about myself when she needed comforting. "All this dull terrible way of living seems quite enough for most people but for others it simply is not the right way for them. Mostly they are trapped before they realise it. Oh dear!" I said, "what a lot I talk!"

"Dear Laura," she said to me, "you're right, I know,

Eva is ashamed really that I am thirty, that I'm not pretty and have no husband and no prospect of being married. But how can I tell you! It's more than that. I get so depressed and feel so hopeless and futile. I feel I can't live the kind of life I'm supposed to live but it's more than that, I can't tell you. Oh Laura!"

"Poor dear Andrea!" I wanted to comfort her so much. I longed to clear away all the sadness she felt. "Dearest Andrea," I said. "Please don't be so upset; let me try and help you. You must believe me, you will feel better. Remember, you have been ill and when you are really better everything will seem easier. Later on, when you are better, we'll invite them all out for the day, up here, and then you'll see for yourself, you'll get things into proportion. You'll really understand that you can't measure yourself by their ways when you see them here."

"Them? Who? Who do you mean Laura?" she asked.

"Rodney Glass and his wife and the Forts. I usually have them up for one day before the hot weather comes, while the flowers are still out. You won't mind? You'll see what I mean. It will help you to sort yourself out, I'm sure of it!" How could I explain to her what I thought I already knew about her, I tried to say things without hurting her. I longed really to stop talking and just to take her and nourish her with love, kiss away her troubles and stroke her lovely young body with my hands.

"Just one day out for them," I said. "And then when they've gone we can forget all about them again. I always forget them between visits. We don't need to measure ourselves against them. You don't need to be mixed up. Let's forget them for now. Sometimes it's best to dismiss things, forget them till it's easier to think them out. It's a kind of personal discipline."

"You had to forget once?" she asked quietly. "You had to forget?"

"Yes," I said. "I had to forget Eva and Jake once. I have forgotten! It belongs to a time which has gone for ever. I'll tell you about it, but not just now." I felt I couldn't talk about it to her then.

"Oh Laura, I'm sorry. I didn't mean to be curious."
She began to weep again, "It's because I'm depressed,"
she said. "Do you ever get depressed?"

"Dear Andrea! Don't cry, please don't cry. Of course I
get depressed. Everyone does. This kind of melancholy,
yes I've had it, perhaps it follows naturally after certain
things. It's like the melancholy of the earth, sadness
and relief, after a fierce storm." I slowly stroked her soft
hair, gently parting it away from her face.

"You haven't forgotten then?" she asked.

"No of course I haven't, how could I forget. I think
about it all the time. Dear Andrea," I said, tenderness
for her nearly taking away my words, "How could I
forget something so precious!" And then she said something so sweet,

"Laura I want you to love me again." She unfastened
the buckle of my belt.

"And I want to love you so much," I took her close in
my arms and we kissed each other, a long deep kiss.

"I'll take you back to bed," I said.

We stood together beside the big bed.

"Do you think you can forget troubles for tonight," I
asked her.

"I want to forget everything except you," she said. She
was shivering.

"I will warm you," I told her, I was shivering too.

"Come into bed Laura," she whispered, "Come close to
me. Oh Laura let's forget everything except this."

"Can you?" I asked, I wanted her so dearly. "Can you
forget?"

She lay in my arms and showed me with her hands
where she wanted my hands.

"Oh Laura!" she called to me and I replied with her
name.

She slept then in my arms, her thin cheek and some
strands of her soft hair in the breathing space between
us. Gently I kissed her while she slept, I rested with my
lips against her hair. Small and asleep at last.

Somewhere I read that people never love other
people, they only love themselves through others. I

don't think I believe it. I believe I do love her. I suppose in loving someone it is possible to discover oneself, perhaps it is the only way for the discovery of quality in another person.

I never expected it could be like this. She is my dearest dearest child! She is only a child. I must see no harm ever comes to her. I want to protect her, to give her things and I want to see her happiness. How ardent she is. She is a passionate little creature, she gives her whole self in love. She wanted to please me and she wanted to be pleased herself.

Surely there can be no laws about love. Love like this cannot be a mixed up thing. It is so right. I am grateful for this, so grateful. When she called out my name "Laura" during those moments I was grateful and it is this gratitude which spreads quietly through me now and comforts with the glow of satisfied desire.

* * *

Andrea

"Screwdriver!" Laura shouted this morning. "Screwdriver!" and she hunted in the drawer she has in the kitchen, she tipped everything out, nails and everything, all on the floor. She was really mad because she couldn't find the screwdriver. In the end she found it in the knife and fork drawer and went off out quickly not even stopping to clear up all the mess she'd made. She gets angry quickly over things like this and forgets just as quickly and I suppose living alone as she has done for such a long time it doesn't matter if she leaves a mess like this morning. Sometimes she notices that I have tidied up and is very sorry and other times it's as if I'm not here at all.

Everything smells of kerosene.

This is a house of long silences with the quiet moods of living and working alone, forgetfulness, haphazard meals and hours passing without anyone near and without words. Sometimes the whole day passes and there is no voice or human sound of any sort. It's terribly lonely. The days go by slowly. There are no shops and so there is nowhere to go. I am used to being very busy, to being among people in London and in Ceylon and in the house in Kingston Road. Christopher's house is in a suburb where people are hurrying to and fro and the shopping centre is crowded all day. Oh Christopher's house! I suppose it's because I miss him or miss the person he used to be. But how can I miss him when I'm with someone like Laura. I felt imprisoned in his house and yet I was happy when I heard his key turn in the lock when he came home even though he looked for the Meringue Pie when he came in and not for me. That's what I ought to remember, that loneliness. How can I talk to Laura about Christopher. I wish I could tell her, if I could talk to her perhaps it would all come right somehow. But I can't.

I've been watching her from the window of this big bare room. It's wild weather outside, cold and wet. Too wet she says. It's cold in here. She doesn't feel the cold till she stops working and then she comes in and makes a big fire. I like it when she pulls off her boots, it's almost a ceremony and if I unfasten her belt, she pulls it off, coils it on the table and waits for me to kiss her, and then she kisses me. She makes the house comfortable when she comes inside. She is a woman of the privileged and sensitive sort, privileged because she is not bound to any sort of drudgery and so is able to do the work she wants to do and is able to further her talents. I wonder what she was like as a doctor. She can never be a doctor again. I wonder if the life she has now can make up for the one she did have once. A woman like Laura demands life on her own terms, but her own terms limit the kind of life she can have. Though I know she must have limits I am not sure what they are. Perhaps I am afraid her understanding may have quite reasonable limits. No understanding goes beyond all limits.

I can see her on the far horizon, a lonely figure in the rain right over by the sky ploughing a ridge of this land which seems so very important to her. I could be there with her but I am not. It is my choice. Last night she suggested I cook something, so some of this long day I have been preparing vegetables and trying not to think.

I want to talk to Laura. I want to be happy with her. She is good to me. She smiles when she comes in and takes off her boots and notices that I have washed the kitchen floor. When I washed her clothes she was embarrassed and said I wasn't to do those things for her. She was used to doing them for herself.

The plough keeps on stopping and I can see Laura bending over it. She looks thick-set in her working clothes. She takes her land very seriously, it is everything to her, she says so; it pleases her to try to produce something from her land. She is trying to work faster than the season.

"Can't Mr Murphy do the work," I asked her one morning but she just said that Mrs. Murphy was ill again and in any case Murphy's way of doing things was not her way. Sometimes Laura does not speak for hours, she is used to being alone and just goes about what she has to do. And then she suddenly remembers and is sorry because she has neglected me and she gives me fruit and cheese and wine and tells me things. She explains how she is trying to get up the long grass, the wild oats and the cape weed and put it all round her fruit trees while it is still wet so that the roots will be kept moist for longer. She loves the summer but dreads the heat of it because of her young fruit trees. She is always out before I wake up in the mornings. I suppose I ought to help her; I think I could get interested if I was free in my mind.

This room is stern like Laura's nature. There are saddles and harness and bridles heaped below the unwashed windows, and calico bags of seed litter the table. And, as her stern nature can suddenly become very tender and full of understanding, this room changes too when she comes back into it. She can, when she chooses, bring anything to life, a house, a person, some music, a book, even a piece of cheese! This room is suddenly soft and comfortable with the harmony she brings with her after her work.

"Where's the kero?" she asks when she comes in from

work. "Kero! our 'life blood'!" She often lights the lamps early. It's all kerosene, lamps and stove even the refrigerator. Fortunately the smell of kero does not make me feel sick!

It's stupid that I miss Christopher so much. He always made me laugh but of course not when Margie Meringue Pie was around, really I should remember that if I was back at the house in Kingston Road it would be intolerable there. Being with them is not at all what I want and I can't spend my life with Christopher alone. I do think of him such a lot; it's not the immediate thing I miss, that's how Laura would say it, it's something from before, before I went to Ceylon, like the times I always got his breakfasts. I should never have come back from Ceylon. I was happy there really. I suppose I'm thoroughly displaced. I must try and make my place here.

Laura is coming back to the house soaking wet, she's left the plough over there, something is wrong she's wiping her eyes and her face with a rag.

"Laura! What's wrong have you hurt yourself?" I really am afraid. Whatever shall I do if she's hurt. God! I'm frightened! I run out to her.

"Andrea," she's laughing! "You'll never think I could be so stupid. I opened the oil sump with the engine running, you understand, the hot oil's sprayed all over me, into my face too, you never saw such a mess!"

"Oh Laura you're burned!"

"It's not hot really, fortunately for me! Just warm. It's moving, d'you see, all the time. I was a fool!"

"Oh Laura you gave me a fright!"

"Oh Andrea! I'm sorry! It gave me a fright too. I never thought of it being under pressure. How silly," she's still laughing and smearing her face with the oil rag trying to get it off.

"But you're getting wet!" she says. "Quick let's go into the house. Have a warm shower and change and I'll do the same. You start, and I'll build up a big fire! You'll see, we'll be warm and dry in a minute."

"No more work then today?" I can't stop shivering.

"No more work!" and she smiles that kind smile, "Hurry up into the shower," and she goes into the wood shed.

The water is lovely and warm.

"Laura!" I call her. "Laura the hot water won't last. Hurry up! and bring the scissors I want to cut my hair." She comes in her dressing gown.

"Come on!" I urge her. "Come under the hot water quick! before it's all used up." She hesitates.

"With you? Really?" She seems shy.

"Why not! Hurry!"

Her face is all black with the oil. We are laughing together as the water pours over us. It is the first time we have really seen each other naked. She looks at me tenderly and I soap my hands and gently wash her face.

"Close your eyes."

"But then I can't see you!" she says, laughing.

"You want the oil off?" I ask and lean to wash her so that our bodies touch and I soap her all over and gently the water rinses us both.

"Don't cut all your lovely hair," she holds me close.

"Just a little trim," I say. "Hope I don't block up the drain. I'm just trimming the ends." She steadies me with her strong hands.

"We'll see to drains tomorrow," she laughs, "and to our wet clothes," and then she is quietly serious. "Andrea," she says. "You're so lovely."

Laura's body is strong, not thin exactly, perhaps a bit thick, I suppose it is her age, about the hips, and her thighs are long and strong. I read somewhere once that a woman who wants another woman always looks at her thighs. Women notice thighs. I can see why this might be true. I notice hers. I don't know what Laura notices about me. If only I could love her as much as she seems to love me. Really love, I mean, not just a hope to get out of the terrible muddle I am in.

In the lean-to bathroom Laura sings, her voice is low, like a gentle bird.

"What's that you're singing?"

"Oh, was I singing? Of course I always sing in here,

just one of my bad ways!" she says. "It's Schiller, the Ode to Joy, happiness you know, Beethoven. I'll play the record for you afterwards. But just now you know what I feel like? I'd like some fruit cake and beer, let's have some! What a mixture!"

After the Beethoven she lies on the couch in her study and I sit on the floor in what she calls my Asian position. She likes me to sit like that. She strokes my hair gently and the back of my neck and is quiet as if she is thinking about something else. Then she says quite suddenly, "When you know more about some of the things in my life you will understand why I live here alone as I do, that is, if you are not bored to know."

"Of course I'm not bored," I say. "I can't help wanting to know about you but I'm not questioning, Laura, I am simply enjoying staying here with you. I'm really having a wonderful rest. I keep wanting time to stay still so that it won't be time for me to go." I feel I would like her hand to go on stroking my hair and neck for ever.

"You don't have to go," she says very softly. "You can stay for as long as you want to," and again she looks at me with this tenderness she seems to have for me. No-one ever looks at me like this. She talks about the Beethoven, she says the first phrases of the Ninth Symphony are like the very beginnings of love in two people, shy and quiet and hesitating, like the unfolding of the sky and the sun and the fields and woods and mountains in the very beginning of the world. Everything slowly opening and coming to life in the first warm light of the sun and this was the way love happened between two people. I hear her voice and feel her near.

"Really to love someone and really to be loved is rare," she says. "Did you like the beat of the ode? The introduction to the ode?" she asks.

"Yes I did."

"I thought so," she says. "You know it's like the rhythm which goes before the perfection of the climax," she says. "I hope you don't mind that I said that!"

"Of course not." How could I mind! Laura sees only the harmony and rhythm, she doesn't know any other way. She wouldn't see feelings as being terrifying in urgency and completely lacking in all the ideals she has. Perhaps she does know this but refuses to acknowledge it. I don't think she really knows as much as I know.

"I've written things which explain my life," she says after a little pause. "You can read anything, any of them, if you want to so that you know all about me! You can read my contributions to surgery and obstetrics too. Fascinating!"

"Oh Laura don't be bitter," I want to comfort her. I know things went wrong for her. I heard Mother talk or hint about them at times. But what could be as bad in her life as in mine. Her life and the things which happened have gone by. Mine is now.

She leans over me so that her face is in my hair, I wish she would kiss me.

"Oh Laura," I say. "I know I keep on about being mixed up. I really am you know. You are so good to me, perhaps if I know more about you, though I don't want to seem curious, I'm not you know, but if I know more of your life perhaps mine won't seem so bad! If only you knew!"

"Don't hide your dear face Andrea," she replies gently. "I know love is not always kind and I know that the birth of the world is not really a gentle unfolding. Birth is ruthless and inevitable and cruel even if the amniotic membrane is shot through with superb colours! Human beings are tough, or should be if you judge them on the struggle for birth; but sheer physical toughness is not the only necessary thing."

I can't say anything to her, tears are pouring from me. I'm frightened when she talks. I don't want to hear some of the things she says. I put my hands over my face and the tears come through my fingers.

"I'm so unhappy Laura," I can't stop crying. "I just want to forget, and be happy here with you."

"Andrea," she says. "How can I best help you? Dear little Andrea, tell me what will help you. I'll do anything."

100

"Laura, could you put off the Forts and Rodney Glass and those people? Could you write and make an excuse, say we have bad colds or something? Could we have a bit longer time before we have to see them?"

"And your brother too Andrea? Don't you want to see him? I thought as you are very fond of him I'd ask him and his little family too."

I have stopped crying thank God! God! Christopher! up here with Laura!

"Yes Laura, put him off too. I don't want to see anyone!" I say this with such emphasis I am afraid I have surprised Laura. I have surprised myself.

"Perhaps you do need more rest dearest," Laura says. "I'll write tonight and alter the arrangement."

She asks me a few things about myself. There is something clinical about the way Laura speaks, I suppose it's because she's been a doctor. When she asks me about myself she really searches into me, turns me inside out; I could feel embarrassed. I think it is because she is so shy and reserved herself. I can't quite tell her the truth, but I think I will be able to later so I begin to feel better.

"I don't want to see Christopher yet." I get up and sit close by her in the curve of her body resting on the couch. She holds me in her arms and I feel safe.

"Perhaps I can help you," she says. "Can you try and talk to me?"

"Yes Laura I can, Dear Laura." I am surprised at my own voice. I seem to be pouring out words, "Please help me Laura!" And I tell her everything how Mother put me and Christopher in the back of the car when they went out and how Christopher was frightened in the dark and I used to cuddle him and comfort him and play with him. "This is how it all started," I tell her and she listens and doesn't seem at all shocked and she doesn't ask me any questions only holds me close to her all the time so that I have the courage to tell her how this comforting and playing turned to something else for me, something much more serious for both of us and there seemed no possibility of giving it up, only a searching for more opportunities. Eva and Jake were often at the beach cottage or out on the boat and we had the house to ourselves. I looked after Christopher, I made his breakfasts. I tell Laura how he tried to break away from me how he lied to me and then always came back. I wouldn't, couldn't let him go; and then all the hurts of his lies. I tell them to Laura, and the mean things I did to keep him and the terrible hurt of him going to meet Margaret Fort and the whole goddammed thing and when I finish talking she says, "And this attachment still means a very great deal to you," just in a plain voice, a statement as if everything is just all right as if there is nothing shameful in it at all.

"Well, it doesn't really," I try to explain. "And yet I can't get it out of my mind. I want to . . ." I try to say more.

"Go on," she says and I can't tell if I'm hurting her by telling her I love Christopher when she loves me so much and thinks I love her. How can I tell her I want Christopher!

"Oh Laura it's you I want," I cry to her. "Please Laura hold me again like the other night. I want to forget everything except that I am here with you." I turn to her and kiss her, just a little kiss and I feel her body move to mine as she kisses me. We kiss each other again long and deep; her breasts are soft to mine.

"Sometimes, you know," she says in her low voice, "If you try to forget something like this it doesn't always succeed. We must be careful. What we have together is so beautiful and precious, we mustn't lose it!" She explains very softly, stroking my hair at the same time, how she would come to my bed every night, that she wants to but doesn't, because she wants to keep things rare and special.

"If you had a diamond," she says, "you wouldn't wear it all the time." I have to agree with her. My dress is not buttoned and she looks tenderly at my breast. I am close to her. She fingers the pendant I wear.

Her fingers touch my neck and my breast very lightly and very shyly.

"Andrea," she says in her very low voice. "This thing, this love you have for your brother, I think I can explain a bit about it. First, I don't think you must worry yourself so much. It might sound hard of me to say this, but it does seem to me that he is either getting himself free from it or has in fact done so already. If he hadn't, d'you see, it would be so much harder," she paused a moment and then goes on speaking, "I'm not saying that loving Christopher as you do is a bad thing. I suppose it is just that it doesn't work out well, it doesn't in itself make a life for either of you." All the time she is talking she is holding me close to her and her hand is caressing me very gently.

"During the search we all have for ourselves," she says, "all sorts of things happen to us and we go from one experience to another, this stepping is essential. We must go on." She laughs. "I sound like one of Dr. Esme Gollanberg's chapters," she says. "She had tremendous theories and I studied them all! I could give you a whole course of lectures!" she says, she's laughing. "I'm not laughing at you," she says, "I'm laughing because I love you so! Dear Andrea, it is our responsibility now for you to step from him away from that experience."

"But Laura if I step from him will I have to step from you too then?"

"I'm afraid so, Andrea. But don't do it yet. Not yet!"

It's always me who starts the love-making. She waits till I want her. She waits till I undo the buckle of her belt, she says it's like a little ceremony every time and she waits for me to kiss her.

"I love your little kiss," she says. "I love your invitation. I accept!" And then she kisses my hair, my ear, my neck and then gently with her finger tips she begins to caress me.

"I'm so happy with you here Andrea, I can't imagine how I ever lived without you! One day when you're strong enough, when you're better I'll tell you all the awful things in my life, and then you'll know the worst!"

I want to ask her about her life. I want to know the

things Mother hinted about but I'm afraid to ask. I'm afraid of making the happiness end.

"Happiness is so short," Laura says. "There are so many things to take it away. I had awful times," she says. "I've been in prison. So you do see, don't you, I've known bitter and hard things."

"Oh poor Laura! It must have been terrible."

"It was!" she says. "But now at this moment with you here, nothing is terrible, nothing is hard or bitter. I want to love you. I want, more than anything to help you, and, Andrea, I do want you so much."

How can I tell her how much she helps me, I want to tell her, I try to talk but she starts to help me take off my dress, very gently she unbuttons the front of it and peels it down over my shoulders.

"You're lovely," she whispers and she puts her hands over my hair and down over my shoulders and, with shy reverence, she gently strokes my breasts. And then she throws off her dressing gown and takes me in her arms.

"It's as if we're in the garden in the Lebanon," she says. "Time stands still for us, there is no time, only now and we are alone here together. I'll misquote something," she lies down and draws me down too.

"Make haste, my beloved
And be then like to a roe or to a young hart
Upon the mountains of spices."

And laughing softly she pulls me on to her breasts, saying, "I'll tell you about the loquats when they are in flower, cream and gold, little clusters of blossom, palomino coloured, and the air is sweet with the smell of them. And I'll tell you, the acacias will be splendid."

"I think I'll like the acacias," I'm kissing her, the quick little soft kisses she likes so much. "How do you feel?" I ask her still kissing her.

"Magnificent!" she says. "I feel everything. But most of all I feel you."

* * *

Laura

A delicate adventure in incredible tenderness. I can

104

look at my hands and at my body and see in them new purpose and meaning. "Are you smiling, Laura, in the dark," she asked me during the love we had in the night. "Are you smiling, Laura, in the dark" she asked "when I touch you and kiss you in these secret places." It is beautiful like a poem, I keep saying the words over and over to myself to keep the delicate night with me forever. "Are you smiling, Laura, in the dark —"

I think now she will really feel happiness here. Perhaps this afternoon we'll go to the Palomino stud.

Yesterday the light and shade changed in the house and, in her presence, the empty corners were glowing mellow and soft and we sat and lay together on the couch most of the afternoon and evening. We seemed to love each other for hours into the night both putting off the climax exploring and touching with our hands fresh sensuality till the moments came and there could be no more putting off. I think after our talking and after our loving some peace came to her for she slept soundly. I love her so dearly for this.

This morning tender tributaries swell the dark and penitent earth. The land is swollen with all this rain.

While she slept against my side I listened to the rain and thought of the places where water collects and flows. I have been carrying earth to make islands in the flood of the rising stream. I hope these platforms of earth will hold the roots of my tender trees.

I thought of the details of our living, the small details which are determined by people who are no longer alive. Because of the way the path was made, years ago, she can watch me come up from the orchard. And when we sit in the kitchen, because of the position of the little window there, we can see how the first light from the sun touches the white bark of the wandoo trees and makes the wet scrub sparkle.

All night I thought I would live forever. This morning I know I will not. I am sad and tender, happy and melancholy too; loving brings these things, and the morning has the knowledge of them and the realisation of mortality.

All along the top paddock birds rise suddenly, a tawny flight of doves flying up with a clapping of wings, a tiny scattered applause. I stop my work to look at the birds.

A bit later I stop my work to listen to the water running in flood and to listen to the frogs.

And again I stop, pausing, leaning on the shovel, to think of her, to think that she is up there in the house and to realise how happy I am and grateful.

I must find Murphy. It's a race against the passing seasons. Almost at once the heat of the summer will be here and it will be too hot and too dry to finish ploughing the fire break and there won't be a chance to burn out the dead trees along the stream.

It's like a quartet, the four seasons taking up and passing on the growth and the work of the land; it's like the four instruments taking up and passing on the theme and phrase of the complete music. All four seasons make the whole, cherishing and nourishing the seed, the root, the branch and the flower. The season changing, the sowing and the growing and the harvest brings the explanation from the earth.

Somehow it seems impossible to help Murphy. As soon as I see the Murphys, I know my time will at once be taken up and wasted with their unending troubles. Murphy has a bad eye today, it is all swollen and terribly painful. He can't work. Mrs. Murphy looks so yellow and ill. She asked me to see to the eye but of course I can't. It's illegal for me to practise medicine of any sort. It's just one of the many things Mrs. Murphy, in an uncanny way, knows about me, that I was a doctor once. If something happened to Murphy's eye because of my lack of skill and the right equipment I could not bear the consequences. I am too frail for anything like that. So first thing, there was nothing else I could do, I had to drive Murphy to Queens Meadows to the hospital and wait there two hours while the Sister irrigated his eye and removed splinters of burned wood from under the upper lid. I suppose it's no use trying to find Murphy, he can't do anything today.

106

There were letters for Andrea at the post office and a suitcase at the railway station. She will be glad to have her things. I can't help wondering who has written to her. I suppose her brother might have. There is nothing I can do except love her tenderly as I do and hope she will be able to love me completely. She gives so tremendously of herself and it seemed last night after the intimate talk we had together that she took tremendously in love.

Often people who love each other have qualities which are not equal and do not match. Our equality is overwhelming.

Everything about her interests and enchants me. I suppose this is what the chemistry of love is about. I know so little about her and yet love her dearly. I hardly know anything about her work abroad and yet I have in my mind from the few things she has said, a clear picture of the little school where she was and of the children. Everything she says and does is important to me. This is what love is; it must be, it can't be anything else.

When I brought Murphy home I took a box of oranges to the children. They were very pleased. I must do more for them. The pigs have come, but Mrs. Murphy complains that they will be expensive to feed. Everything I do to improve things seems wrong. In spite of the Murphys I will get the top acres cleared and increase my stock and I'll have some geese even if Mrs. Murphy can't stand them about the place.

All morning after coming from the hospital I have been moving earth down to the bottom orchard. I'll stop now and go in to her. I told her she was to stay in bed and rest all the morning.

* * *

Andrea
The table is all piled up with newspapers, medical journals and catalogues. Laura says she's going to have a good read later on. I'm unpacking my case. Laura fetched it with the mail and some groceries she'd or-

107

dered from town. It's so nice to have my things.

"I'll play my record for you," I say to Laura. "I have one, it's Indian music, you'll like it."

I read my letters while Laura is putting drops in her eyes. Her eyes are often troublesome she tells me.

"Mother wants to come!" I say to her. "Christopher writes to say she wants to come. Whatever shall we do!"

"I haven't seen Eva for years," Laura says slowly. "Really not for years! I suppose she wants to come to see you, it's quite understandable that she's anxious to know how you are." She stands by the window, very still and thoughtful. "I haven't seen her for years," she says again. "Years! It was a different life, another life then. Another life, I've left it behind."

"I don't want her to come," I say.

"You mustn't worry about me," Laura says. "I can manage. It will be all right if Eva comes. Let them all come! We can manage anything and everything together!" She laughs and puts her hands over her eyes. "Oh! these eyes! they smart." I'm not sure whether she's crying really.

"But I don't want any of them to come," I say crossly. "Really Laura it will ruin everything, the quietness of the place and the loveliness. I like being here with you. I don't want them. I don't want the intrusion. Imagine Mother here! Let's put them all off for good!"

Laura laughs again.

"I know just how you feel Andrea," she says, "We'll give ourselves a bit more time. We'll ask them all a little later on."

"You're sure it's all right to put them off?" I ask her.

"I'm not sure about anything except one thing," she says to me in a low voice. "I love the peace here. I love having you here with me and I hate the thought of an invasion! I have to ask them sometimes but I must say I had never thought of inviting Eva!"

"Eva could have thought to come years ago," I say. "But as she didn't, there's really no reason for her to come now!" It seems to me that Laura looks suddenly older and very tired. She steadies herself with her hands on the window ledge and I see the pulse beating hard in her neck. I pull things out of my luggage into an untidy heap so that Laura will not think I am seeing how she is. "I'll show you all my treasures," I say to her scattering my cheap clothes and beads and my few books on the floor.

"It's a new life now," Laura says as if talking to herself. "Nothing from the old life can spoil this one," she smiles at me.

"You haven't read your other letter," she says picking up my dresses and folding them crookedly, her hands are shaking and she doesn't want me to see, but I do see.

"Oh yes I have," I say. "It's just a note sent on by Christopher from the Headmaster of the school 'to wish my health better'," I laugh and don't tell her what the letter really is. I don't tell her because I can't.

"Oh I see," she says and I put up my hand for her to pull me up from the floor. She smiles at me.

"Let's walk over to the stud," she says, "to look at the horses."

"What about work?" I ask. "Another day off?"

"Just a half day," she says, "We'll wash up and tidy the house when we come back."

So we walk together down the sun-warmed slope to cross the flooded rushing stream on the crazy bridge made of four weathered railway sleepers. It is just as Laura described it, and up the other side through the trees to the place where the horses run.

Very shyly Laura takes my hand in hers and holds it close by her side. It is the first time she has ever done anything like this.

"Oh Laura be careful! Someone will see!" I tease her.

"Who? Who can see us here! We are safe here," and she laughs and keeps hold of my hand pressing her palm to mine. She says her hand does really feel my hand and that our hands are beautiful and their behaviour means so much. It is all special.

"I want to choose a horse for you," she says.

"No Laura I won't let you!"

"You can't stop me choosing, can you."

And then we come up to the fence. The horses are running together on the far side of the paddock, cream and gold and honey coloured. Laura calls to a man in the yard at the side of the house. It is some way off but he hears her and comes over.

* * *

Laura

The days are going by one after the other. The summer is coming and long waving grasses line the country roads. The season is a good one. Yesterday Murphy sold most of the sheep and the lambs, the ones I gave him, and mine. For once they looked fat, the lambs, it seemed a shame to have to sell them. Already I miss their crying and the ewes' tender replying. It is suddenly quiet. Sometimes a crow in the distance sounds like a lamb.

"We had a good sale, a good price," Murphy said. It's the late rains, these extra rains and the greater warmth of the coming summer; everything seems to grow for a second time. The wild oats and the cape weed and the wild radish have taken over the spaces between the trees and the only way is to slash them down with the little scythe and rake out the tough stalks. On these warm days the fragrance of the cut grass drying is a reminder of the changing season. I welcome the summer but regret the time passing as every long day spent with Andrea is one day less to have. I try not to think about this.

The trees I thought were dead last summer when I came back from the voyage are alive, new buds and new leaves and delicate blossom, and already the nectarines have set tiny hard dark fruits. Too many of them, Murphy says, for the good of the trees. I suppose he is right.

For the time being Mrs. Murphy is better. She is better and then worse and when she is bad one of us must rush her to the hospital. She is swollen and puffy. Some of her hostility disappears when her face is round with the fluid swelling all the tissue of her thin body. She looks at me with a babyish sort of face and I'm sorry I have no real feeling for her. Her children always stand quietly grouped by the door, their uneven hems flapping round their thin legs. I have promised them new dresses.

Selfishly I dressed Andrea first. I took her shopping and to the tailor. The clothes were made quickly; we only had to go twice. Both times the long drive was enjoyable. She didn't want me to spend on her, but I wanted her to have the things; she seems to have so little even of necessary items. As I thought they would, the clothes suit her, she is slender and graceful in them as in the Indian dresses she likes to wear. She sits well on the Palomino mare. The horse is called Dove. The Dove is in foal which means we can't ride for long unless Andrea will ride my horse, Charger. But very soon it will be too hot to ride in any case.

This morning was excellent. She rides well and the Dove is a proud little horse. There is a warmth and vitality with the horses. The smell of them and the stains from their sweat on our clothes seem to be part of our life. When we gallop from one end of the long paddock to the other the flying hooves throw up the fragrant earth and Andrea calls out to me, laughing, as she passes me. I stop riding and simply enjoy watching her.

There is too a warmth and vitality and a particular fragrance which belongs to our living together. It so fills my house that I can't imagine what it would be like to live without it now.

I have enjoyed everything lately. I have never known so much happiness ever in my life. Everything we do is a pleasure or a joke. She is pleased when I tell her to look at the sky. She watches the nature of the sky now as I do and sees the changing colour and texture of the trees from one hour of the day to the next. Our meals together are lively with conversation, there is so much to say, she is quick to understand and quick to respond and reply, and her golden eyes look straight into mine. She eats her food with obvious enjoyment. She says she's really hungry. Every meal does her good. She looks up from her plate, smiling with her eyes; she helps herself to more and she chews with her lips neatly closed and all the time she smiles with her eyes. The dear child, I love her so when she's hungry!

I hardly ever go to town, but we went twice to see about her riding clothes. I never thought I could enjoy shopping so much. During the long drives she sat up close by me, sometimes her hand was on my thigh, "I'm just keeping you awake," she said. We spent the time in town buying things and didn't think or speak of people we ought to have visited.

I feel so well too. I haven't felt well like this for years. It is the lovely sleep we have and the waking up. All I know about loving is from her, and yet she says all she knows about love is from me.

So this is how love is, quite unreasonable, and yet at the same time full of reason and tender happiness.

She invites and I cherish. On the ship I thought I was the one to invite but it is the other way about. I always wait for her invitation. It's because I'm so much older I couldn't bear to do anything out of place. I like to cherish, so does she. This morning she brought me tea, she put in the sugar and stirred it. We are so equal, I wonder how it can last. How long will I be able to have her here? How long can I hope to have her love?

My whole house is different because she is here. She laughs at my flower pots and tins, "the audience" she calls them. "Have you watered your audience?" she calls out to me. "Why do you have so many jades and rosemarys and myrtles?" she asks me quite often. I tell her it is because I want to propagate and this is the only way I can. I love to see her laugh.

This morning she looked radiant. I have seen this radiance coming as these days go by. Her skin glows now. She is smooth and glowing all over, she has a lovely young body, creamy skin, rose tinted, and her bright hair shines. Her golden eyes shine too and in the half light of the early morning I have seen her white teeth shine when she smiles and laughs.

She has so few possessions and no money at all. What she has she treasures. She says she has all she needs.

"You'll need more things," I say to her, and she replies, laughing,

"I'll play my two records for you, when you've heard them you'll see I don't need anything else."

I think I am afraid of her radiance. I like her to look as she does but I am afraid all the same.

* * *

Andrea

Sometimes Laura cries just a little. Yes she weeps, but only a few tears. I see them force their way from under her closed eyelids. She says it is gratitude for being caressed. No-one has touched her body for years except Murphy once when he put his hand on her arm to steady her out in the paddock when it was raining in the night.

"And I'm not sure that he did touch me in any case," she says laughing to get her tears away.

I want to tell Laura about the letter I've had from Irma. I want to tell her something else too. If only Laura would tell me she'd made love to her grey horse or something then it would be easier for me to tell her what's on my mind. I want to tell her the whole god-dammed truth. How can I tell it to her, the whole thing about Christopher and me without shocking her and hurting her. If only I knew what she'd done years ago, I just need some little piece of knowledge to use just to remind her so that what I have to tell her will seem simple compared with what she's had in her own life.

"Did you ever love anyone?" I asked her last night.

"My father," she said.

"No I mean someone not your father," I said.

"I loved your mother," she said in that low voice.

"You loved Eva!"

"Yes," she said. "Don't be surprised! I did love Eva very much. And I'll tell you this; she was a very devoted mother. And she needed very much to be loved." This shut me up for a bit but Laura was very gentle and held me close in her arms.

"Don't be upset by what I've just said," she said. "I'll

113

explain it all one day. There's nothing about it you can't know."

"Did Eva love you?" I asked her, wanting to ask her more.

"I suppose in her own way she did," she said. "But if you want to know of someone who didn't really love me but wanted me, there was a certain wardress in the prison—"

"Did she try to have her wicked will on you then?" I asked her and we laughed and kissed each other. The kisses mean so much to her and I feel her heart beat hard and I think she is a bit embarrassed by it.

"Well," she said. "I think she might have but I got this horrible infection in the prison hospital, do you see, and she was afraid of it."

"So you escaped."

"Yes I escaped. But I don't want to escape any more." That was last night. She was very sweet to me all night.

Mother said she'd killed a person, I can remember Mother talking about it, but nothing in the end was really ever said in public about her.

Laura herself, at the time, said she'd killed this person. I don't know how long she was in prison, I can't really ask her about it but if she killed someone I'd like to know why. She would never do anything without a reason. I could never see a reason which would be her fault. I wonder when she will tell me and how she will do it. I wonder if she would kill me if she knew all there is to know about me.

She looks really something in her riding boots, I told her the sight of her striding about in the boots sent me and she didn't know what I meant. She kept adjusting my new clothes, she said they were becoming, such a quaint old-fashioned word.

"The shoulders are a perfect fit," she said stroking them. The cloth of the riding jacket is good quality. I thanked her for all the presents, the lovely clothes and for the beautiful horse and the saddle and bridle, all of them expensive things. She said I mustn't thank her, it was the other way about, she wanted to thank me. She

114

said she had never ever been so happy as she was now. She loved having me to stay with her she said and it gave her pleasure to give me these things, therefore it was she who must thank me.

"But all that money!" I said to her.

"Father owned a lot of land along the river," she shrugged her shoulders. "And Uncle Todd, they were the only brothers."

"They were both doctors?"

"Surgeons, yes, Uncle Todd did obstetrics mainly."

"And then you?"

"Yes until I was struck off. There are plenty of other surgeons!"

"Poor Laura!"

"Well never mind, as I was telling you. Don't interrupt! I had the good fortune, in a way I suppose, to have a lot of valuable land left to me, especially valuable, the land by the river and Uncle Todd's enormous house down there too, all very desirable, and it sold well. Uncle Todd married his old housekeeper and she died soon after him and I was the only one to inherit. So you do see don't you, I like to buy you a present. Please be pleased and don't be worried. Even if I lose some money trying to run this place I don't need to worry about it. In time I may even make something of it."

"I'm pleased, very pleased," I told her.

I know she is hoping nothing will happen to spoil our lives here. I wish nothing need happen. I like to be here. The loneliness drives me mad though. I keep hoping something will change and I will be able to draw and paint and really settle into this way of life. When it's so quiet all my troubles come in on me and seem unbearable. When Laura is out working the only noise is the ticking of the clock or the tap dripping in the kitchen. When they were still here I heard the munching of the sheep as they came cropping up the long paddock which is alongside the verandah at this end of the house. When I say it's so quiet Laura at once tells me it is not quiet.

"There are a thousand sounds," she says to me. "Listen to the frogs and to the rushing of the water, these noises never stop till the hot weather comes, you can hear the wind sighing in the trees, then there are the horses thudding across the valley and the roosters from Murphy's yard. Oh God yes, and Murphy's children and those mad dogs. The cicadas are starting up and soon there'll be bees and very often I drown everything with the gramophone or the chain saw or the tractor!"

Laura doesn't realise what a lonely noise the tractor is. Behind the tractor engine there are acres and acres of terrifying silence. A silence filled with all my fears.

I am afraid.

Everything is going to have to change so what's the use of trying to be interested in anything, my books or the things I liked to do once.

How ever am I going to manage? I wonder if Laura will be hurt beyond comfort and I wonder when Laura is hurt if she will want to throw me out of here. I wonder what she will do. I don't know what Laura is like when she is hurt, and I don't know what her anger is like.

I can't have Christopher come here and I don't want to see Mother.

* * *

Laura

This morning I went all round the fruit trees, very early in the fragrance of the withered grass. When I go round to the trees doing delicate things to them with the pruning knife it is like going round patients. I know every one of them, details about them all, it is very intimate really because they are, to a certain extent, depending on my care as my patients once did.

I suppose I am troubled about the visit. I have invited them all for Sunday. I can't leave it longer as it gets too hot here for visitors. I have left it late for the wildflowers though there still are some. I suppose I am afraid. I suppose I don't want to see Eva. I stopped wanting to see her years ago.

How easy it is to say "do not think" when it is impossible not to think. I have not thought about Eva for years and now I shall have to see her.

116

Andrea and I don't really want these people to come. They represent another world outside the one we have here and neither of us wants this other world and yet we must take our places in it.

"Maturity is being able to blend oneself, one's life, with these other things," I tried to explain to Andrea. I told her I had to invite Rodney Glass and his wife and the Forts. "They helped me," I told her. "During the hard time I had. They were my colleagues once and they had respect, love perhaps, for Father and Uncle Todd. If I did not invite them they would come uninvited and I don't want that." I think Andrea understood this. "Up till now," I said to her, "they have respected my privacy and leave me alone except for the invitations which have an easy regularity."

To avoid an extra invitation I have asked Christopher to come and to bring Eva. So they will all be coming. Eva with her lack of discrimination is sure to bring someone else as well, her mother perhaps, who must be getting really old, or that terrible Myrtle.

Andrea does not speak of it. She seems very quiet. She looks well, her skin has changed. She has a new soft bloom of health which is more evident every day.

"Your hair shines so," I said to her at lunch time and she smiled. I wanted to tell her how lovely she is but I didn't. I am always afraid to say too much.

"Yes," she said, "It's even curling a bit along my forehead," and she lifted her hair to show me the tiny soft new curling hair along the delicate hairline. I longed to kiss her sweet face.

"You feel well?" I asked her. "You do feel better don't you?"

"Of course!"

"You aren't eating anything. Look! I've eaten everything! And my stomach shouldn't be made to bulge!"

"Perhaps I'm not hungry," she said and then she gave such a long terrible sigh, I have never heard such a long sigh, and she pushed aside her plate.

"Andrea!" I said. "What is it? Is something the matter?"

117

"Oh I don't know," she said. "Oh well!" If you must know, I suppose it's the thought of Sunday. I really can't face it!"

"But Andrea," I said. "Sunday is only one day out of all the days we have. And they don't arrive till just before twelve and we'll serve lunch and they'll sleep and leave in the evening. It won't be so bad. You'll see!"

"I worry about you, Laura," she said.

"I'll manage," I said to her. "I am used to everything now. Sometimes I say 'no' you know. I was invited to Margaret Fort's wedding, I didn't realise who her husband was at the time. I dislike the vulgarity of big weddings — satin dresses and velvet coats; champagne disagrees with me and I loathe stupid speeches so I didn't go and they left me in peace. This invitation is the smallest thing I need to do, just as going to Rodney's to dinner is a small thing too. I keep it like this and it is the easiest way. The only thing which is not easy is you being sad. We'll help each other on Sunday. You'll find it easier to give up Christopher if you see once and for all he has tried to give up you." She put her head in her hands and I thought I had said too much.

"You know I'm quite looking forward to Sunday," I said, "especially to the time when they have all just gone and we are alone here again, just us together. And then there'll be another Sunday and after that another Sunday."

She only sighed and kept her head down in her hands.

"Andrea!" I said. "You're not feeling ill are you?"

"Put them off Laura!" she whispered. "Don't have them come!" She clasped her hands, the fingers seemed thin and white as they were when she first came to me.

"Please Laura! Please put them off for my sake!" she said.

"Look Andrea! I tell you what," I stood up, "let's go riding this afternoon. Sometimes as grown women, and in my case I'm not a young woman, we have to say 'no' when we want to say 'yes' and the other way round. So with this awful truth in mind let's forget the whole thing and get changed and go riding." She looked up quickly.

"You're not going back to your work?" she asked, she seemed as pleased as a child. "A half day off?" she asked. "Do you mean that Laura?"

"Yes, we'll ride, would you like that?"

"Oh yes!"

"Come on then let's leave this mess. We'll have a grand clearing up later on."

While we were changing she came over to me and put her arms round me and rested her little blonde head against my shoulder and I held her tenderly in my arms. She seemed to hold herself away from me as if to keep her body and her breasts from being touched or pressed. I already had on my clothes and perhaps she was afraid of the buttons hurting her.

I keep thinking about that now instead of giving myself up to the enjoyment of being on horseback. Perhaps her breasts are tender as they are at times in young women. Another thought occurs to me, another reason, which I am afraid to think of. I must think about it however. I am of an age where I have to think of everything and this thing will be so inevitable it will have to be faced.

We are riding back towards the long paddock and she is ahead of me. Usually she calls out to me as she passes, this time she did not call but went on by. Her little horse takes the long paddock at a gallop and I am coming slowly, I am thinking too much to ride well. She is going like the wind. The Dove is a sturdy brave horse and is galloping as if she had no rider. The horse has turned the width of the paddock and is flying down the far side.

"Andrea! don't ride like that! Andrea! The foal! Remember the foal!" My voice is lost in the wind and the thudding of the hooves. My own Lucy trembles and quickens as if sensing the frantic gallop of the Dove. I can see Andrea's face, expressionless white and small, her whole body is strained as if she is hurling herself into the movement of the horse.

"Stop Andrea! Be careful! You'll hurt yourself!" She

119

can't hear me at all. The honey-coloured horse has turned and is gone again.

It seems that Andrea is doing this on purpose but I don't understand and I don't know how to stop her.

The Murphys are all lined up along the wire fence just outside their place. Even Mrs. Murphy is there in her blue dressing gown. Andrea said the other day "Blue Blue Candlewick!" and burst out laughing. The way Mrs. Murphy stands she could be standing in a hospital corridor. All the Murphys are watching Andrea's ride.

"Laura! Get out of my way!" and Andrea has gone by me again. And then she turns and comes back straight towards me and turns her horse aside at the last moment.

"Oh God! Andrea! Stop! Stop!"

I try to follow her, urging Lucy who is perplexed but obedient, and we are both galloping up the paddock and, to my horror, Andrea tries to jump the pole fence. It is much too high for the little horse and Andrea is thrown.

"Oh my God! Oh Andrea!" I am there beside her. Murphy is there too. He caught her horse at once, he was quick. He has both horses tied to the fence. The grass is coming up to me in waves on all sides, a terrible dizziness. I am afraid Andrea is dead. I am afraid to look. How weak I am suddenly. "Oh my dear little Andrea, don't be hurt, please!" it is like a long moan coming from somewhere inside me. I gather her up in my arms, she seems light, she opens her eyes.

"Laura? Oh Laura!"

"Yes, I've got you safe!"

She looks at me and then closes her eyes again.

Murphy has pulled off his coat, he is kneeling on the grass. "Lay her here," he says to me and I am glad of his authority and his surprising strength. "Lay her here, we'll carry her up to the house, better the two of us."

* * *

Andrea

Laura's hands. Laura's hands are holding me. Sometimes her hands are warm and sometimes they are cool, sometimes they are covered in soap and all the time they are gentle and firm and kind.

On the way back from the hospital where she took me for X-rays and an examination I watched her hands on the steering wheel. She controlled a skid. "Some grease on the road," she smiled at me, "We'll be home soon," she said softly.

She wears her gold watch with the black leather strap on her left wrist. It is very handsome. I love the perfume of the leather. I love to watch her drive.

I am safe with Laura. I am better. It was only bruises, but the pain was bad and I was helpless and Laura never left me. She has looked after me. She has done everything for me; all the awful things that have to be done when one can't get up.

"What about your work," I asked her more than once.

"You are my work," she said. She read to me and sang to me and cooked things, and when I didn't want to eat anything, patiently she reasoned with me.

I told her I rode hard on purpose but I haven't told her why and she has not questioned me.

Laura put off the visitors, they are coming next week.

"The honeysuckle smells so sweet," she puts the jar beside the couch, deep green leaves and pale creamy pointed petals. Her hands arrange the flowers, Laura's hands.

"Laura," I say. "I rode the Dove hard on purpose. I'm sorry!"

"The Dove is quite well and her foal is unharmed," she says so gently, "and she has some months yet, no harm has come to her. But tell me," she asks even more gently, "did I hurt you in some way? Were you really riding at me? Have I hurt you? Tell me!"

"Laura it was not against you I was riding. It's something inside myself. I was riding against myself."

She is so good to me, she looks thoughtful.

"You don't have to explain things to me just now if you can't," she says.

I suppose she is wanting to get back out on to her land. I suppose not telling Laura hurts her. Whichever way

121

telling her and not telling her, both will hurt her. She is hurt now and I don't want to hurt her.

Laura must be sixty or more. She is the innocent one. For all her knowing things, the way she has read and studied, I am the one with the knowledge.

She lies there in the evenings listening to the music. One night she told me she likes to listen to the music fitting it to what will follow. She thinks about me all the time she says. She has let me teach her all sorts of little things about love-making. Without saying anything she asks me to teach her. She is too shy, too afraid of being indelicate or ridiculous.

"You mustn't be too careful," I told her once and she laughed waiting for me to undo her belt.

"I'll be careless then," she said.

When we are loving each other I can get her to forget everything, I can get her to give herself up completely. It is then that I think I do love her, perhaps it is her love for me that I love. I am so muddled I don't really know what love is except that I really do feel her love and her care. If only I could tell Laura everything and get some of this burden off me.

Laura has been out working today for the first time since I fell off the Dove. Her back is quite brown.

"Summer is here," she says. The tan suits her, it suits her grey hair which she has short and brushed back away from her face.

"You look very distinguished," I tease her and I take my drawing block and pencil. "Sit still I want to draw you."

"Do you!" she says and she gets up from the floor where she has been lying and sits on the edge of the couch. She takes a handful of the honeysuckle flowers and holds them in her cupped hands and breathes in the scent. "I would like to be drawn by you," she says. "I love these flowers," she holds her hands for me to share them.

"Oh Andrea!" she says. "I love you so dearly. Can I ask you? Do you?" she asks very softly and shyly, "Do you love me?"

"Of course!" I say and I bite her finger and we both laugh.

"I mean something more than biting," she says. "I know the orgasm is terribly important, I've written about it so often, it must matter! But it's not the only thing." She puts the honeysuckle back into the jar, we are both sprinkled with water.

"But you see," she says, "I shouldn't ask you that when you don't really know me. When you know everything you might hate me! There are things you don't know and which I suppose you should know. After all, there are a lot of years between us which for me are filled with things I have to forget."

"Dear Laura," I say to her, "I do know a lot about you, perhaps what I know from living here with you is enough." I put my hand gently on her strong sunburned back and stroke her, her fragrance is of lemons and spices.

"Your back is so smooth, you got quite burned today." I say to her.

"Yes and the flies were intolerable, yes I know you know a lot about me, all the secret things, but there are other things, could you bear to know them? You'll be on your own here all day tomorrow, it might be a very long day as I have to see about the new machinery and some sort of truck and I want to arrange about some calves, fattening calves, you know, there's more money in calves!"

"Ugh! It sounds so cruel!"

"Well that's farming! People have to eat meat! We like it too! Murphy'll be coming with me."

"A day on the town with Mr. Murphy!"

"That's right," she hesitates a moment and then asks, "Would you like to know about my life? While you're by yourself all day you can read everything about me! Some of the things I've written myself, that is if you want to. I don't mind your reading them. It might be easier than talking. We can talk afterwards about everything. Everything there is about us both!"

"If you really want me to know," I say to her, "I'll read them, Laura, but are you certain?"

"I want to be certain of you," she says.

"It's so hard to be certain of anything," I can't help saying this.

"Let's be certain of each other." That's so like Laura to end the conversation like that. 'Let's be certain of each other." It sounds so easy.

* * *

Laura

On Sunday Rodney Glass will walk out on to my high verandah to throw his chest out. Every year he makes the same joke, Andrea has not heard it yet. And later on he will fall over a pail and say he did not expect to have to come all the way up here to kick the bucket. I am looking forward to the time when they have left to go back home and I am alone again with her. Being with other people must surely bring lovers closer together. What a strange party it will be, it will include Christopher and his wife; Rodney's young son, the mistake, they call him, he is still a schoolboy; and it will include Eva. A painful party for Andrea and for me too but I suppose it is necessary.

I can't think about Sunday. I have to think about today. It's hardly sunrise, yet the sun is up and it's going to be hot. I told Murphy to be ready early as we had a lot of things to do in town. I have to call at more than one place and have some important things to buy.

I seem to be so often in this quiet mood of working alone and knowing she is up there in the house for me when I get back. It is unthinkable that it would ever be otherwise.

I am down in the bottom orchard. Murphy has to change a wheel. I have left Andrea asleep like a child in the big bed. She is prepared to be alone, she knows we may be away for part of the night too.

I am too hot down here, the flies are already in my eyes.

"The late rains have certainly given the pasture good

heart," Murphy said when we met this morning, he has a poetic way of putting things sometimes.

The late rain has made the weeds grow. While I'm waiting I have pulled up cape weed and rye grass and put it round the pears and quinces. The quince trees I was so sure were all dead blossomed this spring, delicate perfect little flowers, and soft green leaves and now tiny velvet fruits are setting; they are a very pale green.

The delight I have on seeing these dear little fruits, the first quince I have ever grown, is not quite enough to steady me. Crouching down, weeding, on the earth, I can't help being afraid that when Andrea has read the things which will explain my life to her she will not want to stay. Last night she told me she wanted to be here with me and nothing, she said, could change this. I want to believe this. I want her to stay here more than I have ever wanted anything. I will promise her everything she wants. She can travel, or we can travel, to any place she chooses for a holiday, she can go on with her painting or anything else she wants to do. I will share this place with her, I'll get it all repaired; some parts are very shabby and the paint is flaking off in the kitchen and bathroom. We are always sweeping because of this. Last night she took out her drawings and we were both sketching, nothing serious. I kept trying to draw the barn and she was drawing me. It is the first time she has really done anything.

When I think of it I can't expect her to stay or even want to stay. I must be out of my mind! And yet I plan to build stables so that we can keep horses, she could have the horses. Perhaps she would stay for one year and have the money from the horses though in one year there would be no return. Everything takes so long to come from the land.

While I am weeding, I try to sort out the confusion in my mind about her. I want her to stay and I must want her to go. I even think I could be more disciplined so that it would not matter so much. I could live without these nightly excursions into tenderness. I could refuse to accept her invitation so that I do not need her and at the

125

same time she would want me more and not want to go! She might get tired of me. I am afraid of loving her too much.

Yet I know that if tonight, when I come home, she invites, I will cherish and love her. Last night the fragrance of the honeysuckle was intoxicating, it somehow became part of our love-making.

When I come home this evening everything might be different. She will know things she did not know before. I also have something to find out. I think I know it already.

From the edge of the quiet forest the magpies send their voices in a shower of sound filling the yellow grey morning. I gently finger the tiny nipple-like fruits of the quince and, thinking of Andrea, I experience pleasurable sensations all over my body. I would like to go back up to the house to where she is asleep. I want to go and wake her and tell her I love her. I want to love her, the desire in me is so strong I start to walk up the slope back to the house. Perhaps I'll go back to bed and spend the day there with her. Perhaps I should stay with her today and not go to town.

"They reckon there's no market for quince," Murphy has come down to tell me the car is ready and he walks ahead of me breaking all the bright spider webs as he goes.

"It's a lovely morning," I say to Murphy sitting beside him. He turns his head to look, I see his thin cheek and the bones of his forehead under his hat.

"Nice enough now," he says, "But it's a troubled sky yonder," and he jerks his head towards the house, which is the west, to indicate the direction.

* * *

Andrea

Last night Laura said something like "It's not the immediate thing you miss but something from before."

I am not quite sure what she meant but she was so tired and wanted to sleep so I did not go on talking. Living alone as Laura has for so many years has made

126

her not selfish exactly but perhaps self-absorbed, no-one could call her selfish, she is quite the opposite. But put it this way, if Laura wants to sleep she does so or if she is hungry she pulls out food and eats, sometimes she is hungry for special things — salmon, ham steak, pears and so on — and if she wants them she has them or if she wants a raw carrot and dry bread she has that. But she is gracious and graceful, she never does anything ugly or uncontrolled. Even over the Dove, the fall I had, she knows I did it on purpose but there has been no ugly word or look from her, not a vulgar thing said in haste. Control if it is unbroken could be dangerous; I suppose this is what I am afraid of, afraid of Laura losing her control because she is hurt or angry. Even in her love-making she is controlled, she waits for me; very occasionally, on purpose, I have made her lose control of herself so that she can't help herself and when this happens and it is over she is terribly sorry. Once she wept and was afraid she had hurt me physically. I suppose it seemed so violent to her. Love-making with a woman is different. What seems violent to her is not to me. She knows nothing of the full violence of it, she doesn't know the hardness of a man's body and the weight and the fierceness of a man's passion.

"I don't want to crush you," she says very softly, she is afraid of her weight, she makes me turn and lie on her so that she takes the weight. But woman loving woman is all turning; in any case, she is not heavy.

"Gymnast! Contortionist!" she calls me. "Rest on my thigh," she tells me. "Put your dear head on my heart, lie as close as you can. I do love you so much!" Love-making with Laura is something quite beautiful, she makes it so, she makes me feel as if I were the beautiful one. She tells me I am fragrant and smooth and cool, but it is she who is like this.

I have never known this sort of love before. I don't know whether Laura suspects my lack of innocence, she is so innocent herself. As she says she has written books on every aspect of woman without really knowing her subject.

127

"Write one now," I said to her. "Write a best seller!"

"I don't have time just this minute," she said. She kissed me softly on my hair and face and neck. "I'm far too busy," and we both laughed so much, laughing with pleasure. With Christopher I laughed sometimes, with relief, when the urgency and the fierceness of the passion were gone. With Laura it is only urgent when we want it to be, with her it is the care and the caress that matters. This is what I have learned from her.

Sometimes, while we are laughing, she reaches over and I see her strong sunburned arm against the white sheet as she reaches for the lamp to put it out.

"Oh electricity would be useful in this place," she says. "I keep thinking how I ought to have it, it's creepy sometimes with candles but the lamplight is so soft and pretty."

I love this moment when Laura has just put out the lamp, the darkness is kerosene-scented and comfortable and she is so tender then, and loving, and says such sweet things to me and our two bodies are close in nakedness. We are so alone together in the dark in this half empty old house. I love the high old bed; it's soft and spacious and heaped up with pillows.

But the other night when we were laughing just as Laura reached for the lamp, Mrs. Murphy, who is really too sick to be out, knocked on the kitchen door and called out, "It's only little old me!" and she was suddenly in the kitchen and Laura jumped up and quickly pulled on her dressing grown. I know how she feels about her nakedness. She is used to privacy.

"I just popped over to see how your friend is," Mrs. Murphy said, her eyes poking all round the house. "You had the lamps on so I thought as somepin could be wrong." She sounded quite hopeful.

I could see Laura was annoyed by the way she frowned and her hand whitened at the knuckles as she held the bed post to steady herself. But she showed no anger in her voice.

"Miss Andrea is very much better now, thank you Mrs. Murphy. Thank you for coming over. But you know you shouldn't have come so late at night in the dark, you might have fallen! You are not really well yourself, you know."

"Doctor, Miss Laura, I wonder if you've a packet of tea and a bit of sugar?" Mrs. Murphy whined looking all round to see as much as possible. "Just a bit of tea and sugar to spare?"

"Yes, of course. I'll come over to the fence with you." Laura had to go out then to take her home.

Mrs. Murphy has a strange effect on Laura.

When she came back she wasn't laughing any more. She sat on the bed beside me and drank off a double Scotch without any water and then said, "Goodnight Andrea dear, sleep well!" and went off into her study and closed the door. She must have been reading or writing for ages, I could see the light under the door, it was still on when I fell asleep, the line of light was the last thing I saw.

Laura hates to be spied upon and she did say once there was something about Mrs. Murphy that made her feel dirty as if she, Mrs. Murphy, had smeared her with something.

Last night we were not disturbed by anyone. "The honeysuckle, the perfume!" Laura said and took me in her strong arms. "I am your victim!" she whispered. "Kiss me," she said. "Because I want to kiss you so much. Tonight I can't wait for your permission!"

Laura wants me to read so that I'll know all the awful things about her. I will always feel the same about her whatever I know or don't know. I'll read everything as she says and then I'll tell her everything.

I can't really get Christopher out of my mind. Seeing him on Sunday might change things. Laura says I must give him up, or rather let him go. I know you can't love two people at once but one of these things isn't love. I wish I knew which was which.

And there's something else I'll have to tell Laura sooner or later. I wish I didn't have to. Perhaps if this other thing didn't exist I could really try and make a success of being here for a while and then start afresh somewhere.

Now to go back into those other years. I remember her dark brown hair and that she wore brown clothes, smart neat suits, with good quality shoes and stockings. Mother always said she was very elegant. I often sat naked on her lap, I remember it. I must have been about six years old, small for my age, Mother always said. It must be well over twenty years ago . . .

PART 3

THE CARDBOARD DIARY

Andrea

The house is empty and quiet standing in these quiet paddocks with the still quiet jarrah forest beyond. I am more used to the stillness. I have come to like it at least I try to think I have.

In her study on the wall next to the portrait of the poet Schiller she has Saint Jerome in the mountains. It is a lonely picture and beneath the rocks Saint Jerome is so small. I wonder why Laura has this picture. On her desk she has left the packages marked in order of reading. There is a note on the top, it is addressed to me.

Dearest,

It seems strange to write a letter to you when I have just left the bed where you are lying so sweetly asleep. I will be back late tonight, don't wait up for me unless you really want to. I hope all this reading won't turn out to be too tedious. I certainly hope it will not be hateful!

I think it is necessary for us both that you should have all the "material" if you can bear it. I love you so! I am afraid to presume that you love me. I must be sure.

Perhaps when you know all there is to know, the best and the worst, you will let me know you more. There are some things I do know about you already and, when you want to, we'll talk about them. I just want you to know I shall love you always, for the rest of my life, forever. And I want only the best for you.

All day while I am with Murphy doing things I have to do I shall be thinking of you. Take care of yourself my own Dearest. Always I am your Laura.

How tenderly Laura writes to me. I have never ever had a letter like this one written to me. Is it possible that she has guessed my predicament and can still write to me like that!

The Cardboard Diary

I bought this book the other day in town, it was reduced in price because of the year being half gone. I shall have to write the date at the top of every page as it is already the seventeenth of April and this first page is dated January the first, New Year's Day. The book has cardboard covers, that is why I have written *The Cardboard Diary* on the front.

This is Wednesday 18th April
A year ago today my Father died. It is my birthday. I am thirty-six. He died on my birthday after dinner. As usual we ate the meal in silence. To please Mrs. Platt my Father praised the vegetables. I sat opposite him and towards the end of the meat course he said,

"It's your birthday today Laura. Many Happy Returns of the Day!" and he raised his glass to me and finished his wine. I said,

"Thank you Father."
On that night we sat together after dinner in this room which was his study and is now mine. Father slept and died in his chair. Mrs. Platt had gone when I discovered he was dead so I had to leave him in his chair till the morning. I am glad he died like this. Though I have missed him very much I have not been lonely, at least not lonely in the expected way.

132

The house is very quiet but so it was when he was alive. My study is like a green cave curtained with a trellis of roses, sadly neglected I'm afraid, it is on the point of collapse. Sunflowers, like little trees, grow on either side and the whole house is hidden in a ring of trees, flame trees, kurrajong and Norfolk Island pines. And in front is an overgrown hedge of hibiscus splashed all over with scarlet and pink like a hedge in a child's painting.

Mother died when I was eleven and we have lived alone here since then. Mrs. Platt has been coming all the years. After Father's death she has been coming less. I like this arrangement and so does she. I like living alone here in this old house. I love my work and I love this place.

Tonight I'm so tired. Even my hot bath and these comfortable new clothes do not refresh me.

I suppose I am afraid.

The day has been a very long one. Uncle Todd was operating and we had a long theatre list. Rodney Glass was away today so I could not leave. I'm tired and my back aches dreadfully. I'm cold this evening and it seems to me that I'm wasting precious time. I never have enough time and tonight I am wasting it!

Eva has just telephoned. I suppose I was really waiting for this. She invited me round for drinks. I have refused the invitation even though I want to see Eva so much. I find lately, I cannot stand Jake and his friends. I want to avoid him, in fact, I can't stand him.

At one time I was always at their place when I was not working. The house is comfortable with the smell of roasting meat and the fragrance of the little girls. Sometimes it is crowded with noisy visitors and sometimes it is quiet there with Eva's mother sitting and knitting and repeating her platitudes in a monotonous voice.

Since I have refused the invitation I won't be able to see Eva. I'll be on the verandah and give all my attention to Bach and the moonlight and the sweet night-scented jasmine.

Mrs. Glass has telephoned. Rodney has 'flu so I'll have to be at the hospital before eight in the morning. Mrs. Glass is very charming but seems nervous of me, this amuses me. My colleagues often invite me. I think they are sorry for my loneliness. They only know conventional loneliness not the real loneliness of being as I am, entirely alone.

I've tried just now to write some more of my chapter for inclusion in a general textbook of obstetrics and gynaecology, my contribution is some elementary surgery, rather dull and pedantic.

I wish I'd gone up to see Eva, even if it meant putting up with Jake and his friends.

Thursday 19th April

Last night I went to bed early because of the eight o'clock list. My hands shake if I don't sleep enough.

Monday 23rd April

These cold nights I wear Father's old cloak, its warmth is comforting. I went in the dark to fetch a lemon. How fragrant the lemon is and the tree has fruit and flower at the same time.

I have not described my work in this new journal. I have kept journals for years and have written about all sorts of things, mainly about people. Though I am detached from people I am concerned about them. At the same time, I'm cautious. I dread hurting anyone and dread being hurt myself. If I ask myself why am I keeping another diary now, I think I would tell myself with honesty, perhaps it's because I want a place where I can write about Eva. I want to think about her and write down my thoughts privately.

This is Easter. A long peaceful weekend with only one visit to the hospital. I called at Eva's place on Easter Sunday but all was closed up and the blinds were drawn. Then I remembered Eva had said they were going to a hotel in the hills. She said she thought the hotel there had a television lounge.

I walked round the harbour, people walking, couples, cormorants fishing in pairs and dolphins, always two together side by side, diving and swimming through the waves. I mended the rake and burned some leaves. Later I read Uncle Todd's article, on the anxious, unwilling multipara, he wants me to suggest a suitable title for the series. Tried to think what Father would have suggested.

Tuesday 24th April

I bought white Chinese silk pyjamas for myself. I love these expensive well-made clothes. I called at Eva's but no sign of anyone being at home yet. I wish I could remember how long she said they would be away. Rats very noisy in the roof, heavy rain and of course I have not had the roof seen to. Several leaks.

I'm terribly tired, back worse than ever, cold and aching. An emergency appendix and a motor cycle accident. Uncle Todd operating and cursing, Rodney still ill, I assisted Uncle Todd, the boy badly mutilated. No lights on in Eva's house when I drove by. I had nothing to eat because I didn't notice Mrs. Platt had left something for me in the oven.

Thursday 26th April

Because of being so tired I'm depressed as if all the pain and illness and suffering rested on me and what I can do for it. It seems to me that other people's faces are well fed and smooth and completely without expression. There are deep lines on my face, I'm always pale and my hair is going grey already. Life seems futile and I'm restless.

I am pleased with the pyjamas however, the blue trimming is pretty and the mandarin style collar is very neat.

I have seen Eva today. She is well. Radiant. Yes there was television at the hotel. We had only a few minutes together, I called in on my way back to the hospital. I assisted Uncle Todd with a hysterectomy, the wife of a friend of his. Eva is worried about Angela. She asked me to sound her chest. Angela, who is thirteen, was very shy about unfastening her dress. I couldn't hear anything in such a hurried examination.

Oh, I long to step from the life which is so full of the children and Jake and the household. I long to step off into the other world which is at the side of our busy lives. It's the world of loving I want to step into. I want to walk in some lonely place with Eva where no-one can disturb us. I want to be alone with her. I want to talk to her and to have her talk to me. But restraint has become a part of my life. I am my own wardress. That is why I am so tired. I never relax this self-imposed discipline.

I am disappointed in Eva's return. What did I hope for?

Saturday afternoon 28th April

The distant sounds of cars and buses remind me of Eva, I think of the main road winding up the hill by her place, it's as if all the traffic is making its way to her. The afternoon is very still, only bees and the caressing song of the magpies. When I was a child I thought if I could only burrow through the leaves and grasses I would emerge in some magic place. I feel just now as if some magic place is just beyond my reach.

Angela is fourteen today. I took a small present for her, a tiny jewel on a gold chain, the kind of things most girls like. I hope so. Eva is always busy, she does too much. I always call on the birthdays. It seems hardly any time since it was Angela's tenth birthday and little Andrea sat on my lap after her sleep. She was naked, soft and warm, silky to hold. Eva smiled then and told Andrea, "You are lucky to sit in Laura's lap!" I have never forgotten Eva's smile that day.

I want to listen to music with Eva, to listen to every phrase of the music and to know she is listening too. I want to tell her of the love and the tenderness in the music and of the discipline necessary for two people in knowing of these delicate things and being able to be dignified and in repose. I want to be with Eva without the little girls in between us and without the bruising rudeness of Jake when he comes in and shouts for towels and clean clothes after his boat has turned over.

I hate Jake and I dislike the house he has built for

Eva. It's all concrete and glass and he uprooted all the trees. His garden is made of coloured slabs. Eva says it's easy to keep clean. It's strange to think I've known Eva so many years and we don't really know one another.

Monday 30th April

Perhaps this rapture is the beginning of disaster.

Eva, how easily my pen glides over the paper when I write your name. Eva.

Last night she came to see me. I was in bed when she came. Her coming was something of a shock. I thought something must be wrong but I must confess here in the diary, I was so pleased to see her it did not matter to me what her reason was.

She cried. It was a strange deep happiness for me to have her in my arms while she cried. That seems selfish of me, I can't help it. Jake had been drinking she said, and he had behaved like a brute, those were her words, it was a scene she said in the bedroom without any love and as soon as he had gone to sleep she dressed herself quickly and ran down to my house. She was afraid her mother and the girls might have heard their quarrel and she was ashamed. She was afraid she would be pregnant again. She was afraid of that. She did not want another baby, she was very emphatic. How she cried my poor little Eva.

I thought of all my smiling pregnant patients, self-satisfied, asleep in their well-kept homes, secure, protected by layers of brick and tile and well-manured rose beds, marriage and reticulation, double fronts, double garages, double beds and double faces. How many of my smiling pregnant patients were sick with distaste at the moment of conception. I wondered.

For some time I listened and I comforted her. As it was so late I locked the door and persuaded her to lie down in my bed. She seemed small and frail. I think I have never felt so fond of her as I did then. I put out the light and lay on the bed beside her and cradled her all night in my arms, next to my heart.

Of course we overslept. It was a laughing mad rush to

my bathroom which, in the mornings, is full of sunlight. It's like being in a tree there as branches, twigs and green leaves force their way through the window which will no longer close. I would have liked to stay in the sparkling morning forever with Eva. I had to leave her at her gate without breakfast and with hardly a word spoken as I was expected in theatre before eight.

Always on the drive to the hospital I feel competent and serious, sometimes tired and thoughtful before the day has really started as if in preparation for what lies ahead. The road curves round along the placid river. The buildings of the city are indistinct, blue in misty repose and the sky is gentle, tender and sad.

Later in the day I had the chance to telephone Eva. The relief I felt at hearing her voice is an indication that this call will be the first of many. I know that when I speak to Eva on the telephone the conversation has to be limited because her mother is never far away and she listens to everything. My restraint is gone and my peace of mind is lost. Already twice tonight I have telephoned Eva's number and, both times, when Jake answered I put down the receiver without saying anything.

Friday 11th May
I love Eva. I love Eva as tenderly as only a woman can love another woman. I have just told Eva to lie down on the couch by the window so that I can see her as I sit at my desk. Eva is here with me. Today my room is like a pool with golden green varying depths of light and shadow. There is a stillness and a tranquillity here, and there is, too, a quiet vibrating secret happiness. Eva will be staying till tomorrow. She is not quite well and is pleased to lie down. She thinks I am working at my chapter, instead, I am writing in the cardboard diary. It is exciting for me to write about her and about our being together for the night and about my happiness. I'll have to visit at the Infirmary and at the Nursing Home in the morning but I shall come back as quickly as possible.

Tonight I have allowed myself to step into my other world. I wish I knew if Eva will come there with me. I

138

admire her so much. Her hair shines, she is so fair and her skin is smooth and unblemished. She is round and soft and fresh and very dear to me. I want to spend the whole night holding her close in my arms and telling her all the things I feel about her. I want to laugh with her and I want to run into our happiness.

Sunday 13th May

I'm wretchedly cold. I have a headache and a backache. I don't want to write but I must write all the things I would rather forget. Eva is with her family and friends, they are having a barbecue. I was invited but I am not going. At one time I would have joined in simply to spend the day near Eva.

I have discovered an unpleasant thing about Eva. I have discovered that the night she came down to me so distressed she was only pretending. She is obviously pregnant, several weeks of pregnancy; I could see this at once. Why should she lie to me? She's quite advanced.

And I have discovered an unpleasant thing about myself, it's this, I no longer have my own discipline to protect me from Jake and Eva's mother and her insufferable friends. When I kept my life a secret I was safe. When I did not expect too much I was more content with my life as it was. Now I am both restless and afraid.

We never had our night together. Eva is nervous in my house, she is frightened of ghosts and spiders. She is nervous of my bath heater because it is old and makes a noise as if about to explode, so I prepared her bath. To make the night seem longer I put off going to bed. I played some records of Glück's opera Orfe and Eurydice. The parts are sung by two women. The contralto, Orfé, in particular, is very rich and satisfying and the voice is so sustained, I wondered if Eva noticed this as I did. "Vieni Vieni con me O Caro," I wanted to sing, "Vieni Vieni con me O Caro!". I wanted to take Eva and lead her through all the ways I have known, safely and tenderly, if only she would come.

Then I was called out to the Nursing Home. It's always the same, childbirth starts for me with the disturbance of the telephone ringing, the voice of the sister in charge, my car in reverse and the quick drive through dark and night-quiet streets. A kind of urgency to which I am accustomed but often there is more time than there seems to be, as there was the other night. Eva was afraid to stay alone in my house, there was quite a little scene with me trying to persuade her. I had time, after examining my patient, to return and drive Eva home and then I went back to my patient, a breech delivery. So far this has been my most difficult case, I was not home till five. I slept and went back to the Nursing Home at noon. Everything very satisfactory, I am relieved about this.

Eva telephoned and, in a very ordinary voice, asked me to the barbecue. Life seems one long barbecue for them. I asked her if she was all right and she said "yes". I thought she sounded hesitant. "Is your mother there?" I asked. "Right here," she said, so there was nothing we could really say to one another.

Sunday 20th May

I have time to walk about in the seclusion of my garden and see the grapes withered on the vine. I lit a fire in my study, the first this autumn. Outside it is damp and fragrant with grass and leaves. Uncle Todd came. He told me I should take a holiday. I am very relieved that he thinks I am simply over-tired. I am so afraid of Uncle Todd or Rodney and worse, Mrs. Glass, or any of them, probing into my secret world.

I don't really want to go away though in the past I have enjoyed the complete solitude of holidays. I always wrote to Eva when I was away but always they were conventional disciplined letters. I could.not write her such a letter now after holding her in my arms as I have done and after telling her that I love her. I want to go on telling her, I'd like to write pages of love to her and I want to show her how I love her and how much.

Uncle Todd asked me to dinner next Saturday. There was no way of refusing. I'll have to tell Eva in case she thinks of coming that night. I could not bear for her to come to an empty house.

Monday 21st May

Today I wrote to Mrs. Grant at Great West Bay to ask if she can have me for the second fortnight in June. It's where I have often been. Even though I like going there, I feel very depressed about it. I wish I could stay hidden in my house.

Sunday 27th May

Bach. Harpsichord and orchestra. The quality of reason is not in harmony with my mood. I have to make arrangements to have the house rewired and the roof repaired. I dislike thinking of the intrusion of workmen however necessary. I have forbidden Mrs. Platt the study. She was upset and said, "But Doctor, what about all the dust and mess in there?" and I said, "I will clean the study myself Mrs. Platt." I am afraid of Mrs. Platt finding out something about my secret world. I am continually afraid that I will forget to lock away my diary and she will find it and read what I have written about Eva.

My hands are shaking badly and tonight I have to do the post-operative dressings for Uncle Todd's surgical patients.

The dinner at Uncle Todd's was very dull. Mr. Fort and his wife, who have just come from England, seemed ill at ease as if not used to dining with men like him. Mrs. Glass admired my embroidered dress, she always admires my clothes. My clothes deserve admiration because I dress well. I never wear anything cheap because I can't. Mrs. Glass does not know this, she only admires because she does not know what to say to me. Mrs. Glass and Mrs. Fort in vulgar dresses, ugly, but if they knew this they would be hurt, they are not vulgar on purpose.

Privately, Uncle Todd told me he was going to marry Miss Beverley. She has been his housekeeper for thirty-three years. Uncle Todd said too that he had more regard for my ability and competence than he had for the work of either Fort or Glass. Sometimes I do wish for the old world of Father and Uncle Todd discussing their patients and their work.

I did not want to go on thinking unpleasant things about Eva so today I endured the terrible boredom of the barbecue in the hills. I went because it was my only chance to be near her. Angela came in my car. I am patient with Angela and her incessant chatter only because she is Eva's. It's always the same people, the same rocks, the same bush and the same interest in the food and the drink and keeping the children from fighting.

Eva is looking so pale and tired. She admired my new jacket. I have not told her yet that I am going away. All day I have been sad seeing her and not being close to her.

Once years ago Jake hurt his hand during one of these all day outings, and someone suggested that I, as a doctor, attend to it. I have never been able to forget Jake's coarse laugh and his even coarser joke about me and the rough laughter of the others at my expense.

It is time to go to the Infirmary. The hospital at night looks like a great ship forever in harbour. To me, the lights are a reminder of the pain and suffering within.

Monday 28th May 4 a.m.

This is not a usual time for writing but I want to write that Eva is going to come away with me on the holiday next month.

I had only been home from the hospital ten minutes when Jake telephoned asking me to come at once because Eva was very ill. I went at once. Jake met me in the drive, he said, "Eva has tried to take her life. Aspirins."

He rushed me into the house and into the bedroom. Eva was not unconscious. I sent Eva's mother and Jake out of the room. Never have I counted anyone's pulse so tenderly. She cried and told me about a quarrel she had with Jake and that she had tried to poison herself. I longed more than anything to take her in my arms but instead I washed out her stomach. Later when she was warm and comfortable, sweetly asleep, I had a talk with Jake. He said he wanted her to take a holiday, she badly needed a rest he said. Like many men he is sentimental about his wife because of her pregnancy. I told him I was going away and I suggested she might like to come with me. Jake seemed relieved and I tried to hide my pleasure at the thought of the holiday with Eva.

I have written to Mrs. Grant to tell her there will be two guests instead of one.

Still Monday 28th May

I have visited Eva four times today. I lay beside her on the bed this afternoon while her mother was out. I was so tired I could hardly keep awake. I almost did not hear Eva's mother coming into the house. I jumped up quickly, just in time. Eva is pleased about the holiday.

Thinking about Eva has become a great part of my life, now I can think with unspoiled happiness that we are going to be together alone for two weeks in a lonely place.

Tuesday 29th May

It is very sweet to question Eva intimately about her health. And it is pleasant to have the right as a doctor to be alone with her. Today I bought a pretty nightdress for her. The shop assistant was very bored with me giving the impression that she disliked me simply as a type to be disliked. I am often hurt because of this sort of thing. I know these people are of no consequence but I am afraid of their scorn.

I don't expect to give Eva the present. Eva's mother is the kind of woman to extract things from Eva. She might extract the present and, with it, the knowledge of my love and drag this noble tender feeling through her tattered gossip. I am afraid of Eva's mother, she finds out everything. She is always first to get to the telephone when it rings.

Monday 4th June

A kind of intoxication, a quiet happy excitement. A lot of people are curious about someone like me. I don't want to encourage their curiosity, I am afraid of it. Oh Eva, it's nearly time to go. I shall not even think of Jake, not once. How can I sleep when, in a few hours time, I shall be fetching you.

Friday 15th June

Eva is sleeping. I have been perfectly happy watching over her sleeping. It is pleasant to lie here listening to the falling waves and the long sigh along the shore which follows every fall of the full sea. Fresh cold air seems to seep through the weatherboards. It is a wild night with fierce winds and sudden storms of rain. The heavy rain on the iron roof is like the last movement of Beethoven's Seventh Symphony. It is raining now as if it could not rain any harder, rain, rain and more rain. It is a wild passionate music this rain and this wind and this sea. Mrs. Grant's old house creaks and somewhere close by a shutter bangs to and fro. It is as if everything gives way to the passion of the storm. There were wild nights like this years ago when I came with Father for our holidays. The house seems to overflow with Grant children, they stare at Eva and me. Mr. Grant is away, his work takes him away for weeks. Eva and I have the large room at the back. "Mrs. Grant will bring us hot water" I told Eva and I showed her the primitive arrangements in the yard. Getting used to these is not so easy.

All evening before the hot fire I was nearly asleep. I was tired after the long drive. Eva and Mrs. Grant talked on and on about their husbands and their children. I was longing to sleep. "I want to sleep but you must dance," as the poet says.

Eva has the big bed and I have a small folding bed. It is not comfortable and I am horribly cold. Since coming to bed I have not been able to get my back warm.

Eva enjoyed the journey, tucked in a tartan rug, she said she felt safe with me. I liked that very much. The country on both sides of the road looked sad and dark, rain-soaked, and the road seemed to go on and on into the banks of cloud ahead. Eva and Mrs. Grant were

144

friends as soon as they met, that is Eva's way. She found pink hair ribbons for the Grant girls from her own things and she had birthday tea in the kitchen with them. That is so like her, I felt very much on the edge of the day really, that's why I'm sitting in the cold night writing.

Tuesday 19th June

The days of our holiday dissolve in Mrs. Grant's household, this is Eva's way, it is what interests her. We have had very little time alone though one thing happened which is very sweet. Eva said to me to share the big bed because of the cold. This is something I look forward to, there is an intimate sweetness about sleeping and waking beside the one you love.

Today we walked on the shore. Several Grant children, who are not at school, followed at some disance. Eva was for calling to them to accompany us but I said no and I sent the children home. We saw Mrs. Grant appear in the distance on the beach and she took them back to the house. I don't want the children with us.

It was rather cold but the sun was hot and in the shelter of some rocks we bathed naked in the sea. Eva was shy at first but I persuaded her. I let myself look upon Eva, her pregnancy is advanced, her breasts are full and heavy. The white skin of her breasts is delicately traced with fine blue veins in a strange design belonging only to Eva herself. Today I looked upon her with wonder and with reverence and with love. I thought, could I reach her soul if I put my hand over her hand and kept it there, or, if I stroked her hair very lightly and gently. I felt a great tenderness for her. She gave a shy laugh and said,

"Oh Laura don't look at me that way," and she burst into tears. She begged me then to get rid of her baby, she says she doesn't want another baby. She hates the thought of it, it's embarrassing she says when her other two children are so big now. She says she hates Jake and her life with him; she wants to like the things I like, books and concerts and plays. She cried so bitterly. I can

145

see now, in loving Eva and in telling her that I love her, I am doing her harm. This evening I have made up my mind to help her to accept the baby and to be pleased about the birth and to help her back to her life with Jake. I have to give up Eva but first I'm going to be happy with her in this separate world which is our own and after that I'll help her to go back to what is hers.

We are about to go to bed, there's a lovely fire in our room. I have been writing and Eva is addressing post-cards to Angela and Andrea. She has on her pink lace nightdress and I have my white silk pyjamas. We are alone here and it is the night.

Friday 22nd June

I am wondering how to speak to Eva, she is avoiding me and is so busy about the house with Mrs. Grant. They have much in common both being pregnant unwillingly. I am quite desolate not knowing whether to go out by myself or not. This atmosphere with Eva tossing her head and being so offhand makes it very hard for me to write or study. And if I go out to walk by the sea I might miss the chance of Eva wanting to come out with me. A person has no right to make another person so unhappy. The last two nights Eva did not ask me to share the big bed; apart from the cold, there is the unhappiness of being uninvited.

It occurs to me that Mrs. Grant and Eva have read my diary. I might have left it out by mistake. If they read it, they would not understand. And then I think they are far too preoccupied to want to read anything I have written. They talk endlessly about clothes and children and recipes. Eva seems really happy with Mrs. Grant. Perhaps she is only my friend because we have known each other since school, and she is sorry for me. Perhaps she has read the diary and is disgusted with the intimate things I have written. I am tormented that Eva, knowing about the diary, will tell her mother about it. Once her mother knows, everyone will know, her friends, my colleagues and my patients. Gossip gets everywhere, enlarged of course. I will be dragged down by my own passion!

Saturday 23rd June

How well and how deeply Eva sleeps. I suppose it is her condition. Children too sleep well and wake refreshed as she does.

Things are better between us. I have brought Eva into town and am waiting while she has her hair washed and set. It's a sordid little shop but Eva is delighted with the hairdresser. Later we are going to a film because Eva says she adores Dirk Bogarde, whoever he is.

Sunday 24th June

Eva's hair is a mass of little rolled up curls. She is very pleased. She wanted to go to church so we have driven into town again. She has not been to church for ages she says and had a great wish to go. I never go to church and would feel awkward so I am waiting in the car for her. I am absolutely convinced now that Eva would never read anything private of mine. We have had a very tender conversation in which Eva said she was sorry about her behaviour towards me. She said she thought she ought to get back to Jake,

"The only way I can get back to Jake is by being mean to you Laura," she said. This is how she thinks it out and she is sorry. If only there was some way of having our strength and depths of friendship and still be able to be what other people need us to be. But it does not seem possible to combine the two things.

I'm waiting in the car quite peacefully writing and thinking. It is the peace that comes from being asked to share her bed again. Last night was the coldest we have had. Eva used the cold as a reason for asking me to come into her bed. How can I write of the longing I have for her. When I have the chance I am afraid to say all I want to say and she is so very quick to fall asleep. I could wish for a night of wakefulness for us both. I was awake alone in the night next to my dear Eva who slept so soundly. I kept thinking of the nearness of the ordinary world and

147

how we would soon be back in it, and this kept me from sleeping.

When Eva comes out of church I'm going to take her away to a secluded place along the shore, a hidden beach where we can be together undisturbed.

Sunday 24th June Still Sunday. Very late evening.

I've been walking alone at the edge of the sea for miles. The sea today was drab, monotonous and had the minimum of movement and the sky reflected the monotony.

Eva, once I looked into your eyes and I thought I saw all the light of the western sky reflected there. I wanted to ask you, would you smile if I kissed you and touched you, would you smile? In the softness of your lips Eva, is there an unexpected coolness? I thought if I followed desire I could never come to emptiness. You are not here. Everything is very quiet. I have been sitting watching a lazy spider fall and start to spin again its broken web.

Where are you Eva?

Eva came out of church with a little group of people, relations, down here on holiday. Jake's cousin Doug, and his wife Myrtle and Myrtle's sister Alice. I was introduced but not invited to join them. If I am honest, I did not want to be invited.

"We'll deliver her safely tonight, Miss," Jake's cousin put his big laughing face in at the car window. Eva hardly looked at me, her eyes avoided mine, she gave a little wave and a tiny helpless shrug as if to say, "they've taken me, what can I do." The women were on both sides of her and I could hear her voice telling about Jake, Angela and Andrea.

I am waiting Eva for you to come back.

Tuesday 26th June

I am entirely unable to do anything. I can't write and I'm afraid to go out. I am seriously thinking of packing up and going home, the concentration of driving and being in control of the car would be good for me but there is the thought of the bleak journey half done, especially if I keep thinking that Eva might come back here and be all alone. Every mile would separate us. She might be ill or it is possible there has been an accident and that is the cause of her not being here yet. I am listening for the sound of a car but all I hear is the long drawn out sigh of the sea.

I listened for Father's car at school years ago. One of the staff had said she'd heard he might be coming to visit me. I stood outside the school where fallen leaves lay withered all over the wet grass and, in clean clothes, I waited hearing his car approach, even seeing it come, more than once, round the distant bend of the empty road. He never came but I waited and waited wishing more than anything to hear the sound of his voice. How I wished to be with him just for a short time. As the afternoon wore on I kept telling myself even if I only had ten minutes with him it would be enough. Other girls who had been out started to return and still I waited hoping he would come. Dusk was early because of the rain clouds and I was forced to understand it was a mistake and, without his voice, I wept in the endless repetition of the loneliness of the boarding school.

Mrs. Grant has just brought me tea and a telegram from Eva. They will be coming here tomorrow. Tomorrow is Wednesday and we go home on Thursday. Simply, I would like to pack up and leave now.

But what of Eva if I do this, I am so afraid of losing her.

Later the same evening

They are all here. They are playing canasta and are laughing at private jokes. Mrs. Grant is busy making room for them for the night. A woman doctor makes some men feel awkward. Jake's cousin laughs because I embarrass him.

Eva looks so well.

"Why did you bring them?" I asked her quickly and quietly.

"Oh they just came!" she said, laughing, "they are good fun, Laura."

I have never heard Eva laugh so much as she is laughing this evening.

We have all to share the big room as Mrs. Grant has only one other tiny room which is for Jake's cousin. I can't bear to think of Eva in bed either with Myrtle or with Alice yet how can I lie beside her in their presence.

Myrtle is good-natured. "Don't mind us dear!" she says. The room is full of women and the smell of them. An unpleasant lack of privacy.

"Oh Laura, don't disturb your work," Eva says to me, "we have our hair to do yet." She is already undressed and in bed. Myrtle says, and I agree with her, that the folding bed will not take her weight.

"Make room for a little one," and she climbs into bed beside Eva. Her good-natured red face is shining with cold cream. They are reading magazines and pay no attention to me, I feel very out of it all. I wish Eva could be ill so that she would need me. I should not wish this but I do. My only claim is a professional one. As her doctor I could claim privacy but she has no reason to ask and so I do not have any excuse.

The only comfort is that they will be gone tomorrow. Eva and I will be together and we shall be alone for the last night.

Wednesday 27th June

We have Alice with us. She is to travel with us tomorrow. Miles and miles of Alice! She is a friend of Eva's mother. "She's got a heart of gold," Eva said when I had a chance to protest privately. "She would do it for you Laura," Eva said, "if you needed the ride." So there was nothing I could say.

Early this morning I went up the yard to the lavatory. I thought I could smell cigarette smoke and was about to go back to the house to wait when Jake's cousin, Doug, emerged. He peered at me in the half light, tucking his shirt into his trousers.

"I see you're no fairy after all," he laughed and stumbled back down to the house laughing as if he had said something very funny. I cannot stand this kind of humiliation, I'll put this carboard diary away and go to bed.

Thursday 28th June

My house has been severely disturbed. It has a strange smell from the building repairs which are unfinished. The house seems withered and not like my house at all as if the life has gone from it. Perhaps it was like that before but I did not notice.

Eva's family were very pleased to see her and Alice. I stayed there about two hours, it would have been better to come straight home. I had a bad headache after the drive. It rained heavily for most of the journey. The sky was dark with rain and the countryside uninviting and dejected. I'm tired and depressed this evening. Tomorrow I shall be at the Infirmary by eight o'clock, it will be as if I had not been away at all. The river and the sleeping city will be unchanged. I shall continue with my work. The loneliness of my house begins to wrap round me but without any comfort.

Last night it was cold. When Alice was asleep I sat on the edge of Eva's bed. She was cold too, she had given Alice the extra blanket. Quietly I lay beside Eva and we talked in little whispers. I wanted to ask her why she chose to be with these other people instead of with me, but I could not. Eva told me in the night that she had not really tried to poison herself. She had wanted to frighten Jake, she said. She had only swallowed a few aspirins and it was easy to pretend after that. She told me she was sorry. Of course I forgive Eva because I love her. But I am desperately afraid that she will tell her mother and Jake and they will make a silly joke of it at my expense. I would not want my patients or my colleagues to know that I was taken in by her pretended symptoms. Why should Eva do something like this to me?

At school the other girls and Eva too often did things to make me look stupid like the time when they pretended Eva had a haemorrhage from her lungs and I rushed off to fetch the matron. And, when I had brought

151

her panting up all the flights of stairs there was no blood on the floor and no sign of Eva or the other girls in the dormitory. When the matron had had her outburst of anger and left, the girls and Eva jumped out of the clothes cupboard laughing. I felt I would never forgive them because, in her anger, the matron said, "You deserve all you get Laura, you deserve all you get!" Yet by the evening I had completely forgiven Eva.

Eva is in very good health. She could pretend to be sick and send for me at any time. I do not think she will do this, there are so many things she is eager to do and so many people who want her. She says she is hoping for a baby son. She asked if I would deliver the baby and I have agreed to do this, she is to come at the necessary intervals for examination. I find it incredible that this happy multipara, Eva, is the same lost little Eva who wept so bitterly and hopelessly in my arms.

Eva has brought with her through the years something of the endless summer charm of childhood. Her life is strewn with little fragrant posies and pretty fragments of sewing and embroidery, dainty and unfinished. When I first came to school Eva was already there. She was small and bright and fair and everyone liked her. Wherever she was there was laughter and bright colours and the warm intimate scent of apple blossom soap. The sound of the piano and of girls' voices singing in harmony was the background to our little private talks. When I sang at school I wanted my voice to reach Eva and when I played the piano I was playing for her. I tried to resist the attraction. In my seriousness and my devotion to studying, her laughter and her way of looking at things was a relaxation, a pleasure.

Once years ago, Eva said to me,

"Laura, did you know you have such a kind face when you smile." Our friendship continued after school, offering and asking on her side and with this discipline and restraint on mine.

And now that I have given up this restraint, I have nothing.

Friday 31st August

I have not written about Eva for some time but she is always in my thoughts. Everything I do is in some way connected with her and yet has no connection. I slip into a perpetual dream about her so that I do not know what is real about our lives and what is the dream. Her brief visits are real and are confined to a few remarks on her health which is excellent. I can never prolong these ante-natal examinations because she is short of time and I, of course, have other patients waiting. It is no use for me to telephone because her mother always answers the call and Eva is always out. There is never a chance to really be with her. Perhaps it is better like this. Oh Eva.

Evening of the same day

Eva's appointment was at the end of the afternoon. I wished for her to stay a little. Of course it is not possible to speak to her of my unhappiness. She invited me to a party at her house tomorrow.

"Oh Laura, please do come," she said, "I hardly ever have the chance to see you these days." She couldn't stay as she had to fetch Angela from her music lesson.

I have accepted the invitation.

This evening I have been looking at my own lonely body. Naked, it is creamy white and entirely unknown. It has a certain strength and its own secret quality of possibility but, as it has never been looked at or touched by anyone, it seems to have no meaning.

Saturday 1st September

Russett is the colour of autumn and that should be my colour, it is the colour of my long dress. I have come home without going to Eva's party. I am all dressed to go in this perfect frock. There are a great many people at Eva's house, the cars are on both sides of the street and round the corner. All the house lights are on and there are lights in the garden, the laughter and the voices can be heard for some distance.

I found a place to put my car and I started to walk across the sand to the footpath when, all at once, I knew

I could not enter that house and be among all those people. Some of them would be acquaintances but there would be a great number I would not know. I felt I could not face being introduced to people with Jake's coarse remarks and laughter, and worse than being introduced would be being left to look after my own introduction. Suddenly I was horribly frightened of all those people. Their laughing voices seemed to be louder and louder and I felt I must get away before I was seen by any of them. I felt hunted by their laughter and their curiosity. I wanted to get back to my car as quickly as I could. The situation was both ridiculous and terrifying. I was afraid of some kind of exposure, some kind of cruel joke at my expense; I told myself it was stupid but I was shaking so much I could hardly start my car and reverse and drive home. That I must get away was my only thought.

I did not want to see Eva in those circumstances, that Eva is not my Eva.

It is a relief to take off this dress and to be quietly alone here in my study. Eva will not miss me. Such a large party must have been arranged for some time and she invited me yesterday. I am thankful to be hidden here away from all that.

Perhaps I'll walk outside in the dark garden and wait for some wisdom to come to me from the fragrant stillness. In the shadow of leaves and petals and soft earth yielding a more settled happiness I can think of the soft touching of fingers and of gently murmuring voices. Everything reminds me of you Eva but I must leave you to your home, your husband and your children. I know that you do not need me for anything. I am quiet and I am grateful for the quietness. An emotional storm yields no rain only a devastation against the devastation of the seasons. I must endure to know new things.

* * *

PART 4

FROM EVA

Andrea

God! Oh Christ oh God awful! I can't stand the stillness! Oh Laura. Laura how quiet it is here without you, it's hard to come back into the present time after what I've been reading, yet all your things are scattered about, your clothes, shoes, books and even your belt is here over the brass rail of the bed. I feel I've been reading for hours and yet hardly any of the time I've got to get through without you has gone. I've still a lot more reading to do.

I'm telling myself right now, straight away that I know from loving Laura and being loved by her, physically I mean, that she has never made love to Eva and I know no-one has ever made love to Laura. If Laura heard me say that, she would say I am jealous and she would say that I have no need to be.

I've been reading about her longing to be loved and her even greater longing to love, that's what her cardboard diary is, it's her work and her music and her writing but even more it's her deep longing to express what she feels she must not express.

It seems incredible to me that someone like Laura, with all her intellectual qualities could love someone like my mother. Eva is a stupid woman in many ways, but I suppose Laura would see her qualities and love them, or even put qualities into Eva and love what she has put there. I suppose Laura knows really what Eva is like but she does not despise her for being what she is. Laura can see and recognise all the small phrases which make a whole whether it's a person or a piece of music by Beethoven. She knows and accepts that all people are not equal and that some are wasted on others yet she can't seem to see this in regard to Eva. That's what I find so hard to take.

Oh! I want you back here Laura, quick. I want this long day to be over. I want to talk to you and to have you talk to me.

My God Laura! How could you have lived like that waiting for Eva. Of course Eva admired you physically but how could you be pleased with such safe superficial admiration, a kind of non-event admiring. Eva could and would safely admire your strong wrists and your exceptional hands and your long straight legs and well-formed feet, but what does this mean when put beside the deep knowledge and admiration which comes from within? Eva would keep on the surface always and it's nothing special, Laura, if Eva says something nice about you, the chances are she'd forget the next day that she said them.

Of course Eva's not so silly really. She's always kept herself safe. And this is a clever quality in any human being. Laura, you would agree with that. Of course Eva admired you. Years ago, she liked to be known as Laura's friend. Eva would have tried to climb into your mind, that's what she was trying to be a part of. Your thoughts. Since she's never had an original thought of her own, she's always been in the habit of repeating the last thing she's heard as her opinion. That's why I had to get away; well, that's not the only reason. Living with you has made me more honest to myself. But don't you see, Laura, she needed your mind couldn't you see that?

156

She could only fasten on and look as though her mind moved in the way that yours could. She pretended to like things like music. She's pretended a great many things.

Oh God awful! Here I am Laura on the end of our bed, not even washed yet, talking out loud to myself. I want you back Laura, quickly, your leather belt smells of your spiced perfume, Laura. I breathe in that fragrance which is yours and I'm missing you so much. This is loneliness your loneliness from the cardboard diary and mine now, I know I'm not alone really, I know this. I'm in your place and I've been reading about you. But how can I read and not want to talk to you straight away. Now this minute! You've had all the tiredness and the disappointments and the uncertainties, I know because I've had a quick look at what's to come. I don't know if I can bear to go on reading.

I want you back, Laura, quickly. I want to feel safe with you safely here. Suddenly I'm afraid, terribly afraid.

On the outside of this next envelope there is a message in Laura's handwriting dated November 9th, today's date.

"This came in my letter box, I suppose it must be about eighteen years ago! It was in an envelope addressed to me but is obviously meant for someone else. I don't know who the person is, I can't remember if it was someone at school with us, a friend of Eva's in any case. I don't know if Eva actually wrote to me too and then made a mistake when putting the letters in their envelopes. I never heard anything from the person for whom this was intended and who might have received whatever was to have been sent to me. I did nothing about it myself. I had become very busy with my work, it was when Dora was housekeeping for me, I was writing and studying and operating and delivering babies and I had a very busy clinic. I was deeply involved with the theories of Dr. Gollanberg. I didn't allow the arrival of this letter to disturb and re-open a wound which, though not really healed, was quiet. I didn't even allow myself to wonder if in fact Eva had written to me. I did nothing."

From Eva

Dear Shirley, Thank you for your letter. I'm sorry I've been so long replying. No I never see Laura now even though we live quite close. If I ever see someone who knows Laura I never ask about her, something seems to stop me just as something seemed to stop me 'phoning her when she didn't turn up to that big party we had when I was expecting Christopher. All these years I've been telling myself that I'm too busy to miss her and though this is true one bit of me does miss her if I'm really honest with myself. If you remember Laura and I were friends at school and we went on being friends. Mum could never understand it and neither could Jake's mum. "Whatever do you see in her?" they used to ask me. I couldn't seem to tell them that it wasn't what I saw in her so much as how she saw me and how she was to me.

Everyone predicted I'd marry the boy next door and I did. Perhaps being friends with Laura was the special thing I needed in my life because I think every person has something that's special to them however stupid it might look to other people. Laura herself has always been used to being special. I mean she was top in every subject at school and she had her music and her writing. She didn't make friends easily and I think I liked the idea of being sort of chosen by her. I couldn't help being friends with her. In a way I'm sorry I never 'phoned her. I suppose I could have 'phoned when I saw her Uncle's death in the paper but I didn't and I let the time go by and then it was too late.

Time flies doesn't it, Christopher will be six next week. Angela's going out with a very nice boy and Andrea has started her monthlies. It's all of six years since I've seen Laura.

At the time Mum said Laura probably forgot about the party and Jake said she was more likely to be so boozed she couldn't find our place. He was so funny I couldn't help laughing. But I've never seen Laura drink too much though she always liked a drink. Mum said if Laura was sick being a doctor she could fix herself up. Me, I'm not so sure and perhaps that's why I've got her so much on my mind specially just now with you reminding me asking about her in your letter. I feel I've got to tell you how things were between Laura and me.

When Laura smiled she could make me feel so special. She's got a lovely smile. When she smiled I felt everything about me looked good and nice and I felt I was beautiful when she looked at me the way she did. Laura could make me want things, anything, a hat, a dress, a car, a house, a leaf, a flower, they seemed lovely when she noticed them.

When I went to see her I could forget about what was going on in the outside world. I wanted to be near her like I was before I was married. She has lovely eyes, she can look at you so kindly, perhaps that's what I miss. I always felt it didn't matter what awful things she might know about me it would not make any difference. At one time I would have done anything in the world for her, and that is the honest truth and it's how she made me feel.

Often I tried to make her touch me with her hands, she's got very thin hands you can see every bone in them, but they're fine and strong. So often I wanted to feel her hands on my hands, on my arms or on me somewhere, anywhere, everywhere. I often sat very close so that if we were looking at a map or a photograph we would be sure to touch. I suppose I led her on like this at school and later. I couldn't help it. Sometimes at school we teased Laura because she was so serious, we tricked her and made her look a fool like the time we splashed lollywater on the floorboards and pretended I had vomited blood. That day she was hurt and angry but by bedtime we were friends again. I went into bed with her that night and we lay there so close together because of the bed being so narrow and we talked for ages and she kissed me and stroked me ever so gently and I wanted to stay with her all night but she said it might

159

be bad for us and we must never do it again and she took me back to my own bed and sat with me till it was beginning to get light.

That was the very first time and for a time she never spoke about it but stayed up later at night reading and studying on her own and only going to bed long after everyone was asleep. Sometimes Laura and I fetched the palms for the school hall. We had to get them from the conservatory. It was hot in there and steamy and there was a spicy smell. Laura said it was an atmosphere where things were forced to grow and because of this she didn't like it much, but all the same it was a secret place and no-one was likely to come in, specially at the end of the afternoon. Sometimes we sat there undisturbed with our arms round each other all through tea time. When we were hidden in the palm leaves and trailing feathery things Laura said the warmth and the quietness made her think too much about this feeling we both had but she liked it this way and I liked it too. She said it was the real meaning of the word tranquil, how we felt afterwards while we took the plants to the platform in the hall. I wanted to talk to her but she seemed to close herself off. That last year at school I often sat on her bed laughing and talking to other girls but all the while teasing her secretly pretending all the time not to notice how she was looking. Her eyes would seem dark and she'd go very quiet, really moody.

As I said Laura could make me feel I was beautiful. I felt in love as they must feel in films. Jake has never made me feel like this, it's a terrible thing to say about your own husband but he has never turned me on as Laura could. Mum has always thought Laura was a bad influence, as she calls it, on me. She says you can't be that clever unless you're completely selfish, I think Mum has a point there. Jake thinks of Laura as someone set apart, he could never begin to understand her, for a start she'd never let him, and he'd never ever understand how I've felt about her.

It's awful to say this but I've got to tell someone,

sometimes I've wanted her and I've gone straight from her, because she wouldn't, to him. How could I ever tell anyone this. You'll have to tear this letter up and burn it, promise!

I don't know why I feel the way I do. I think some people do more than others. I mean I don't think the physical side is everything but if it's there you can't ignore it. I'm embarrassed about it really with Mum and with the two girls growing up. When I realised I was pregnant again I felt I couldn't face Mum and the girls. I felt I couldn't even face Laura, though being a doctor she would have an entirely different attitude, purely medical, and not being married herself wouldn't know the other side of it.

I got everything out of proportion and went down to Laura's one night. I'd had a couple of drinks and Jake had had more than he should have. Anyway he'd dropped off to sleep leaving me right out of the picture. I felt that mad! Anyway I went down to Laura's. She'd gone to bed and the shock of seeing me made her go white. I've heard some queer things about women who live alone. It was silly of me to be afraid of her but I was. She was really good to me and I stayed all night. I let her talk to me and put her arms round me but those drinks really stopped me fully understanding what she said and I've no idea really what happened. Mum said however could I stay there in that dirty house and Jake of course can't stand the way she has bushes and trees right up against her house. He won't have anything growing near the house, it's all cleared round our home and he's set coloured concrete slabs into a terrace and a patio.

Mum said did I sleep with Laura or does she still keep guest rooms like they used to. And she looked at me as if she wanted to inspect my pants though what she'd find God only knows. So I said off hand that Laura knew how to look after visitors and that Mrs. P. still kept the place clean as she had done for years.

I went to lie down as I felt sick and Mum came and asked me why I didn't ask Laura to get rid of the baby. She really took me by surprise, she said, "Laura's a doctor and she's your friend. She could do this easy for you and no one be the wiser!" And I didn't know she knew.

Even though that's what I wanted, I howled for ages and Mum did all she could to stop me. In the end she went to the shops and bought some lamb's fry and some white lawn and there and then started on the gowns for the baby. I managed to keep the lamb's fry down and Mum seemed so pleased and kept thinking up ways to please me, I told Mum I felt a heel for not telling her before and she said, "Oh Evie I know when you're unwell and it's twice now you've missed your time of the month. There's something about you gives you away."

Mum ran up a lovely little two piece for me, pink with a white Peter Pan collar and adjustable waist bands. It was really nice. Jake had to go off on a job and Mum suggested having some friends in for a game of cards. She loves a game. But I said no I'd rather go down and see Laura about what she, Mum, had suggested.

So I went down very late. Laura was, as usual, at her desk. She was very pleased to see me and she was pleased to leave her work she said. I lied to Laura about the pregnancy knowing full well I'd missed the curse twice. Laura seemed amused and pleased and we teased each other and Laura changed completely and was so serious and said she was afraid for me. She talked me nearly to death and then she walked me up home.

Mum said, "Well did you ask her?" she was waiting up for me. And of course I hadn't asked Laura to do what I'd gone there to ask her, and I hadn't even told her I was pregnant. Mum said Laura being a doctor would know for sure that I was pregnant. All I could do was burst out crying and in the end Mum made some tea with rum in it and came into bed with me.

All the week I was in a tizzy with Jake away and there we were starting to make baby clothes and I hadn't even told Jake and the girls and it was Mum's idea that I go and stay the night at Laura's and try once more.

So I went down there and Laura seemed really ever so pleased to have me there. She looked after me as if I was a precious jewel, not that Mum doesn't look after me, she does, she spoils me. And I never want for anything from Jake. We just about have everything there is to have. I wanted Laura to smile at me. She was laughing a lot and there I was trying not to be sick. As far as Laura knew I wasn't supposed to know for sure whether there was a baby or not. I had to tell her I didn't feel well and she said she could see that and that she'd run the bath for me. I'm scared of her old bath heater and really her whole house is scarey at night. The upshot of the whole thing was that she was really kind, reading poems to me, playing nice music, she really loves her music, and she brought me hot milk in bed, and then just when she was coming to bed and I thought I'll ask her now, the 'phone went and she had to go out to a patient.

I wasn't going to stay alone in that house, not on your life, so I got dressed quickly and Laura drove me home. So I still hadn't asked her. Mum said later perhaps it was all for the best and that we shouldn't tamper with nature.

Well, the next thing was my attempted suicide. Don't laugh, Shirley, but I play-acted the whole thing. Jake was that scared when he thought I'd tried to take my own life. I fooled him and Mum and Laura with some aspirins I put in a bowl with some water. The end of that little episode was me going off on a holiday with Laura.

Before the holiday I didn't give Laura a thought I had so much on my mind. Mum and I went to town to price brunchcoats and baby doll pyjamas for the girls and Mum bought a lovely white nylon stole she'd fancied. When we got it home we discovered a flaw in the lining so we had to go back to town the next day to change it. I told Jake and the girls about the expected new arrival. Everyone was thrilled and the news seemed to bring us all closer together which in this day and age is a good thing.

The place where Laura took me for the holiday was quiet. Laura liked this quiet but I prefer a bit more going on. Give me a metropolitan beach any time, you've got everything, kiosks, toilets, first aid and surf, the lot. Laura was really moody but I was used to that, she can go for hours without saying a word. Still there was Mrs. Grant to talk to. She said Laura looked unwell and I said not to worry as I knew Laura was on pills and knew how to look after herself.

Well one day on the beach I got up my courage to ask Laura if she would do something about the baby. Mrs. Grant didn't want hers either, she's got seven already. Imagine seven! But before I could say anything Laura had all her clothes off and was in the water nude. She made me do the same, there was no-one around. Of course she could see straight away how far on I was and I could see her looking at me. Of course she refused to do a thing. She said straight off she couldn't think of an abortion for me and she tried to make me see all the good side of having a baby. Looking back now I see that I went on howling and crying because it's awful to ask for something like that and then to have to carry on knowing the other person knows what you wanted and has refused what you've asked for.

Even when she helped me to dress she was so careful not to touch me anywhere even though I'm sure she wanted to and I wished she would. I felt I had had Laura for good. And by the night time I couldn't stand that ricketty old bedroom and the noise of the sea got on my nerves so did the sheer loneliness of the place. Just fancy an old house on the shore miles from anywhere! I couldn't stand it. I went along to the kitchen for my hot milk and Mrs. Grant and I got talking again. She was really unwell, her legs were terrible and her back was bad, she said she couldn't be more fed up than I was. So I said how about we persuade Laura to do something. When Mrs. Grant got my meaning she was thoroughly shocked. She said she'd known Laura all these years and Laura's father being such a gentleman she couldn't suggest such a thing. And then she said, "What would we need?" All I could think of was hot water and gin so we filled the black kettle and all the biggest pots and put them on the stove. Mrs. Grant pulled out all the dampers and the stove roared up really hot.

"Any gin?" I said and Mrs. Grant fetched some and we both had a drink for confidence. I pulled the table up nearer the lamp and I put a chair by it with a wash basin on it. It looked right somehow.

"We'll need towels and pads," I kept my voice down because of the children being asleep so near the kitchen. "We'll bleed," I said.

"It'll be painful I suppose," Mrs. Grant whispered, and I felt afraid of the terrible thing we were doing. I told her to shut up and sent her to get another storm lantern and the soap as Laura would be sure to want to wash first. It was pretty hot in the kitchen and I felt queer so I had a bit more gin, so did Mrs. Grant. The kitchen looked so changed. It was the preparations, the washbasin on the chair and the white sheet Mrs. Grant had spread on the table, the oil lamp hung down low and seemed much bigger and full of meaning; the kitchen looked like there was an operation going on already.

"We'd better go up to the toilet," I said. So we went together up the yard; it was dark and stormy and we were glad to get back into the house again. We dragged the bath in from the verandah and we filled it with hot water and put more water on to boil and by the time this was done the kitchen was so full of steam we could hardly see each other.

Well, then I went along to our room to get Laura. Imagine how I felt when I found her in bed asleep. I had a job rousing her; finally I got her up and told her to come to the kitchen as Mrs. Grant was ill. Laura couldn't seem to wake up, it's my belief she'd taken pills. She was really shivering.

"Get your bag and instruments," I told her and Laura said she hadn't got them, they were in the car.

"Well you'll have to go out and get them," I said. I did feel annoyed with her for seeming so stupid. Somehow I got her to the kitchen. When she saw everything she looked really upset and frightened and I said to her, "Laura, Mrs. Grant says your father did an operation on her once and you must do the same for us." I was surprised at myself, really I was. "Your father gave Mrs. Grant a miscarriage," I said.

Laura looked very white and beads of sweat came out along her forehead, she leaned against the doorpost. She looked at Mrs. Grant who was sitting down with her head down as if she was going to pass out. The steam was so thick and it was so hot the fire really roaring in the stove pipe. I felt queer and my head seemed to be loose from my body. Laura looked straight at me.

"Eva, you are quite mistaken," she said, "so is Mrs. Grant if you think that of father." Mrs. Grant started to howl out loud and Laura came right on into the kitchen and told Mrs. Grant to be quiet because she'd wake the children. She asked Mrs. Grant how to shut down the stove and then she said we'd better hurry up and clear away the things. She said the kind of operation we wanted was not an easy one and not so simple as we thought and could easily go wrong.

"Rubbish," I said, and I said, "wash your hands Laura and do this for us. You must! We aren't letting you leave here unless you do!" Laura seemed paler than ever.

"Eva," she said, "I can't do an operation of this nature in this place and even if I could, you know that I would not. Apart from anything else you are both advanced, it is a skilled operation and if something went wrong where would I get help if I needed it. Eva, you must know that I would never consider doing such a thing." Mrs. Grant started off her crying again and she kept saying she was sorry and Laura told her not to worry and to get off to bed as quick as she could and that she would empty the bath herself.

I really forget what happened, I remember Laura moving about slowly pouring away the hot water. I remember shouting at Laura and blaming her for everything and I know that while I was shouting I kept wishing Laura would stop what she was doing and be angry at me and then be sorry. I kept trying to hurt her, to rouse her anger and I don't remember anything else. Somehow she must have got me to bed, when I woke up she was still asleep on the little bed but she never brought up the subject and I couldn't bear anyone near me in the morning especially Laura.

She never spoke of it even when we made up later. Whenever we made up she was always extra kind and thoughtful. She was good to me and she was a lovely person, I say that now that it's six years later on and I never see her.

The last part of the holiday turned out to be the best. It was a coincidence really. I had this sudden wish to go to church. Laura never goes but she drove me into town, it's quite a drive from Mrs. Grant's place. She sat in the car with her writing. After the service I was just coming out of the door when I heard a familiar voice,

"Long time no see!" and I turned round and there was Doug and Myrtle with Myrtle's sister Alice, a great friend of Mum's, right behind. Doug is Jake's cousin, they were all down there on holiday. Was I ever glad to see them! Laura didn't seem to mind at all when I went off with them. She just sat in her car and she didn't say anything, she never moved and she didn't wave but Laura is like that. You just have to accept her as she is. But Laura between her kindness and her moods had been a terrible strain on me and it was a relief to get back to normal with other people. When I was with Doug and Myrtle it seemed impossible that I ever tried to get a miscarriage and I realised that Mum and Jake and the girls were more important to me than anything else in the world. And now that I've got Christopher it's hard to think I ever thought I didn't want him. It just shows really that we don't always know what's best even when we think we do.

I told Laura in the night, the Wednesday night, it was our last night there, that I'd only wanted to scare Jake with the aspirin lark, I told her it was only the outcome of a lovers' tiff. I didn't want her to think I'd tried to bring on a miscarriage. What I told her wasn't exactly the truth but I was tired out and I wanted to have a sleep and she would keep on talking. You see I hardly slept while I was with Doug and Myrtle. The time went so quickly while I was with them and it was two in the morning and we were still playing Canasta and I had Myrtle's home perm to see to. Her hair takes well and she looked lovely. And we were up early to go fishing and because I was worrying having left Laura alone Doug suggested we all drive over to Mrs. Grant's place, that way we'd all have company and Laura wouldn't be out of it. I needn't have worried about Laura, she seemed perfectly all right sitting with her books and her writing. She isn't an easy mixer and she doesn't play Canasta or any games, but as Doug said we were all there for the taking. Myrtle was scared Laura would notice her legs and tell her she must have her veins done.

After the holiday I really seemed to settle down. Alice stayed for seven weeks, Mum loved having her around. I felt better and really enjoyed life to the full. Mum got busy with the machine and ran up some lovely florals for me to knock about the house in. It does you good to have new clothes.

The last thing we had before Christopher was born was the big party to christen the yacht and Laura never turned up. I suppose I'll never know why she never came. I kept thinking I ought to 'phone her but looking back I can see that I kept having reasons for not 'phoning. I let the time go by and it would have been strange to ring then. I felt so awkward changing to another doctor so late on but I think really it was all part of not seeing Laura and being more settled because of not seeing her. Our lives couldn't mix I suppose, and for most of the time until now I must honestly say I haven't thought much about her. I'm so busy with the home and the girls and young Christopher.

This last year Jake has built on a games room and a big utility area with frosted louvres. There's been a lot to think about matching the vinyl tiles and the curtains. Mum has gone all contemporary and I've got a yen for stripes. It's lovely to have the extra space. And only today Mum discovered some gorgeous material in Lawleys and she's making Wendy blouses for the girls.

They'll be thrilled and I really enjoy seeing them nicely dressed.

If I went to see Laura now I wouldn't know what to say to her. Perhaps it's better to leave things as they are. Mum says it's better to let well alone and though I am really sorry I have to agree with Mum and leave it at that. I think the most important thing in life is your family, and mine certainly keeps me out of mischief.

PART 5

SO YOU ARE BRIDE AGAIN TONIGHT

Andrea

However can I go on! I want to see Laura so much. Oh Laura Dear! I'll have to go on reading. It's still quite early but, because I've had all this life opened up in a way I never expected, it seems as if I've been sitting here for years. Reading about my own home and about Mother is so strange, it's like being back there and not being back there because I didn't know any of it though I do sort of remember Laura coming when I was little. What Laura wrote then fits in a way with how I felt about things when I left home, though I could never have put it into words. How awful Mother must have been! God awful! How still it is here without Laura. These empty rooms seem high up and light; it's as if Laura's house is fragile, not quite real.

If I make a noise with the shower the silence will be worse afterwards but I ought to wash and get dressed. I feel too tired to go on reading but if I don't read, the silence will be more frightening and I'll have the awful feeling that perhaps Laura will never come back.

If I cut the loaf and spread butter it all seems so pointless. I hate eating alone, I suppose Laura is used to it. I suppose I should eat something. I haven't had any food. The idea of getting it ready makes me feel more alone. I wish I could see her now. I wish it was time for her to come back but it'll be hours and hours. How slowly the time passes when she is not here, it's only ten minutes since I looked at the time. I'll try not to look at the clock.

There's more of Laura's life to read. I don't know if I can bear it. She's had such a sad life really and yet she's privileged. I'd like to be with her now here on the big bed. I'd kiss her all over and make her happy and perhaps lose some of my own sadness. If only worries like mine could be got rid of so easily!

Oh Laura come back quickly. You are made for loving and kissing Laura. It's true your hands can deliver babies but your hands are made for love, for the delicate touching of love. When you are not here there is no life.

This next letter is in Laura's handwriting and she has written something on the outside of the envelope, she has written today's date which is, it's hard to believe, still the same day, the 9th of November.

"I wrote this in prison. I was in the prison medical care department. Before this, Dora had left me to get married to a little nut shaped man. I was in prison for some time, it seemed an intolerable age to be kept alive. I was struck off the Register. All the official papers are in the yellow envelope, my discharge from prison and so on. I must tell you, Andrea, I am guilty of murder, I told them I was guilty. A friend of Father's took the case, there was very little publicity. There seemed to be lack of motive and real proof. It's all neither here nor there. I still think I am guilty of the murder even if she was a sick old woman and was dying in any case. They spoke of my being temporarily deranged, unbalanced because of overworking. I didn't care, I didn't want to live. It was the end of my work and that meant the end of my life. But you can't choose whether you will go on living or not. I had no-one. Rodney Glass and his wife and the

172

Forts were kind to me in their own way and I am grateful to them. They were sure it was just a temporary thing, a mistake because of being tired. It could happen to any doctor. Later I stayed with Rodney and was taken into their world of pastel nylon pleats, plastic picnic sets, small dinner parties with carefully selected company, very good meals, outdoor sports with the children, long drawn out musical evenings with the children singing and reciting and playing recorders. They respected my privacy, never referred to the disaster and never referred to the fact that I was no longer a doctor. Rodney helped me too over the sale of some of the property; he has a friend who knows all about this side of things and he looks after my investments. He helped me to get tenants for the other house. Rodney really helped me to take up what life was left for me. It was his idea too that I should go on the voyage round the world, the self-healing voyage last year, which in the end, brought me on to the ship where fate had put you.

"And then it was at his dinner table where you said you wanted to come to me, Dearest, so you see we have to say 'thank God there are Rodneys!' even if it's the only thing we can say about him. And, d'you see, Sunday is inevitable because of this. Rodney is inevitable and so is Sunday and after this Sunday there will be another Sunday."

* * *

So You Are Bride Again Tonight

This is probably the last time I shall write to you Dr. Gollanberg. They have given me a little wooden table and some sheets of paper. Though the paper is very poor quality I am grateful to have it. The pen they have given me is not as good as my own and does not write smoothly on the paper, so I am not able to improve the ugliness of your name as I used to. I always spent considerable time making a long and graceful loop on the G, it gave me pleasure to make your name beautiful, and I tried to give the other letters delicate Gothic qualities. I spent

173

hours writing to you, studying what you had written to me and then writing and rewriting my answers. And then there were all my questions to your wisdom and your learning and your ideas.

It seems now that the events which led up to the present were inevitable. And you are not in any way responsible for what has happened. The responsibility is all mine. A thousand times I have gone over, in my mind, that one action of mine as if I could in some way change what I have done. If only I could really change the movements of my hands and the choice I made that night and perhaps even now change everything.

Though I have a strong desire to write I find it difficult. Because of what has happened, I am having to force myself to think and the writing has become an act of the will.

Whenever I start to write I remember too vividly and see too clearly the scene and the events of that night. It is as if I can still hear the hoarse sobbing and the desperate voice calling your name. The calling and sobbing went on and on and I tried not to hear it and I'm trying not to hear it now.

You will never read what I am writing now. The love I had for you was spread over many years and took up a great deal of my life because it was associated with my work as well as my life. I feel unable to face the prospect of a life without this work and without this love.

The reason why this paper is so precious is that on it I can write that I loved you. During all those years of writing to you I never wrote to say that I loved you. Now I am free to write that I loved you beyond any measuring of love. I love you. In those three words is the happiness of fulfillment and a profound despair.

For me you wrote out all your experiments and you described in detail all your patients, their symptoms and their histories and you explained all your theories, giving examples, and because of this, I knew beforehand what was to be in all your books and I was able to follow the exact working of your magnificent mind even though we were several thousands of miles apart.

Together we explored every aspect of woman, the physiology and the psychology of women, the lonely woman, women together from choice and those who have no choice. In your work I studied the mature woman, intellectual, deep thinking and capable of great depths in friendship and in love. You wrote everything for me to read and I replied from my heart to the greatness and nobleness of your heart. I lived from one of your letters to the next.

It was as though we were always meeting and never parting.

Why did I try to make your name beautiful with the long and graceful loop on the G? It seems clear to me now when it is too late.

Perhaps qualities can be believed but not given.

My room at the clinic is like an aquarium. It has a greenish yellow watery light because there is a conservatory outside the window. The conservatory is not used. The room is quiet and restful. I always looked forward to showing you this room and the clinic. I often stayed there late into the night reading your letters and making notes from them for my own writing and for my lectures. I tried to look at my patients as you would look at them. Hour after hour at the clinic I examined and advised and treated, all the time teaching and demonstrating so that the students could have the best of my experience and of yours. My subject? The tender beauty of the pregnant woman, her loveliness, sacred in its limitation, the soft rich skin of the breasts, the smooth white thighs and the tender expression in the eyes of the healthy young primapara.

From your teaching, we studied everything from the normal to the abnormal in obstetrics and gynaecology, from the menstrual cycle and ovulation and the gravid uterus to ectopic gestation. In teaching I emulated your technique in every detail, from the more complicated stages of surgery down to the gentle methods you described for the use of the vaginal speculum. Always at the end of my work I came back to you, to your letters, in

175

my room which is like an aquarium, and I often wrote to you before leaving the clinic for the night.

And you have never seen the clinic or my room there.

Every day I left my car at the bottom of the long desolate hill. I always walked up the hill, the wind moans in that derelict part of the town. It is a place of warehouses and yards. Beyond the leaning verandah posts of the Federal Hotel are strange places, uninhabited, and corners heaped up with unknown rubbish. Facing down the street is a clay-coloured church. The clinic is on one side and all round are small houses in terraces with rusty corrugated iron roofs and a sense of overcrowding in the windowless verandahs and the lean-to kitchens. There is nowhere there to leave a car.

I always imagined what it would be like to show you my room. Because I am not able to take you there, I will write about it. To get to my room in the clinic I have to walk between the rows of waiting patients. You will have known the smell of pregnant women. It is a warm oppressive smell. Every day I walked through it. On the last day I found it disgusting and was surprised that I had not thought so before. I was struck suddenly by the passive ugly stupidity of a mass of pregnant females. Have I ever asked you about the smell of pregnant women? Perhaps not, but you are no longer able to answer questions. Something about the washrooms in this place reminds me of pregnancy. Perhaps it is the water running endlessly over the yellow tiles and the sense of community in a place where there is none, only a physical smell and closeness of people together for similar reasons, but other than their predicament, having nothing in common.

The white coats at the clinic are over-starched to hide their frayed sleeves. On the plinths are squares of cheap white paper. Chipped enamel bowls of soapy water are on little tables and faded paper screens provide a doubtful privacy. Everywhere there are old-fashioned copper sterilizers creating in their noisy steam an atmosphere of hot cleanliness. I seemed to spend my life in this crowded and busy place.

My consulting room at home, where I see a few patients, is private and quiet and very comfortable.

Because I loved you something of this love spread to my patients and to my students.

On the day when your letter came to say you would be coming I could hardly believe that you would come so far and so soon. Of course I was pleased, the sadness now is because of what has happened. With my pleasure at your coming was some fear. I was afraid that I might disappoint you in some way. I wanted your approval so much. I worked very hard to have everything in order at the clinic and at the hospital and at home.

In my house I prepared a room for you. I cleared everything from my study so that you could have the large and pleasant room to yourself. Through a communicating door is a small room which I made ready for myself, it has another door opening into the hall as has the study. I arranged the desk in your room so that from the writing table in my room I could watch you at work. You would be for me, during the day, enchantingly encircled by the roses which frame the windows. I made up the bed for you myself. I opened the door between the two rooms and left it wide open. I worked for hours to prepare this pleasant place for you. I felt I was reaching out to you in the happiness of having you come at last.

I exhausted all my energy and lay down on my bed to rest and discovered that from my bed I could see your bed in the mirror on my wall. I experienced in that moment a deep sensation of exquisite pleasure which was at once so complete and relaxing as if you were already with me and very near me. This sweet perfection and the sudden absence of tension caused me to cry. I have never told you about this; about the evening of preparation which was stimulating like the prelude to love-making and the ensuing intellectual, or was it perhaps emotional, climax. I wanted to discuss it with you. During the short time before your arrival I continued to think about it. And of course, I wanted it again.

But when you came there was no chance, and any

desire to communicate seemed to disappear. There seemed suddenly nothing to ask you and nothing at all to hear from you.

I met you at the airport, the weather was bad and it was nearly three in the morning before you arrived. I waited and suddenly seemed surrounded by tired passengers arriving. I searched the white faces for your character, for the forceful gentleness and the intelligence. I looked for someone graceful, kind and clever.

In all our years of writing we have never described ourselves to each other.

I can never forget how I felt when I first saw you. I knew it must be you, there seemed no-one else left for me to meet.

I first saw you, small, thick set and stout, an animal stranded from its hole in the night. Your fur jacket was unbuttoned and you were surrounded by baggage, an untidy heaped circle of small packages.

Your appearance and your age startled me. Because of your work and your experience I knew you would be some years older than I am, I knew this, but I had not thought how many years. Appearance and age could not make any difference to my feelings for you; it was simply that after, as I thought, knowing you all these years, I came face to face with someone I did not and could not know.

I know it is quite unjustifiable that your appearance could suggest that it would be quite impossible for me to know you.

I am tall. You peered up at me through thick-lensed spectacles. I saw your pale eyes, bulging, and the whites of your eyes yellowish and red-veined.

That you might be elderly and not in good health had not occurred to me; not that either of those things are reasons for not being able to continue the friendship and the love of all the years.

Your voice startled me. I have a flat quiet voice and yours shrilled up and down as you spoke to me in the imperfection of knowing several languages without troubling to learn one of them properly. This is not anything against you, rather it simply was not in keeping with my idea of you.

Your marriage was completely unexpected. This was something else for me to have to understand quickly at our first meeting. Your marriage to Matthew. During your flight, you told me, you were married, in Rome. Matthew came quietly from the grey half light and shyly we shook hands.

Now while I am writing I am remembering the drive through the suburbs back to my own house and my fearful impatience to close the communicating door between those two rooms. My eager preparations for your arrival and the tender making of your bed seemed suddenly ridiculous. It seemed that, if discovered by you, these things would expose me.

Your arrival at my house was not at all as I had thought of it. You insisted that Matthew carry you kicking and screaming like a young girl over the threshold.

"Tonight I am bride!" you said. And you revived Matthew with your smelling salts.

I am not used to having people in my house. That night I became furtive. My head ached and continued to ache unrelieved. I am afraid now that the headache might return at any time.

My bathroom seemed to be taken over by your soap, and you had left your teeth in plastic cups on the window ledge. I felt timid as if in someone else's bathroom. I wanted to go to bed but when I was in bed, I could not sleep.

Your voices from the other room disturbed me, first one voice and then the other endlessly, subdued, talking on and on in a language which sounded like Polish or German but was not either.

I woke too early because I had forgotten the blinds and the morning sun, stained purple with bougainvillaea, pours into that room. My terrible headache seemed to come from the top heavy masses of creeper just outside the window.

It came as a shock that the bathroom door was locked.

179

Harsh and exasperated bird calls from the garden and the blue flowers of the jacarandas scattered on the grass and the irritation of having you both in my house and trying to ignore the familiar and necessary actions of living, the private things of the body, to appear not to notice these things but simply ignore them, things which cannot be ignored, and then to speak, as if unconcerned, of the colours of the morning, the strange bird cries and the spectacular flowering of the jacaranda which seemed to fill the middle distance between the earth and the sky. Watching the trees I tried to think of other times when I had watched them and how I had given myself up to this gentle caressing of the leaves, watching them almost touching, almost stroking as the branches moved. Always parting and never meeting.

Waiting for the bathroom I saw no trees.

In the pockets of your loose jacket you had little bottles and various packets of silver foil. Always something to be taken with meals, before or after or in between meals, something for the heart, for the circulation, for the bowels. You showed me the label on the glass tube.

"Vitamin E extract," you said to me, "for senile vaginitis," and you patted the pocket of your jacket, "for everything, a remedy."

Now I think of your pleasure in living and how I was unable to share this with you. Now it seems that I could never have longed over you, wishing for you as I once did, thinking about the cool fragrance of your back and your breasts and your thighs. In my love for you I sometimes imagined your sweet loveliness. I wondered what your fragrance would be. I wondered what it would be like to stroke your hair, your shoulders and gently your whole body lovingly, loving you with my hands. Why did I dream like this over you, for you never told me about yourself.

I created for myself your perfection.

I should have loved you for the pleasure you had in living. You were so happy and so eager that I should enjoy what you enjoyed. I refused to swim and you forgave me at once. I should have been grateful, you were so generous. But I saw selfishness and self-absorption instead of generosity.

"Esme, the wind is too cold for me." Matthew apologized. He sat in his frail elderly skin as far under the beach umbrella as possible.

"Here is something different!" you came breathless out of the sea, dripping water from your white flabby body, three fleshy strands of seaweed in your fat fingers. Matthew, interested, wrote about the unusual weed in his small notebook. You wanted, eagerly, to share the discovery with me, but I, experiencing my first real pain, was unable to share it.

My pain I understand now was jealousy.

Your food intruded. Little dishes of chopped up liver, shreds of fried onion and breadcrumbs covered over with saucers. The bathroom, warm, inhabited by your needs, repelled. The mornings came strangled with the purple creeper and the days followed filled with your desire for life, your wish to live. You wanted all the fruits. You wanted the glowing flesh of the rock melons, the golden apricots, the sweetest oranges and the fragrant peaches. And you wanted the Kreutzer Sonata, you asked for the Kreutzer Sonata; it must be played exquisitely, you said, by two people in love, in the perfect harmony of love.

You said you were a bride tonight and later we would work. Matthew, forgive me, so that I can forget your weeping. Now I would like to lift my head from this table and stare into the long white bells of the datura and breathe forgetfulness. But I suppose these bells are yellow now and rotting and there will never be forgetfulness for me again. Matthew, where are you now? What are you doing now?

I am here in this place, in the washroom or in the yard or obediently eating and drinking whatever is brought to me in here. What has happened to the proud friendship? All those long hours of work? And where are the dreams? Where are my dreams?

I should have been able to love the happiness you had

together. Instead, I despised the constant search for youth, the constant attempts at recreating a youth which so plainly was gone. I should have been able to understand and pity the blotched and wrinkled skin under the coarse face-powder. I should have been able to understand why you spent such a long time dressing and frisking your thin hair over your forehead. Why did I mind all this so much? I should not have minded.

"Tonight I am bride again!" you said.

If only I could have wrapped you round in love, nothing of what happened, could have happened.

Your room in the evenings was white with embroidered pillows, white embroidery on white pillowslips, you brought them from Switzerland. Mountains of pillows and the bed heaped up and prepared as for a sacrifice. Your door was always partly open. I wished to close it.

Is it possible to close someone else's door? In your room I saw Matthew kneeling beside the bed. The veins of his forehead knotted to the veins in his hands. I went by the door quickly, an intruder in my own house.

I thought I heard you moaning and Matthew gently calling your name. I listened and then there was silence. Matthew you came to my door and called me, "Esmé is ill! Come quickly! Quickly, Esmé is ill."

Matthew it would have been better not to call me.

I went in to your room. Matthew had fetched your teeth from the bathroom and on the desk was a plate with little squares of bread and butter.

"Eat something Esmé!" Matthew tried to persuade you. But you lay still.

"Esmé, I implore you. Eat something!" Matthew thought if only you could eat you would be safe and well.

I fetched my bag and I prepared the syringe. Matthew held the phial I gave him.

How your hand trembled Matthew.

Dr. Gollanberg, if I had given you the correct injection you might have lived and you might not have lived. Who can answer this. I never gave your heart a chance to choose. I gave you something where there is no

182

choice. When the syringe was in my hand I did not even hesitate. I could have paused. I could have wasted it and rinsed the syringe and drawn up something else. A thousand times since then I have put out my hand to reach for a second phial and, in my mind, I have gone through the action of filing the end, snapping it off, this other phial, and giving it to Matthew to hold. A thousand times since then I have given Matthew this different phial.

If only I really could do it now and perhaps change everything. Then I did not even consider. Now I am thinking of it all the time and I know I shall think of it for the rest of my life. And the headache, the headache will come back. It is intolerable.

For a time I sat in my room and heard Matthew sobbing as he tried to hold you. He searched in the wreckage of the pillows trying to find life where no life was. I tried not to hear the hoarse voice breaking with grief, the desolate sobbing and the desperate repeated calling of your name.

I tried not to hear this grief and I tried not to hear the silence behind this grief.

I went to the clinic because it would not be possible to work at home. The clinic seemed far away in sinister surroundings. The sterilizers were empty and the enamel bowls all wiped dry, all was still in the night. In the empty silence I unlocked the door to my room. It was cold in there and stagnant and there seemed nothing for me to take up to do. I waited for the morning.

All day I seemed to be waiting for someone. All day I examined and prescribed and advised. I fitted and checked contraceptives. There was nothing special about my work, only the dreary ugliness of the bodies changed and weary with childbirth, stupid and repressed women, narrow-minded in their lack of education.

All day I waited but no-one came.

I went in the dark to my house and listened there. I thought I heard voices talking, your voices, and I was afraid. I listened and there were no voices. No sound of your endless talking up and down. The fragrance of my garden came to me and I rested on the dark verandah. I thought, "So you are bride again tonight?"

If you were stout and noisy and ugly it is my fault, not yours. It is my way of seeing you which was at fault. That is the fault.

I was afraid to go inside my house.

The east wind, restless and unhappy, came moaning towards me on the long hill as I walked up back to the clinic. Something seemed to creep alongside, murmuring, in the darkness.

In the clinic I sat down in my stale cold room and I waited there till someone came.

* * *

PART 6

SUNDAY AND ANOTHER SUNDAY

Andrea

Laura knows everything but she won't do anything about it. Goddam! she won't do a thing about it. Hell!

When Laura sits on the edge of the bed in her night-dress she seems soft and full and rounded in her body and thighs. She is much softer than I thought. She looks so different then from when she is out on her land dressed in her thick trousers and jersey, and when she has those long boots on it is hard to imagine her ever wearing a nightdress. I have to get used to the different Lauras. I have to try to get used to the isolation of the house when she is working hour after hour somewhere on her farm. The house is shabby and empty and the loneliness is unbearable while she is out. Everything changes when she returns.

In the dark when we are together and she is naked beside me in the big bed she is strong and lean in her desire.

"How are you Laura?" I ask her, teasing a bit. "How do you feel Laura?"

185

"Magnificent," she replies. "Magnificent, noble and dignified and Andrea, I do love you so much." And afterwards she is so fragrant and tender. She tells me I am beautiful, it is then that I think she is beautiful and that I love her. I love her love but I am not so good at telling her what I think. Once she said it was strange that this very thing, the passion between two people could make them feel brave and strong one minute and then this same passion could so quickly change into something desperate, tearful, weak and frightened. "I could cry now," she said one night, "and beg you never to leave me, I'm afraid to be without you," she said.

"I'm here," I said. "I'm needing you too."

"Oh yes so you are!" and she held me very close.

I read everything Laura left for me. I wished she would come home.

I read even all the boring things, papers of discharge from the prison hospital, medical documents, certificates describing the progress of the skin infection she had, a report on her blood, on her heart and so on, papers reducing her to figures and symbols of discovery of the normal and the abnormal. There were letters from Rodney Glass, I could hardly read his writing, telling her what he thought she should do. Tentative letters, surprisingly kind and sensible, suggesting ways in which she should rebuild her life.

It seems strange to me that Laura who loves privacy (she hates to be spied upon) is used to living alone and dislikes being watched or interrupted at anything has changed all that and cherishes my being here! She is used to having her own way all these years and yet, with pleasure, wants me to have my way. Except in this one thing. We talked about it this morning. I realised she knew what I'd been hiding from her, must have known it for some time. She's gone off somewhere I don't know where. I want to ask her to forgive me if I can ever speak to her again, perhaps she will never speak to me. Whatever can I do about it. Oh the terrible quiet all round me!

It was so late and such a dark night and the car didn't come and I waited and waited for her to come. There were no lights in the Murphy house and it was so quiet in this one. I kept hearing a car come and then it was nothing. I kept on looking out into the blackest night I ever saw.

"Oh Laura come home!" my own voice in the kitchen gave me a fright.

Last night I must have been half asleep when I heard the noise of the car approaching. In the quietness the car pauses on the bend in the track, the tyres turning slowly grip the gravel and it is as if there is a moment of hesitation and then, it is always the same, the car comes on down and the dogs start up at Murphy's place. I opened my eyes as the head lamps sent this now familiar beam of light right round the room as the car turned and came down the last little bit of the track. Their homecoming is always like this, Murphy shouting at the dogs and then Laura's voice out there in the night. This time it was as though her voice was calling, reaching out from all those years of her life I'd been reading. And then she was in the house, it must have been between one and two o'clock in the morning.

"Andrea!" she said.

"Laura! it's you at last," I think that's what I said.

"Murphy!" she called. "Bring in the boxes for me please! They're just groceries and things," she explained to me. "Things for the kitchen and bathroom, hideously dull but necessary." She told Murphy where to put everything. The house sprang to life at her coming, the boards creaked under her weight, doors slammed and somewhere water was running. She brought a smell of the long car ride and the smoke of Murphy's terrible tobacco. She started pulling off her outdoor clothes.

"I'm so stiff! Oh my back!" she complained. "That's right, over there," she showed Murphy where to put the last box. "Just think Andrea!" she called out, "I've lived all these years and I only discovered something today. I thought I knew everything! Schiller's ode is also put to music by Schubert. I bought the record."

It's only Laura who can buy a tractor, seven calves,

187

twenty-four toilet rolls, wire netting for a turkey yard, a year's supply of soap and candles and a Schubert record all in one day.

"It's a lovely record!" she said lighting the lamp in the bedroom. "I listened to a bit of it in the shop while Murphy was getting a haircut," she turned the lamp down carefully. "Don't get up!" she said softly to me. "I just must see to Murphy."

"Murphy!" she called, "Let's have a drink. I'll have whisky. The same for you?" She was back in the kitchen. From the bed I could see her pulling off the end of the loaf and eating it hurriedly. She handed a plate of bread to Murphy.

"I'm so hungry!" she said. "Cheese?" she asked Murphy. However crudely Laura does something it never is ugly. She seems to have this well-bred easy way with everyone. I wish I had it.

But as soon as Murphy had gone, she changed. She walked to and fro nervously putting away a few things.

"What about you?" she said at last coming to where I was at the side of the bed. "How are you!"

"Well!" I said.

"Sure?"

"Sure."

"The unspeakable will have to be spoken," she said. She moved about impatiently. Agitated and restless.

"Shall I boil the kettle?" I asked her.

"Oh yes please do," she said. "Oh no," she contradicted herself, "Oh no! please stop in bed. I can make a cup of coffee for us both. There's no need to get up."

"Let me please," I put on the water. "Did you do all you had to?" I asked her. "You had a good day?"

"Oh yes and more so," she said. "Very successful day, everything done."

"It was very warm here," I said. I felt shy, both of us putting off the real meeting.

"Yes I do believe summer's here at last," she said. "On the way back the sweet smell of the grass after the hot sun kept reminding me I was coming home."

And then, suddenly, she turned round and caught me

in her arms and held me close. She drew me out on to the high verandah where it was quite dark, to the edge so that we were by the wooden rail and the smell of the withered grass came up to us sharply on the night air.

"Oh it is heavenly here!" she drew breath deeply, her strong arm still close about me as if she wouldn't let me go.

"Oh Andrea!" she said. "All day I have never stopped thinking about you. I was afraid, so terribly afraid. I kept thinking I had made a terrible mistake to leave you alone and expect you to read all through everything."

"Did you say something once about chemistry?" I asked her. "Isn't it something about our chemistry which holds us together? Reading about you only made me love you more."

Laura wept, I felt her tears and I felt her body tremble.

"It's the first time you've ever said anything like that," she said to me. "Please say it again!"

"I couldn't love you more than I do," I found myself saying it and I meant it and now I feel ashamed that I said it because of what I've done to her since saying it.

She kissed me then. A long deep kiss of possession. I wonder how many people have ever known a kiss like that one. Laura's kiss. So much tenderness.

"Let's go to bed," she said very softly, gently, she took me indoors to the soft lamp-light and the comfortable bed.

I think we must have talked all night. This time I did not tease her. We lay side by side talking, our two voices alone in the night. Laura said it seemed strange that two people should talk together, miles away from anywhere and no-one else know they are talking.

"You are so innocent," I couldn't help telling her. "You are the innocent one." I felt burdened by my own lack of innocence.

"Of course I'm not innocent as you call it," she said. "Don't you see it all depends on the kind of person you are. If there can be no surrender of principles and we can remain equal always it's wonderful for me. But that's not innocence. Don't you see," she sat up in bed, "I'm not innocent, it's a strange word to use. It simply is that I can't take any initiative in anything any more. Sometimes it hurts, you know, not being a doctor now, not able to decide things, advise people or help them, I felt so useless that's why I live the way I do. I do decide things here and I'm trying to grow things, I'm making a way to live but il's not because I'm innocent! You must understand, Andrea! I can't put my name or my opinion forward. I write but only for myself, I don't even have a trading name here for anything I might produce and I could never publish anything again." She sighed and I longed to say something wise to comfort her.

"Not even your best seller?" "Not even that," she laughed in that soft deep voice, "not even that. But all the same what I'm trying to tell you is I have the same wishes and the same urgencies and the same body and the same knowledge that other people have and I haven't this innocence as you call it." She lay down again close to me.

"Don't you see," she said, "it's been wonderful for me having you here. I'm not innocent at all. I'm really bad! When I have your invitation, you know your little kiss, it's all so simple. I am older than you and supposedly wiser, more experienced? I should only want what's best for you but I'm not like that, I want for myself too! As I can't impose my will on you, I must not! But if I can't and then you show me your will, your wish, then it's all so easy and right and you set me free to love you. And, Andrea, you must know I do love you so very much. All day I have been realising how terrible it would be if I came home and you were not here. I am quite afraid. I'm afraid that soon you will leave and I love you too much. I want you too much to let you go!"

So then I asked her,

"Laura you're not angry with me or hurt about how I am about Christopher?" I didn't manage to ask her the whole thing. "I wanted to tell you," I began. "So often I've wanted to tell you."

"Dear Andrea!" she said. "How could I be angry! St. Paul says somewhere, 'Can the clay reproach the potter with what he has made of it'."

"I'm afraid I don't know what you mean."

She laughed. "I think I was being pompous! How could I be angry with you or hurt! I understand or thought I did when I saw you leave the ship and go to him. I didn't understand quite how close you are to him but I think I know and understand it all now. I knew some time ago there was something we'd have to face. I couldn't help realising, you must remember it was my work once. I know your body so well and the changes that have taken place, I haven't ignored you exactly so I'm well aware of your condition. I couldn't help realising could I but I didn't want to be clumsy about it. I was hoping that when you knew things about me it would be easier for you. Life does not stop with one experience!"

I found myself asking, repeating myself.

"Laura, are you sure you're not hurt or angry with me?"

"Again!" she said. "How could I be! I love you. I want you for myself. I want you away from him. He so obviously wants to get free. Perhaps he hasn't found it easy but he has chosen to be free from you. He has a wife and a baby and will have more babies, he wants this other life and he wants to get on in the acceptable way. Being attached to his sister is of no use to him, he mustn't be hampered by an older sister! He can't be blamed for what he has done, this pathologist, this doctor brother of yours. We must help him. We have to let him go free, it is his right Andrea, and your right too to be free from him. You must be free from each other.

"You must try hard to forget and you must try hard not to be concerned over him. There are so many experiences in our lives, he is one of the experiences. Do please try and see it like that and do please let me help you."

"I feel I've done something so terribly wrong," I wanted to say so much to her. "Possessions and ordinary values have always seemed to mean so little —" I tried to explain. "What I mean is, I don't want possessions and now I've done this horribly wrong thing and I'll need to have possessions — do you see what I mean?"

"It seems so unprofitable to talk about wrong," she said to me so gently. "I do see exactly what you mean," her voice is always so dignified and measured, I began to feel comforted. "You mustn't be so upset," she said, "I want you to see that you haven't done any more wrong, as you call it, than is being done all the time. There are things which are one's destiny, I do feel this, you see it all the time, it's fate, it's destiny and it can't be helped. This struck me very forcibly years ago when I was in practice. Listen to me Andrea!" she leaned on one elbow, leaning over me a little. "Remember the blossoms of the frangipani outside all the temples in Ceylon? Do you remember the sweet pure scent of those flowers? And d'you remember all the worn shoes left in little heaps outside the temples and the crippled beggars on the steps and at the door? I often think of all these things," she said.

"And do you remember those tall palm trees along the curved beach where in the early morning the sands were pink beside a pale blue clean sea? That sort of thing Andrea, Ceylon, India, Europe, London, all the ancient beauty and the present day glamour; and we've seen the small pretty things as well as the fine and noble. Necklaces, jewellery, paintings, statues, things made of glass, mountains covered with snow, great wide rivers which seem to have no far bank, we could talk all night about those things. And we have both seen something of the suffering of the world. Things like poverty and disease can be seen so plainly but there are the other things too, both of us are quite aware of these other kinds of suffering. Perhaps loneliness is the worst of all the other suffering. It seems silly of me to talk so much! Some people feel more than others, some have experiences which are quite unknown, unthought of by other people. Simply, that's how things are. Some people never appear to suffer and others suffer everything. How do you think I came to give Esmé Gollanberg the wrong injection, the fatal one? D'you see now what I mean?"

I thought I saw what she meant, now this morning on the bed I've been crying and crying because of what I've done. If only I hadn't! I've been staring at the white painted door of this room as if I'd never seen it before, I never noticed it had a gold brass door knob. The more I think about Laura, these last few weeks and last night, the more hopeless I feel and now after this morning! However did I come to do what I've done.

All the jade and rosemary, the mint and myrtle, the little pomegranates and the tiny fragrant herbs in their rotting tubs and rusty tins, the audience undulating on their warped benches, are just outside the door to remind me of her.

They are her people, she told me once she talks to them, reads aloud to them sometimes and opens the window so that they can grow with Brahms and Beethoven.

In the night I asked Laura, we had been quiet for a little while, not asleep, but not talking or moving, she had her arm across me and one hand holding me very gently, "What about our love? Is that wrong?" I asked her.

"I thought you'd gone to sleep," she said softly. "How can anyone answer a question like that. How can love be wrong," she almost seemed to speak to herself. "And yet it does not always work out," she said. "Well neither of us is lying here in bed saying that grass is red. We are not making any laws. Our world together is an isolated one. We are not imposing a structure which is harmful to anyone or out of harmony with other structures. Simply we are living here together. I am managing my small farm and you are having a holiday to recover from the illness brought on by malnutrition. We have come to know one another very deeply. I can't see that there is anything wrong; you seem horribly concerned with right and wrong. To me it's not so easily divided, one from the other. I don't see that right and wrong come into it. It is more as if two halves of a whole have come

193

together. And when two people love as we do it seems to be the two halves recognizing each other and becoming one. It was the neo-Platonists in the Renaissance who held these views."

And then I asked her,

"What about my problem? Laura whatever shall I do about it?"

"Yes," she said. "I'm thinking about that too. I have been thinking about it for some time."

"I don't want this baby," I heard my voice cry out. "I don't, I can't have Christopher's baby!"

"Cry if it will help you," she said, but I couldn't cry.

"Whatever shall I do! Oh whatever shall I do!"

"It's happened this way," she held me close, "I'll help you. Don't be upset please! We can discuss it all and sort out the problem, if it is indeed a problem. Do you think you could sleep a bit if I hold you like this in my arms? Esmé Gollanberg, strange I can talk of her quite calmly, had a theory. I'll tell you about it. Come lie up close beside me, I'll hold you so that I can feel your heart beating."

This is what she was like in the night, so good and kind. She told me to listen to the rooster and she asked me if I could smell the sweet smell of the grass. She told me she was sorry she talked so much. I was to sleep she told me, it was nearly morning. I was so dazed with all the reading. Laura slept then but I did not.

* * *

Laura

For the first time I've failed her. Perhaps it isn't the first time. We have had such a disagreeable unsatisfactory conversation. The first one we have ever had. I am trying to get my thoughts into some sort of order. I have walked across the valley to the stud but instead of going to the stables to see Charger and Lucy and the little Palomino I have stopped by the horse fence. It is quiet in the little clump of trees by the smooth round poles of the fence. I don't want the men at the stud to see me, they might think I want the horses saddled up and I don't. It

194

always looks so serene over here when I look across from the rail of my high verandah to the neat paddocks and the haystacks of the horse country.

We hardly slept. It must have been daybreak when we stopped talking. I heard the morning noises of the Murphys and gave myself up to sleep. I held her tenderly as I always do, one hand holding her small firm breast. Perhaps we should have made love together instead of talking so much. We lay quietly by each other talking. It isn't that I think an orgasm is the most important thing to happen between two people. Certainly trying to have one and failing doesn't improve a situation. Had we loved each other completely we might have been closer and more relaxed this morning. We are both very over-tired. I have the affairs of the farm on my mind but none of these worries can equal what must be uppermost in hers.

I want to comfort her. I want to clear her mind and heart of all that hurts her. We aren't able to say anything to each other just at present. I don't know how to speak to her in her present frame of mind.

Yesterday was an extraordinary day. I tried to do too much and I left her with years to cover. We didn't sleep enough. Uneasy sleep and uneasy dreams. Sometimes I dream horribly, in my dream I am back in the prison, the same women are there. The wardress whose name I can't remember, perhaps I never knew it, she had "ninety-one" embroidered on her overall, often comes into my dream. In the dream I want her even though she is repulsive to me, swarthy and solid. I was afraid of her in the prison. She was sometimes quite harsh, cruel even, to me. I suspected her of brutality though it never came to that. Sometimes she neglected me like failing to let me go for my wash and then she would fetch me late and push me along the tiled passage and knock me against the wall because of being in a hurry, and then would show me an unexpected tenderness, a rough caress on the shoulder, perhaps as near to being fond as she could manage. I shrank from her. She was afraid of my illness, I was afraid of it too. I don't despise her for that. She, it seemed, needed to hurt before she could show affection. People are like that. I can't believe Andrea needs to make a wound that she has to heal in order to deepen her feeling for me. I am so deep already over her. I find it hard to see it like this but this may be part of the explanation for what happened. She is over-wrought. She is four months pregnant, possibly a little more. She has tried to hide her nausea from me. Her breasts are tender, I have known this for some time, she tried to hide this tenderness too. The poor dear child, I should have said something as soon as I realised, I was afraid to, I have been so very careful with her, too careful I suppose. Her skin glows and she has the radiance of the healthy prima para. It isn't my love which has brought about these changes. I knew this. No amount of wishing on my part could put me in the desirable position of being entirely responsible to her and for her. It's no use my regretting myself!

My love for her goes beyond any of this. It hardly seems to matter now after I have been thinking about it so much. In a sense the greatness of my feeling minimises everything else. If I can care for her while she needs my care then nothing else can matter.

Even the unexpected thing that happened this morning seems unimportant if I can get back to her. I want to eradicate the failure we had this morning. There is so much to talk over with her. I suppose she was afraid she was pregnant when she came to me and I suppose she has hoped all the time that I could do something about it.

There must be more to her being here than that. Last night we were not able to talk over everything. There is a certain amount of shock.

The house was already filled with the light and open-ness of the late morning when we got up. We took our coffee out on to the verandah looking down the long paddock. The morning was endowed with that promise of summer which for me holds something of menace. The warm fragrance is intense. The earth, leaf-laden for such a long time, shimmers with eucalyptus vapour. On the edge of the forest magpies swoop with their voices falling into the stillness of my valley and follow one another from the antlers of one dead tree to the next.

I put my cup on the table.

"I think I can see a wedge-tailed eagle," I said to Andrea, and I was about to go indoors for the binoculars.

"Laura," she said stopping me by her tone. "Apropos of reading your cardboard diary, it seems to me that though you are consistent, you are so obviously the same person you were then, but you are in fact different now." She set her cup on the rail and pushed back her hair.

"How so Dearest?" Her sentence didn't seem to make sense really.

"Well," she said. "What I mean is with the years going by and you getting old, certain resistance, restraint perhaps, which you once had you no longer have. What I mean is, one way you have changed is the way you don't imprison your passion now as you did then. Have you also changed in outlook? Don't interrupt! You do talk such a lot I never get a chance! What I mean is, if you have changed, and you refused to help Mrs. Grant and my mother with their unwanted pregnancies when they needed help, when they asked you to help you refused, that was all of twenty odd years ago. Times have changed and you have changed, in your changed ways and outlook Laura, the way you are now would you get rid of this baby for me? Laura I want an abortion. Will you do it? You could still do it couldn't you. Will you do it?" She spoke so fast she was incoherent.

While she spoke her face changed and was small and drawn tight, pale greenish about her mouth, almost grey. She looked as she looked the night we met across Rodney's dinner table. Her fingers seemed suddenly pale and thin again, she twisted her hands together nervously and pushed her hair back from her face repeatedly. I couldn't believe it. I stepped towards her, her words shocked me and it was the tone of them too! She looked as if she would either cry or vomit or spit at me.

"Andrea, my dearest child —"

197

"Shut up Laura! with that 'my child' stuff. I may be half your age. All right you are an old woman! Twice my age, perhaps more but I am not a child and I will not be looked upon as a child. I have been about the place a bit earning my living. I've probably experienced more than you have. Men for one thing. What men do you really know! And you call me child! Old woman. Will you do this or not. Times have changed you know or perhaps you don't know!"

I really didn't know what to say or do, the "old woman" hurt but I suppose it's true, the true things really do hurt.

"If you call me old woman," I said, "Then you mustn't mind if I call you child." I tried to speak lightly not to show how I was trembling. I moved the jugs on the table to look as if I was doing something. I suddenly felt weak and I had no answer for her. I picked up a plate and put it down.

"I'll be out in the barn for a bit," I said, and I left the verandah at once. I suppose I should have stayed but I couldn't. I've handled the whole situation stupidly. Instead of going back to the house as I should have done, I have walked over here to the stud without seeing her or doing anything.

It can't be Eva all over again. It isn't Eva all over again. Andrea hasn't lied to me. What's the use of all our loving, our equality, all the things we've said to each other in love and what about our hands touching and caressing each other, our bodies responding so sweetly in this love which is so precious. It can't all disappear like this. She said she loved me and she knows how I feel about her. She isn't stupid and I won't believe she's cunning. I'm not jealous. I'll tell her that. I have known the bitterness of jealousy and the bitterness of loneliness and disappointment. I don't forget those things. I'll remind her. She can't have forgotten what I did to my whole life and to someone else's life for some maddened lack of reason, some bitter jealousy? All I know is that I'm not jealous now. I understand what happened between her and her brother. This kind of thing is a kind of destiny, it can't be shaped or prevented, it can't be altered. But I love her so much, I'll go to any lengths. She doesn't need to threaten me or hurt me. She doesn't understand. I haven't said I won't help her. I'll do anything I can for her.

* * *

Andrea

Laura said I was asleep when she came in she said she could see I had cried myself to sleep because my eyes were all red and puffy.

It's true after she'd gone out it all came over me what I'd said and I couldn't stop crying. I must have fallen asleep.

Laura came in, it was already the afternoon she said. She sat on the bed and took me in her arms and held me.

"I'm so ashamed," she said. "I'm really so ashamed I don't know where to begin to tell you," and she kissed me on my hair and my face and I could feel her body trembling. Her eyes were full of tears and I cried too. I couldn't help crying when I saw her tears.

"How silly we are to cry!" she said. "We don't need to!" And she said a great many kind and loving things about us not needing to go back over what had been said, that nothing mattered to her except that I should be all right. And when I said it was me who was ashamed she would not let me speak. She stroked my hair and my face very gently.

"We haven't had enough sleep," she said. "And we haven't had anything to eat. As the old woman —"

"Laura! Don't!"

"As the wise old woman," she persisted, "out of the two of us I ought to know best," she said. "We must straighten our clothes, wash ourselves, and go into the kitchen and open some tins. You can put on the kettle and make the toast. I'll have three pieces."

She kept putting her arm round me in the kitchen. I burned two lots of bread. Fatigue ages Laura very much, her face looked tired and sad and I felt I was the cause of it. I thought I'd be sick if I ate anything. Laura persuaded me though I felt there wasn't any point in doing anything any more. I'd ruined everything, lost any happiness I might have had, lost Laura as well as hurting her by the things I'd said. I kept thinking I was going to throw up and when I got up from the table Laura said to me to sit down and that I was to eat.

"You won't be sick," she said firmly.

"Oh Laura, Laura I'm so sorry," I felt my tears coming again. The prospect of not being with her in the house seemed unbearable but how could I go on being there after those terrible things. "If only I could unsay them," I said.

Then Laura told me she didn't remember what I had said, she told me it didn't matter that we had had a bad time if we were all right now. She said she was terribly ashamed of her own selfishness, that her own life had seemed so much more important. She said she ought to have talked to me more about Christopher and about the baby, straight away as soon as she realised.

"That's why you rode the Dove the way you did," she said. "Oh Andrea if only I had spoken to you then! You must have suffered such a lot, and all the time I was so happy to have you here you have been in this agony of loneliness."

She made us each another cup of coffee and slopped the brandy into hers. She spilled it into the saucer and spilled the sugar too. "I must measure it," she said. "Sometimes it's half a cup in the coffee. I like it very much, of course, but I'll use the measure. I'm having too much. My liver must be in a state!"

"Laura I can't go through with it! Can you do something please?"

"Andrea," she said. "I can't, you know this. It's years since I practised; it's illegal in any case. It's a very bloody thing and dangerous; it's not a simple thing to do. It's irretrievable; when it's done it's so terribly final and this might be your only chance to bear a child — Women often regret —"

"But Laura I don't want a child you must realise this! and specially not this one. It might be an idiot! Oh God!

200

You must be mad. I don't want this baby, not now and not later. I can't go through with it!"

"I really can't do it for you," she said to me. "I'll do anything in the world for you, you know, but not this. If you really are determined I'll ask Rodney if he knows someone who'll do it. You'd have to go into a nursing home, it's quite unsuitable here. I love you so Andrea," she said. "I don't want you to go. I couldn't bear to have you go in this unhappy state. Please rest now and think about it carefully. You know I'll help you all I can. I don't want anything to happen to you."

"Oh Laura!" I couldn't say anything else.

"Andrea," she said gently. "Stay with me, let me help you please."

"I can't bear being pregnant!" I tried not to shout.

"It can be a very special time," she began to say.

"It can't be for me! Never. Never!"

"Yes it can be!" and she kissed me. "It can be a very lovely time. We'll make it so," she spoke so earnestly and kindly. She explained it wasn't always possible to perform an abortion; and when I asked her what people would say about my having Christopher's baby, she said, "What people! Andrea! There are no people to look at you and say anything. What would these so-called non-existent people say about us if they knew all about us! This is what I mean when I tell you not to measure yourself against false standards. There are times, d'you see," she went on, "when we have to look beyond ourselves. There are these times when we simply have no choice; we must go on and make the best of what we have to do." She was so serious and I could see she meant what she said.

She promised to help me. "Stay with me," she said. "You don't need to go. I'll keep you well and comfortable. I promise everything will be easy. I'll get a good nurse in. I'll get someone, a trained nurse from town whose job is simply to look after the baby. Let's think ahead, Andrea, to making a good home for the baby. After all it's not her fault she's being born is it. This house will make a good home. I'll have the whole place repainted, Andrea, I'll get electricity put on and we'll have stables and a swimming pool. I'll do anything to make this a good place for you," Laura talked on trying to comfort me.

"D'you see Andrea, we'll expand the farm. I'll clear the land beyond the top paddock. There are all kinds of things we can do to improve and enlarge the farm. I'm planning to rebuild Murphy's house, clear away all that rubbish and the asbestos. We'll have more sheds, plant more trees and a second vineyard, and our life needn't be all work. After your baby is born, Andrea, we can travel. We'll go wherever you like, do anything you like, lead the kind of life you want."

"What kind of life do I want Laura," I asked her hating my voice, it was like a spoiled disagreeable child speaking.

"Who knows what kind of life they want," she said. "Mostly people do not have any choice and mostly they have to fit into accepted ways, jobs, marriages, friends even their choice of houses. I didn't choose certain things in my life but I do choose now to live in the way I do and I'm offering you to share what I have, I'm offering you complete choice. Will you take what I can offer?"

"Dear Laura, I don't deserve your kindness."

"It isn't kindness. I need you. I don't think I could live without you! If you accept my suggestion I can give you and your baby love and security forever," she was so serious.

"Oh Laura it sounds as if you were proposing marriage to me!" I laughed and her brow darkened heavily into a frown.

"No," she said. "That isn't what I'm doing. You know what I think about the loveless lives so many married people have, the obvious relief that the so-called loving time is over, we don't belong to that. I'm simply asking you to share what I have to offer for as long as you want or need to and the same for the child."

"Oh God! Child!" I said it aloud, she was waiting for my reply. I didn't say anything and she went on.

"If you want an abortion I'd have to explain some sort

of story to Rodney and get him to fix something. I'd rather not d'you see, he'd find it hard to refuse. It puts him in a very difficult position. And of course, knowing them as I do I am not sure of your privacy in the whole thing. Of course I'd say nothing about Christopher, you realise that. If that's what you really want you know I'll do anything for you." There was another long pause while Laura waited for me.

"Laura, I don't know; I think I want to stay with you. I think you are too good to me. I don't know what to do!"

"Come," she said getting up from the table and putting out her hand to me. "Come along Andrea, we are so very tired. It might be better if we stopped talking and thinking for a bit. Why don't we have some music. Let's lie down and rest and go to bed early. There'll be plenty of time for talking tomorrow. Let's rest, I'd like to and I'd like to listen to one of the quartets.

That's how Laura is. So kind and generous and loving. She is impossible too, all her qualities combine to make the person she is, that's how she is. A Beethoven quartet, the passing of one phrase of music from violin to violin and to violin cello and to cello can absorb her so completely that nothing else matters.

* * *

Laura

She says she can't go to her mother while she is pregnant. She told me she left Eva and Jake years ago because she couldn't stand life with their attitudes. That's why she went overseas to work with the foreign aid people.

"I wanted to go somewhere and teach children," she said last night. "Where it would be of some use." She told me she felt guilty about going; it was just after Angela was killed in a car accident. "But I had to go Laura," she said. "It was because of Christopher. I've already told you. I should never have come back."

She is docile today after her weeping, I am so exhausted too. It is suddenly very hot. The long walk and the unhappiness of yesterday have tired me. I have

203

been trying to comfort her today. In spite of her boyish appearance, she has screwed her hair up into a knot, she is very much a woman. The pregnancy is evident but can be concealed for Sunday. We have Sunday to think about.

I am afraid she will leave. I want to keep her here. While she is pregnant she has nowhere. I wish the months to go slowly. But while she is here, the time goes so quickly. I want her to be happy with our life here. I want this life with her. I have been talking to her about the farm again and telling her the plans I have. I must get her really interested.

I tried to tell her things I have thought about.

"We can make a happy life together." I tried to tell her, "Happiness is worked for and made by people, but joy just comes by itself." She said she knew what I meant. I told her "Moments of joy are mysterious, they come unexpectedly, quickly and they go quickly". I'll tell her later that I've never known such joy as these times when I'm with her. The farm, the fresh air, the horses, the fruit trees, all the things which are part of life in this place seem more important if I'm doing them for her. I must tell her I believe people are made for joy and it comes at any time and in any place. This place and with both of us here.

This evening we are together as before. Perhaps even closer than ever before because we have talked about the coming of the baby and of the ways in which we can really accept the situation, to overcome the things which seemed such problems to her. If we are together it seems there is no problem, the two of us can share this life and our friendship, we can share the seasons and the harvest, and the birth of the baby could be part of the joy we have together. This is how I have reasoned with her, very tenderly.

We are listening to the Beethoven quartets, this evening another of the quartets, the music seems filled with poetry and contemplation and the acceptance of sadness and grief and the ability to understand happiness. Andrea is here beside me. My eyes are closed and

I'm thinking of her saying she loved me and I feel the joy of her saying it. There are tears in my eyes even though they are closed.

"The poet Blake said something like this," I say to her.

"Oh Laura," she says. "I thought you were asleep."

"Was I snoring? I hope not!"

"What does Blake say?"

"Well I can't remember the whole poem but it's something like

'And we are put on earth a little space
That we may learn to bear the beams of love.'"

"What does it mean exactly?" she asks.

"Esmé Gollanberg," I say. "Esmé had theories."

"Tell me," Andrea says.

"Come up here beside me." I make room for Andrea on the couch. "Lie up very close," I tell her. "Blake means either that we bear the beams of love like the warm rays of the sun or we bear the burdens of love, you know the deep cares which loving another person brings, at least that's what I think it means. Esmé, Dr. Gollanberg, among her theories, believed that two people could achieve a deep spiritual relationship by touch and she maintained that two people, who were fond of each other, man and wife, two men or two women, could have a deep emotional experience by simply lying close and stroking each other's arms or legs or their hair or their faces. She wrote extensively on the subject and I was very interested; more than interested. I became involved with the theories by correspondence, by literature, if you like to put it that way. And that's perhaps why I ended everything the way I did."

Andrea very gently strokes my hair and my face, "I understand," she says and I know that she does.

Time has no meaning.

Even Sunday holds no fears.

There will be this Sunday and another Sunday and another after that. We'll be together.

"I'll never have any time when you're not in my mind," I tell her.

* * *

205

Sunday

Andrea

Laura loves the cello.

It doesn't matter what she's doing or how tired she is, if she hears some music it lifts her out of the depths, it sustains her, especially the cello. She says this so often. It means a great deal to her.

She wears a sort of cotton shirt without sleeves when she is out working in the sun. I told her I liked these shirts and she laughed and told me to wear one too.

"I made them d'you see, it's furnishing material that's why they're such lovely stripes, orange and green and black and purple, I can't do sleeves or collars and since I never can get a hem straight I don't put one."

How different this place seems when there are two strange cars parked over by the wires of the Murphy fence. The little girls with their tattered hems and unkempt hair are standing and staring across. Laura said that though Mrs. Murphy is so ill she wouldn't miss any of it, she probably had a chair just by the turned up bit of curtain. No magpies, just people and their voices suddenly all round us.

"I must just walk to the edge of the verandah and throw my chest out," Rodney Glass has said what Laura said he would say. He fell over the pail in the yard and said,

"I never thought I'd have to come so far to kick the bucket." He makes everyone laugh. He takes Laura's bush hat and fly veil on the way to the verandah.

"Where's the wheelbarrow Laura? Is it far away?" he calls. "Is the crowbar handy? And where's your rifle Laura dear? If I could have them, please, I'll be ready. Where's your gun?" His voice is full of laughter.

"It's in the corner by my desk," she calls to him. We're in the kitchen getting drinks with ice blocks for all the guests. Vermouth, whisky, brandy and dry ginger, Laura has them all ready.

"What's he going to do?" I ask Laura quietly.

"It's for Rodney's rural photograph," she whispers back. "Every year he has one taken in the hope that he will be written about by someone and with the information he hopes they'll want a picture! So he likes to have an up to date one ready!" She pushes the tray into my hand. "Here take these round, I won't be a moment." She is talking to Peter Glass, Rodney's youngest child; he is fifteen and is hungry after the drive. Laura is spreading thick bread and butter for him; quickly going from one thing to the next.

"What's the healing process of a fracture Laura?" Peter asks.

"You're surely not learning that at school," she says.

"No, but we're doing a sort of first aid course with some anatomy and physiology. I'd just like to know how a fracture mends, really it's an extra for an essay I'm trying to write," he looks at Laura very seriously through his childish spectacles.

"Well," says Laura. "The bone breaks and there's some bleeding from the tissues, I'll just tell you in a simple way," she laughs. "D'you see it's a long long time since I've thought about fractures; well, a blood clot forms at the site of the injury and granulation tissue starts to form. Granulation containing osteoblasts which make a soft bone substance called callus which gradually hardens into bone like the original bone. Will that do?" She hands him more bread and butter.

"That's great Laura thanks!" he dashes off.

"Don't forget time," Laura calls. "Put in a sentence about time, it's such an important thing in the healing process, always remember this, nothing heals in a moment."

"I'm surprised they let you have a rifle Laura!" Cheryl Glass calls as she lifts her vermouth from my tray and immediately she claps her free hand over her mouth. "Oh! now why have I said that! What have I said!" she moans. "Now, why do I always let out things like that to Laura or where Laura can hear!" she murmurs looking anxiously all round. "Every time I have to make a silly fox's paw like that!"

"The faux pas is necessary at times to release tension," her husband replies, he is posed on the verandah steps with all sorts of long-handled implements clutched about him.

"I'm bristling with tools!" he says. "There are situations m'dear, where the unconscious demands this sort of expression. Laura does not mind. She can take it. She'd even explain to you why you said it, if she'd heard what you'd said."

His wife looks grateful. She and Mrs. Fort have already changed into their halter tops. Rodney put chairs for them at the edge of the verandah where they are sitting now in the widening strip of sun.

"Should get a good tan started today!" he tells them. Already the bedroom, our bedroom, smells different with their clothes and their handbags; and their shoes kicked off for comfort straight away, seem out of place there. Laura tidied her things a bit this morning and pushed the worn saddles and all the harness straps and bridles to one side.

"I really ought to do something with all this, it's old and incomplete and I'll never use any of it. Museum pieces!"

Laura always prepares the same meal for them, she makes an Irish stew and last night she showed me how she removes the fat with a piece of newspaper. "They like a country meal and I put in the mint and parsley and the other herbs right at the last mìnute, this really hides the defects in the cooking!"

How can I help liking her, loving her, she has such lovable ways which outweigh anything stubborn or selfish in her character. Just now she is laughing with Rodney, they started arguing as soon as she came from the kitchen.

"Nothing is sustained in perfection," he is saying. "There's good and bad, Laura, you can't get away from it both in literature and in music — Eroica for example," Rodney says, "the first and second movement, superb — but as for the rest — Poof!" he snaps his fingers.

"The Fifth Symphony," Laura says, "has perfection throughout, you can't deny this! For one thing, think of the economy. The Beethoven Economical!" They are laughing. Rodney picks up the pruning saw which Laura has forgotten to put away. "Beethoven Economical Bargains!" he says.

"Laura will now dance," he announces. "Lara Ward will now perform her 'Sabre dance with Pruning Saw'!"

When I see her laughing with her visitors, carrying on polite and amusing conversation, handing them refreshments and being such a gracious and conventional hostess, it is strange, almost impossible to remember that last night I lay naked along her strong naked thigh. The night was so warm we didn't need bed clothes and the steady moonlight stripped the room of reality. We seemed to only half-sleep all night. Laura stroked the whole length of my back over and over again as I lay there close to her with my face against her soft breast. We hardly spoke but once Laura said, "You are so cool and smooth."

Together we experienced the deep sensation and calm Laura has told me about, and she said, "This is the ultimate," and after a little while she said, "Esmé Gollanberg wrote about this quiet closeness between two people, she wrote with such sensitive thought, her writing was beautiful. And then when she came, d'you see Andrea, I simply could not reconcile this person who was here with me with the ideas I had formed about her from her books and articles and letters; we had a very deep and thorough correspondence. It was simply that. I shouldn't have done what I did but it seemed it was already there for me to do." We lay without speaking and then she asked me, "Are you happy?" and I said I was and she said there weren't enough words to describe how she was feeling. And after a little while I asked her,

"You believe very much in fate Laura don't you?"

"Yes I suppose I do," she replied. "And if you are to be my fate, my destiny," she spoke so quietly, the words disappeared in my hair, "Then I want to believe in this fate, this dearest destiny!"

My Laura is the same Laura but is so hidden from these people and yet they seem fond of her in a way which makes me realise they see her qualities. They tease her too about the farm. I was afraid they might tease her too much.

"When are you going to clear this part," Rodney asks indicating the carefully cherished little fruit trees. "It's very untidy Laura," he says, "Don't you know you can get plastic grass by the yard? Green all the year round! And plastic trees. Now a little set of self-glittering Christmas trees would be tres gai here, you could get rid of all this ugly real stuff. Just look at all that wispy straw!"

"Well I think Laura might as well have plaster ducks and hens and what about a gnome or two?" Cheryl Glass joins Rodney's game.

These people were fond of her father; of course I realise this but they do seem to care for her for herself. They seem light-hearted today, as Laura said, it is a day out for them and they are here to enjoy themselves.

"Ah the country experience!" Rodney is breathing hard.

"Don't take all the air!" Michael Fort joins Rodney at the verandah rail. The two men, relaxed, seem close in their friendship. I had never noticed this before.

"I wonder when the others will get here," I say in a whisper to Laura back in the kitchen.

"I expect they'll be here soon," she replies in a low voice. "Christopher," she says. "And Eva." She gives me a bunch of knives and forks.

"Are you worried too?" I ask her.

"Perhaps just a little," she says. "We'll manage!" Secretly she gives my arm a squeeze and the feeling of her fingers stays with me and comforts me.

I am afraid to see Christopher. I don't want to see Mother. I suppose it's hard for Laura to see Eva again after all these years. I am afraid for myself most. For years I haven't got on with Mother. She is disappointed in me because I'm not pretty, because I didn't turn out like Angela. How can I speak to Christopher in front of Laura now. Whatever can I say to him in any case, in public or in private. What have I got to say to any of these people.

They have arrived. We are making so much noise on the verandah we didn't hear their car come though the Murphy dogs are proclaiming the arrival as Laura puts it.

Christopher, after these weeks seems to be very thin, careworn even. He is bringing Mother carefully through the house and on to the verandah. How slowly Mother walks.

"Eva has had a slight stroke," he explains to Laura, he is always quick to speak, to explain. When he was little, "I'm just going," he always said or "I'm just coming —." Christopher continues, "Possibly because of Father dying suddenly, it's thought she had more than one stroke but they were unnoticed because they were so slight. This time she fell on the back steps, that explains her black eye and bruised lip."

"Hullo there!" Rodney Glass is hearty. "We can see the little lady's been in a fight, haven't you m'dear, who've you been beating up!" Everyone laughs.

Eva smiles slowly and crookedly because of her swollen face, she doesn't look like Mother really. Christopher helps her into a chair. I can't help thinking how all the old ladies will love him, the fair young doctor! He has an attentive way with people. Not with me but then I'm not an old lady. Not yet! In any case he just turns it on, it's not real.

"Here's Laura Mother," he says to her in a loud voice. Mother's a bit deaf," he explains, and we all watch as he settles her with a cushion.

"Laur-ah it's be-en a lo-ong ti-me!" Eva speaks slowly, with difficulty and with some emphasis, the words slurring as her voice is not clear. She holds out the hand she can move to Laura and Laura takes it lightly and looks steadily at Mother, she smiles slightly.

"Eva," she says and I listen for some tone in her voice but there is none. Christopher goes back to the car at once to help the Meringue Pie bring her baby and the bag with feeding bottles and orange juice and rusks and the other bag with nappies and plastic things and another bundle which turns out to be the wrong shawl for Eva.

We are safely over the arrival. I look at Laura to see some reaction but like the controlled quality of her voice I see only the same control in operation in her whole bearing. Because of all the noise we can't hear the magpies or the calves or the usual cackling from the fowl yard.

I see Laura looking at Eva and I think Laura's hand is shaking as she holds a plate of salted biscuits. I see Mother turn her swollen face and her bright but stupid eyes to Laura and smile a slow childlike smile which is recognition without real remembering.

Both the Forts are so pleased to see their very own Meringue Pie and their fat grandson though it's clear they were all of them together yesterday for what they call "roast tea at Mum's place"; how that phrase made me sick when I was staying with them. How far away all that seems now, but the sight of all that baby gear makes me remember how things are with me and I want to go off somewhere and howl.

I watch Christopher. Laura's right. Poor Christopher but he isn't poor. Laura's quite right! Christopher has got where he wants to be on the ladder. In a few years' time he'll be qualified, he knows the right people, he's married them. He's got one baby, for prestige he'll need more but that's no trouble to them. Laura's so right! Christopher wants them more than me. He needs them and he doesn't need me. Goddam the whole thing. I help Laura to serve the food.

"The smell of kerosene is delicious," Cheryl Glass has been to the shabby old lean-to which is the bathroom, "And the water tanks are so quaint," she says. "It's like a holiday house!"

"Really Laura," Rodney says, "You should get the electricity put on and the water." Laura agrees with him.

"Perhaps everyone would like to sit down for lunch," Laura pulls the painted wooden chairs up to the big table. Rodney helps her. The verandah is quite altered by so many people being there.

"Oh Laura! No wonder Andrea looks so well. Just look at all these dishes. You two must really be living in the lap of luxury," Cheryl Glass moves to the table. "I must just pinch a teeny sausage," she says. "Even though I'm supposed to be on my weight watcher's diet!"

"It's the usual spread," Rodney approves. "Worth coming two hundred miles for eh?" And he goes off to fetch his present from the car.

"A little wine for you m'dear," he comes back presenting a carton, staggering a little as he can't do anything without a bit of a show.

"Oh Rodney! thank you!" Laura is pleased and pulls out a bottle. "The favourite claret!" she says. My ever obliging brother opens the wine for Laura. He is ready to assist Laura, to place Meringue Pie gently wherever she wants to be placed, and he sets Mother up himself with a little tray and a dish and a spoon and ties a napkin under her chin which I notice is wet with saliva all the time. Poor Mother.

Laura tastes the wine. "Thank you Rodney," she says again.

"You can give me a kiss later on when they're all asleep," he says. And I wonder if Laura has ever kissed Rodney or been kissed by him. As if it matters really!

Everyone is eating. Even the saint, my brother, has a plateful of food at last. I feel I'll throw up. Perhaps Laura has guessed how I'm feeling for she looks at me quickly, just a little secret look with her eyebrows raised and a tiny half smile. I look away quickly and watch Michael Fort. He talks a lot, surgical or boating things, he eats quickly, fussily, chopping up, separating, moving small amounts of food from one part of his plate to another, his knife and fork are never still and he talks and does not notice what he is moving about on his plate it is all of no consequence, as he is of no consequence.

I want to be alone with Laura. I can't stand all these people. Then Peter Glass speaks, Peter Glass, the "after thought", "the nuisance" as Rodney calls him or "the mistake" suddenly tells a joke. Up till now he has not been noticed, he is a quiet boy, the only child left at home after the four other Glass children have grown up and gone. Peter suddenly tells a joke.

"What is brown and crawls up your leg?" he asks across the table.

"Heavens!" Laura rises to the occasion. "What is brown and crawls up your leg," she repeats the riddle. "What is brown and crawls up your leg, some kind of lizard wouldn't make it a riddle." she thinks aloud. She gives a quick look round the table to see that everyone has all they need.

"Andrea made the bean salad," she says. "It's delicious!" "Now about this riddle, I'm afraid I'll have to give it up. I'm never any good at this sort of thing."

"You give it up?" Peter Glass asks, his round spectacles catch the light so that his eyes are hidden. Everyone agrees they can't think of the answer. And Peter Glass says,

"A homesick shit."

For a moment there is a horrified silence and then Rodney Glass tells his son to leave the table and to leave the verandah at once.

"Go and sit in the car!" he says, anger and embarrassment making him inarticulate. The boy starts to leave the table, his face is flushed.

"Wait a minute Rodney," Laura intervenes and everyone is suddenly hopeful. It is her well-bred good humour, her sense of the moment. "I don't want to fly in the face of authority, Rodney," she seems to sing the words in that deep soft voice she has sometimes. She has her hand over Peter's hand as if by accident on the corner of the table so he is obliged to stand there. I notice this, I don't know if the others do. I know this caressing quality in her hand and voice. "Rodney, if you agree," she says, "I think Peter should stay at the table. It seems to me he can't escape from having all the qualities born in him, inherited qualities, for the making of a surgeon. In a few years' time, you must agree, he will

214

be a tremendous asset at the Faculty dinners, so perhaps he need not be penalised now for his qualities." There can be no doubt Laura is not joking, she is serious, she wants to save Peter from this embarrassment. "Look at his hands Rod," she says smiling. "You have only to compare his hands with your own, you must surely agree with me!"

"Dear Laura," Rodney Glass is smiling. "It is impossible to disagree with you. I can't argue with such a gracious and charming hostess," his voice is quiet. "Laura wants you to stay at the table, Peter," he says. The boy sits down quickly.

"You can't go," Laura says to him. "I've made a pudding for today, a caramel custard, it took hours to bake, and the others may not want to eat custard. I am relying on you! So you see, your presence is essential."

"Thanks Laura," Cheryl Glass says. I suppose I am the only one to notice that her neck has reddened under her tan.

Rodney goes to help Laura with the coffee, I can't help overhearing their voices and I wait just by the kitchen.

"Sleeping all right Laura?" Rodney's voice is low.

"Oh yes perfectly, thank you," Laura's reply comes back in that personal intimate tone she has sometimes. "We've been riding a lot d'you see, it's been good for me!"

"Aha!" from Rodney. "That's good! Now, which cups shall I take? Who's for coffee!" his voice comes back to the verandah.

I never knew until today that Laura keeps a gun; it's loaded. I heard Rodney say to Michael Fort that he could see by the way it was kept that Laura's gun was not just an ornament.

* * *

Laura

Just about here at the edge of the jarrah forest there'll be an olive grove one day. From this place inhabited mainly by silence and about to be filled with memories it is possible to look down the long slope to the sturdy yellow-leaved pear trees and beyond them to the graceful cradles of the willows.

My land is lovely today. The day is still and very warm and fragrant. I can look across to the wealth of hay opposite. The little Palomino horses cross and recross the paddock in front of the placid shape and colour of the hay. "All is safely gathered in before the winter storms begin" we sang at school, I don't think I ever thought of hay-ricks then.

Most of my guests are asleep in various places on rugs and cushions and on the bed in my house. After lunch they disappeared one by one to rest.

"Christopher wants to ride," Andrea said to me in the kitchen.

"So does Peter," I said to her. "But don't you think it's rather too hot?" She shrugged. Her shoulders seemed pointed under her Indian dress. She had chosen the wide one so that the folds would hide her rounded shape. She shrugged again.

"I don't think you should ride Andrea," I said to her. "I think you should not, Dearest," we kept our voices low.

"I'll just take him to the stud to see the horses then," she said.

"What about Peter?"

"Oh he can go fishing or something, can't he?" she sounded a bit disagreeable. I wanted to tell her to rest.

"Goodbye Laura," she said and was gone from the room so quickly. I watched them, brother and sister, walking down the slope and up the other side of the valley. They were lost among the trees up there as Andrea did not take him the way we usually go. I saw again that fatal harmony.

It's best to guard oneself against the misdirecting of the frail human heart. Perhaps there is no way to guard against pain of this sort; it is a pain and there is no preparation for it. I knew this day would be difficult. I looked beyond it to the time when it would be over and we would be alone together once more and able to go on with the delicate privacy of our lives. I can't be present at the real meeting between them.

216

"Hullo Jacky," his name for her. "Hullo Jacky," he greeted her on arrival. "You're looking a heap better already," he said and I noticed how busy he was with his mother and how this prevented him from really meeting anyone at all.

I realise now that I avoided seeing how she received his coming. Perhaps we all defended ourselves.

She didn't ask me to go with them. How could she!

There is a pause in the endless rasping of the grasshoppers and, in the stillness, I can hear the thudding of the horses' hooves on the resonance of the bald land across the valley. They are not dressed for riding, I suppose that wouldn't worry either of them. Andrea is quite capable of taking off her dress and riding the Dove naked.

Somewhere, not far away, a jarrah thief starts up a chain saw and all sounds are lost in the drone of the thieving weapon.

This partly cleared little place on the edge of the forest is so small and the bush presses in from three sides. It is hot here. It's too hot for working though I have done some work here during the last few days. I can't burn at this time of the year and I'll have to get Murphy to get the stumps out. It is slow work.

"I like the thought of an olive farm," Andrea said yesterday. I asked her about the idea of having the vines in arbours and this pleased her too.

This little clearing is the beginning of our work together to expand the farm. I am wishing away the season before it really comes, it is hard to work in the heat. Even though I start at five when the east wind is bitterly cold it is not long before the sun is penetrating and scorching and I have to give up. Andrea and I rest during the long hot days on long chairs which have to be moved frequently from one little patch of shade to another. We talk with tranquillity and ease seeing already the delicate greens of the olive trees bending a little to the prevailing winds, and the trodden paths between the new vines seem so vivid though nothing is planted here yet.

217

"What consequence can our talk have in such a wild and lonely place," Andrea asks. We had been discussing world affairs with so much seriousness. "It only matters to the two of us."

"But it would only matter to the two of us if we were on a crowded bus in the heart of London for instance or walking with tourists to look at the churches in Rome—"

"Yes London or Rome or anywhere. Yes, I suppose that's true, it's of no consequence to anyone, our talking or our living."

"People should live without consequence, should be allowed to live their own kinds of lives."

"Yes, I do agree completely."

Our talk dissolves. She looks so relaxed and pretty. She has been eating good meals again and seems more reconciled to her condition and she seems happy.

The breeze, rushing through the tops of the trees, comes nearer and stronger with a sighing noise and then drops. In the sudden silence when the wind stops, the long summer silence and the hot sharp fragrance from the earth is more intense.

We have ice cold drinks in tall glasses and it is as if we are asleep yet seeing the moving shapes and colours among the branches and clusters of trembling leaves. Because of the slowly travelling sun all the colours are constantly changing. White bark is striped and shadowed pink and gold, yellow green, and green all bronzed in the summer light. Black twigs and brittle leaves sparkling and silver edged are always falling replenishing and scenting the earth. And behind all this moving changing colour is blue sky and blue sky and more blue sky. The dusk is brief and suddenly it is evening and we are cool on the high verandah with the cutlery and the plates and glasses, the fragments and litter of our finished meal still on the table.

It is only a few days since we came suddenly into summer and have our dinner on the verandah, yet it seems that for years I have been sitting there with my arm about her shoulders, watching the night, listening to the cicadas and the frogs, both together they are ъ part of the evening. The thin moon hangs behind the frail-leaved eucalyptus and through the trees are long slanting moonlight shadows. I love these evenings as I love everything about her and our lives together.

"What is it about us!" Andrea asked one night when we were sitting like this. "How is it we feel about each other the way we do?"

"The worst service we can do to our story is to comment on it," I said, laughing. "It's so delicate isn't it, it's the ideal of an Idyll," I said. "Transparently simple. Isn't this how it is? Instead of wars and politics we are concerned with a friendship between two women, with the harvest from the land and with the birth of a baby." We sat for a while longer watching the last strip of pale horizon, yellow washed behind the antlers and foliage of the black trees, narrow to a streak of last light as the sun dropped somewhere beyond our sight. She said she was tired and wanted to go to bed.

"You come to bed now too, Laura Dear. You never come. I want you to come now," she said. Lately I have been staying up to write and then have gone to sleep alone on the couch so that I can get up early to work without disturbing her.

We got up from the table and I said to her, laughing and misquoting.

"This is my body of the New Testament which is given for you —" and we went together into the dark quiet house, tenderly to bed, without even needing to light the lamps. There are still these tender nights for us, a mingling of anticipation and happiness held in the noiseless trembling leaf shadows moving to and fro, back and forth across the silent curtains of our room.

From the top edge of my property looking down this slope which has taken so much of my time and strength is rather like looking over my life. It is as if first there was a cradle song by a lake and then hunting horns in the forests of childhood.

" 'Comme c'est triste le son du cor au fond des bois.' Translate!" Eva bent her fair head over her desk and I

saw her lovely white neck flush. She couldn't understand. The class was waiting. "Translate! 'How sad is
the sound of the horn in the depths of the woods'." I
scribbled on a bit of paper and pushed it into her lap.
Afterwards I told her I thought it was beautiful poetry.

"How sad is the sound of the horn in the depths of the
woods," we walked together in our grey dresses, they
had identical white collars and were tied at the waist
with a sort of braided belt. It didn't matter what we
wore, I wanted to reach her soul. I wanted to reach her. I
wanted.

"You're very clever Laura," she admired me.

I loved her. I loved her. Our clothes were the same. My
feeling for her was something detached from appearance, quite apart from our lives as they were at school.

I suppose I was looking for myself in her and never
saw her. That is how it would be explained.

The sad horns and then the passionate and triumphant trumpets, the duo of two minds in complete
partnership, working together communicating so perfectly followed by sustained movements from a full
orchestra, a finale perhaps, something like the last
movement of Beethoven's Seventh Symphony.

It is quiet again just the soft voices of the magpies
falling. I am storing thoughts, happy, sad and tender, in
this place. I haven't long to stay up here. I have visitors
today and I must go down to my house and boil water for
tea and cut up fruit cake.

It does not take me very long to think and certain
quick and unexpected thoughts are complicating the
very simple reasons I gave to Andrea about having
these visitors. I thought she would have things in proportion in her mind after seeing them. She did laugh to
me in the kitchen about her brother, quietly so that
no-one could hear.

"Oh Laura," she whispered, "He's come in shorts and
long socks, you know off-white knee socks and such
polished shoes. You're right, he's one of them! And I'm
not!"

Eva obviously has difficulty in swallowing. She will

lose weight and strength. Already she has passed from one kind of life to another. Her hair is quite changed, it is white and soft. The wisps of old age. There is very little difference in our ages. I am older than Eva, not much. Her eyes are still very blue but it is hard to say how much they see.

"Andrea-looks-so-well-now," she said slowly to me. Concern over her children has claimed the greater part of her life. Concern for them veils everything and this conventional concern carries her on. As she spoke to me I couldn't help thinking that with all her life of concern she is completely unaware of what concerns Andrea and her brother most, a tragedy for the brother and sister, this strange fate between her son and daughter. Eva was always protected, first by stupidity and now by the cerebral lesion.

I suppose I kept myself from a real meeting with Eva. When we met there was no meeting. I am not disappointed nor relieved, neither one thing nor the other. There were traces of the person I knew once but these were so slight they were of no real consequence.

It was agreed that it was too hot to ride. The visit is much later this year so they walked, just a few steps to look at the fruit trees nearest to the house and a few steps beyond the top paddock where a few leschenaultia are still in flower. No-one can really see this place as I am able to see it. In order to see and feel the changes in light and shade and the various qualities of the air it is really necessary to be here day after day feeling and noticing these things as the hours go by.

Just in this little time I have alone I can try to think what I must do. Any plans I have for new buildings, new equipment, a swimming pool, electricity, more fruit trees and more stock all seem too small to be considered in place of considering what her life is to be.

After reading, as she did so thoroughly and with so much understanding about my life, after the first shock of discovery about each other at that time, we have been very close, and fond and thoughful. She has shown me so much love and consideration. She has enriched and nourished me.

Her life shall be my first consideration.

My own attempts at forestry and the apparent immortality of trees makes me aware of my own mortality.

As the years go by by age will add to age and make old age. To see her growing older perhaps embittered and very lonely is too terrible for contemplation. In an attempt to put this off we shall be obliged to travel, to make tours, journeys and voyages. We might quite soon be together on holiday in Europe trying to accept this bitterness and disagreeable boredom which are so inevitably in store because of the restrictions imposed by our relationship. I am afraid of the loneliness and depression it is possible to feel in a foreign country. I know it already. The travel offices and the restaurants and the dining rooms all over the world and the cafes and shops are all meaningless, some dirty beyond words and others clean, sterile even, and so much the same from one country to another. Loneliness sits in art galleries, concert halls, museums and churches and most of all in the hotel bedrooms where we would unpack our elegance and our own peculiar brand of loneliness, for by then we would have a loneliness unequalled by any other suffering.

And what about the loveless time when the loving comes to an end and there will be only the expected bored enquiries about the qualities of separated sleep and the concern and discussion about the functioning of each other's bowels or whether the tea or the soup is hot enough.

"How we soffered!" Irma said describing part of her voyage with Hilde. "I was, do you understand, I was determined to see Stromboli erupt," she explained at the breakfast table, it's just as if as I can hear her voice.

"It was so cold on ze upper deck but I froze there in my determination and afterwards became so ill. Poor Hilde how she had to put up with my illness and she became ill herself, she also became ill! How we soffered!"

"Ach Ja!" Hilde remembered too. "How we soffered!"

Irma and Hilde were not stared at on our ship. No-one nudged or looked at the two elderly ladies travelling with their luggage and packets, their hats and brown polished shoes and the bags they both carried with various essentials for emergencies.

Irma has a way of announcing herself to the world before the world can whisper. This would not be so with us. In our proud and noble friendship there is no quality to equip us for the common-place. In our elegance and difference, Andrea and I would be noticed, even our two voices in conversation or laughter would draw attention. It would be impossible for her. We would both suffer and become intolerable to one another.

My visitors are glad to have their tea. They are all refreshed from sleeping.

When I see Andrea walking beside Chistopher, their youth and light-hearted movement matching, I am touched by their appearance. As they come up the slope their faces are bright and animated turning towards each other in their talk. They both have palomino golden hair. The evening sun behind them makes a halo of light about their heads and they seem to me to be so innocent. It is their innocence which makes me know what I must do. He must live for his young life and she for hers.

* * *

Andrea

Every morning Laura pours a little water carefully, a libation, she calls it, into the tins and pots to sustain her little pomegranates and the myrtle, the rosemary and the jade. Sometimes she takes a bit of one of the herbs and crushing it, holds it in her cupped hands breathing in the fragrance. The water stays sparkling to the brim of every pot for a few seconds and then disappears into the grey sand and in a little while they all look as if they have never been watered at all.

For some reason Laura seems to have lost her enthusiasm. Perhaps it is the summer. This awful heat, for some weeks now it has been hot, really hot. Soon

223

after that Sunday it was hot. This awful heat. Whoever can work in this heat! She doesn't try to work of course, but it's the other things. She's left them. On her desk are all the letters she wrote to the building contractor, the electrician, the brick company and the plumber and the carpenter. She wrote all these letters full of plans for the farm but they are all spread out there, not even folded up into their envelopes. The paint arrived and is stacked in the porch unlooked at. It might be too hot for painting it would kill Mr. Murphy to be up on the roof on days like these. And of course Mrs. Murphy is ill again. Laura had to go over in the night and drive her to hospital. This is quite a usual occurrence but this morning, though Laura said very little, I could see she thinks Mrs. Murphy is dying. Mrs. Murphy seems to nearly die and then pull round and go on living, being a bit better and then suddenly is very ill again.

It's as if Laura can't make up her mind about the place. She hasn't said anything more to me about the ideas she had. She doesn't ever discuss the real business of the farm with me, I don't even pretend to understand it. But she was talking and planning the extra things she would do as part of the improvements. One thing was to be a swimming pool, just a small one, at the side of the verandah here.

"Where will you get enough water from?" I suppose it was a stupid question, she wouldn't have a pool if she couldn't get the water. She said she'd have to sink another well and that she needed new pumps and generators or whatever it is that goes with the pumping of water.

Perhaps she hasn't the money to spend after all. Perhaps she made all the promises so that I'd feel able to stop here and have the baby and be peaceful in my mind. Perhaps she doesn't want to say now she hasn't enough money, as if that would matter so much to me!

"It's no use to demonish Murphy's house till the new one is built," she said one night and then was stuck because when the engineer from the Shire Council came he said the only suitable site for the new house is where the old one is. The unposted letters seem desolate like an unfinished building in a neglected place.

It was after that Sunday her energy seemed to go. It must have been a shock to her to see Eva after her stroke. I must say it upset me to see Mother so changed. But in spite of dreading the day I enjoyed it. Even though Christopher looks the part he wants to play I had a lovely afternoon with him. Margie Meringue Pie and Junior had a long sleep on the big bed. They all went to sleep, I don't know what Laura did. When Christopher and I came back from the horses Laura had the tea cups out and they were all stretching and yawning and eating cake.

Perhaps it's my fault that Laura has lost her energy and interest. She is very pale and seems busy with her thoughts which she doesn't share with me. She is very quiet. Just lately I have been complaining a lot. God Awful! I am really God awful!

The heat is really intolerable and suddenly the hot hot ceiling is so near and there is no air, I feel I can't get any air and I'm thirsty and the water's bitter. And there's no-one here, no people except the Murphys and they are sheltering in that God awful little house. Sometimes they go to Queens Meadow. Murphy drives them; I suppose they all trail into the store there and out again and Mrs. Murphy looks really weak being helped in and out of the utility. If you think of going to Queens Meadow it's no better there, just a few strange country people in the store or the post office and their hot faces and bodies and an economy of conversation because no-one has anything they can be bothered to say if it's too hot to part your lips and speak. And the flies are everywhere. Laura or Murphy drive to Queens Meadow for the letters and Laura has things sent there by rail which have to be fetched from the station straight away. Perishable things which can't be bought in Queens Meadow. Her own trees have fruit coming. She says to wait a little and her peaches will be ready and then, because I don't really listen, she stops telling me.

Laura tries to soothe me. She agrees the summer is

sudden and early and fierce. In the night she came in to me because she heard me tossing about.

She lit the lamp and brought me water. I saw her hands and I turned my head away on the hot pillow.

"I've brought you a drink," she said.

"I can't drink this water," I told her. "It's not nice, there's something wrong with it. It's bitter."

She brought the white jug crammed with ice cubes, they looked nice but I knew they would be bitter too. So Laura cut up some oranges and squeezed them. As she handed me the glass she had a strange expression in her eyes. I suppose I hurt her all the time. I'm God awful to her. Oh God!

The water is so bitter.

"Is it always like this in the summer? Is the water always bad?" I asked and complained at the same time.

"It's not bad, Andrea," she said to me. "It's come from a long way down and has salts of some sort in it I suppose, it won't do us any harm," she said. I wanted some fresh water. The other day she fetched some. She went with Murphy, they took the utility and went to a place where a long hessian pipe hangs over the old railway line. Two drums of water, but quite quickly it got things in it, wrigglers, the Murphy children call them. It's not clear and it smells. Laura says it's all right if it's very cold. She drinks it as the ice cubes melt, but when I do, it draws my mouth and the strong taste makes me feel I'm going to be sick.

In the night she wouldn't drink the orange juice herself. "It's for you," she said. "Drink it!"

"Oh I don't like it," I said. "I've never liked oranges. I want some clean water!" I shouted at her.

"Oh Dearest, you're being so capricious," she leaned over me and stroked my head and bent down to kiss me. But I didn't want her near me. "It's too hot for that," I said crossly. "I'm too big! and I hate being pregnant, so big! It's awful, Laura! How can you think it's anything special! I hate it, I hate the baby. I hate this hot wind! I hate everything!" I burst out crying and made a lot of awful noise. She sat on the side of the bed in her night-gown.

It won't be long now," she tried to comfort me. "Please Andrea, try to be patient, soon it will be all right, you'll see."

It was just then Mr. Murphy came to the kitchen door, it must have been about one o'clock. I could hear him telling Laura something about Mrs. Murphy and I heard his voice break up and Laura had to go with him. I thought how Mrs. Murphy might be dying and I tried to imagine someone having death rigors in this heat and then I thought about having the baby. I wanted to scream but I was all alone and afraid of my own voice in the empty house.

Every night for some time I have been waking up burning hot, my mouth all dry, the baby kicking inside me and the memory of dreams which frighten me and then this reality of where I am and what is to happen to me. Once I called Laura. She must have been asleep but she came in quickly, stumbling across from her study.

"Laura! What's this rotten smell?" I asked her crossly. "It's like old rotten vegetables, it's making me sick."

"I can't smell anything," she said. "Perhaps it's the honeysuckle, its time is over, it might be the last few flowers of the honeysuckle, a bit strong, that's all."

This morning Laura looks tired and old. She is walking up and down the verandah watching the sky for rain clouds and she watches a pall of smoke which has been over the jarrah forest since the day before yesterday.

The skins of the loquats are tough and they are either tasteless or too sharp and mostly it's just stones inside. Laura has them for breakfast. She says she has a melon for me.

"They are very pretty these little rock melons, the ones with the lace pattern on the rind are the best," she cuts a melon but I don't really like the smell of it.

"Eat a little!" She puts it in front of me and then goes on walking up and down the verandah. Her restlessness

227

bothers me. I wish she would keep still. I push away the dish with the melon.

"The clouds come to the foot of the valley" she explains. "And then they divide and go in opposite directions and no rain comes here."

"What about the fire?" I ask. I know she is afraid of fire. She glances towards the forest anxiously.

"That's some way off," she says, and I'm wishing I was not so awful to her, there was no need for me to ask about the fire. I can see it for myself.

It's going to be another God awful hot day. I can feel the hot dry wind. The water pump is going all the time now. The wind carries the noise of the engine away and Laura stops her pacing. I know she is listening all the time for the engine. She worries that it might go wrong. She worries about the water tanks; she never says anything, but I know she is worrying. The faltering beat of the engine comes back to us on this horrible east wind though the motor sounds as if it will give up altogether any minute. It really gets on my nerves. She relaxes when she hears the pump again.

"Let's take a little walk down to the creek," she says. "Before it gets too hot."

"It's too hot now."

"A walk would do you good."

I'm really trapped in this place, every time I feel the baby move I feel caught.

"Really Andrea," she says, "walking is good, you really must not sit about all day." Her voice has gentle authority. I know she's right and I know I ought to try to be more gracious. Something has gone badly wrong that I'm like this, it's as if I could help being like I am and then suddenly it's as if I can't help myself. Hysteria. Laura hasn't used that word but she has told me to try to control whatever is making me behave like this. I would like to be different, to go on as we said we would if only I could! Since the Sunday when we had the visitors Laura has seemed different. It's as if she has lost the energy and the wish to be busy with all the things she was doing. She's obviously trying to write and sits late in her study. Ever since I've been here her study has been a muddle of music and literature, poetry mainly, and farming things. Just now it's as if she's forcing herself to do something. She's got lines of poetry all heavily crossed out and there are pamphlets on things like the incidence of severe congenital deformities in lambs and bacterial infection in sheep from diseased Wimmera rye grass. These are all underlined and marked as if she's making herself concentrate. I don't feel so safe with Laura when she's like this. It's an extraordinary lack of will, an ebbing of energy. Everything seems to have been brought to a standstill. The heat seems worse because of it. And I really can't care about the staggers in sheep even for Laura's sake.

I used to be so glad when Laura came back to the house and brought it to life with her needs. As soon as she came in she threw sticks in the wide fireplace and filled the rooms with smoke, and there would be water running in the bath and she dropped things noisily in the kitchen and all the time she laughed and called out to me, telling me things. Now all her noise irritates me, especially the way she lets the outside door swing and bang. Living alone has made her careless about things like this and she is sorry. I never used to mind but now everything seems worse because of it. It doesn't make it easier just saying she's sorry.

"It's your fault!" I say to her and she doesn't reply.

We walk together slowly down to the baked cracked flats where her little pear trees are and on a bit more through the rustling whispering paper-barks and sheoaks to the creek bed which is all broken up and desolate. It's ugly here and the voices in the trees mutter as if some strange customs took place here at some time, as if some unthought of suffering happened once a long time ago. It's a haunted place.

"I can't bear it!" I say to Laura. She takes my arm. There are oily rusty pools in places in the creek bed and Laura explains to me that it's the water seeping down the slope under the earth.

"The little pools are useful for the ducks," she says.

229

She guides me on the uneven ground. "I wish it would rain," she says.

"Rain wouldn't be enough!" I want to tell her I want more than rain. I find the place and the quietness intolerable. I want people and I want, oh, I don't know what I want. I want to go away.

"I must go away Laura. I must go. I insist!"

"Yes, yes, so you shall, as soon as it's possible," she says. "But just now it isn't possible. Andrea, please do try to be patient. Please let me try to help you. There could be some consolation in the stillness . . . " but I walk away from her stumbling on the hard earth. All round us is the dry baked ground, cracked open in places and glistening with salt. The weeds and grasses she pulled and put round her trees are all yellow and hard, the spikes of the straw scratch my ankles.

Laura waters the orchard at dusk carrying water to every tree in a tin can; I've watched her.

"The bigger trees don't need water now," she explains. But I can't listen to her, the sun seems to be burning down.

"Let's go back up to the house," I say. "It's too hot."

"Yes, yes of course!" she says, and we toil together back up the slope.

It isn't any better in the house. I knew it wouldn't be. I sit down by the window and Laura sits at the table, the dishes are still spread on it. She switches on her little wireless. "I'll see what the weather's going to be."

"Oh, as if we didn't know!" Really I am ashamed of my disagreeable voice. "It's just this hot dry wind all the time." There is some music on the programme, it's quite nice, it's cello and orchestra, I don't know what it is. Laura sits with her head on her hands. I know music comforts her very much. It's a bit too early for the weather report. Laura's hands are over her face and I think she's listening. And then I see that she's crying, the tears are running down her cheeks and she turns her head, I suppose so that I won't see. But I do see and I know how sorry I am. I get up and go over to her. The concert has come to an end.

"Oh Laura, I'm sorry! I really am." I put my hand on her shoulder and she puts her hand over mine.

Outside the window the hot day is standing still and in the room everything is very still. I can see the pulse beating in Laura's neck. She presses my hand.

"Please Laura, don't be upset," I say. "I'm sorry for being so awful. You must be worn out with me!"

After a few moments she dries her eyes, and says:

"I'm sorry too Andrea, I must be tired!" And then she says, "The Jade seems to live for ever, you know, my Jade was here when I came. Heaven knows how long it was there neglected and uncherished before. D'you see Andrea. I have to realise I'm not like the Jade."

"What d'you mean?"

"Just what I say," she says. "Don't feel badly about wanting to go away. We'll arrange for you to go, Andrea, as soon as it's possible."

On the wireless someone is reading the short news and then it's the weather. There's to be a cool change.

Laura gets up from the table and, putting her arm around me, gently takes me to the open window.

"You know, Andrea, I think I can really smell rain coming. We do get a summer rain. It will be very refreshing, you know, it will be very sweet." She kisses me softly on my hair.

"Please try," she wispers. "It won't be for long now."

"I think I will have to go." I let myself rest in her arms, leaning my head on her shoulders. She holds me close and I can feel her heart beating so hard. "I must tell you," I say. "I had a letter some time ago, I never told you . . ."

"Tell me about the letter." Her voice is low. "Tell me everything about the letter."

PART 7

A POSTCARD FROM IRMA

Andrea

"If any person should forget to flush the toilet or leave it in any way embarrassing one simply does not mention," Irma explained this morning. "Simply one goes in with ze little brush and one makes all right and no word said, iss better so," she gave her little laugh and the gold in her back teeth showed.

Her eyes are full of light and her complexion is clear and healthy; it is the same with Hilde. Both of them must be over seventy.

In all the bathrooms are body brushes on strong calico strips.

"One makes like ziss," Irma explained and showed me how to stimulate the circulation after a cold shower. And here the water really is cold, all the year round. I don't much care for the body brushes. When I take my shower I drop the ugly calico thing out of sight. Irma has explained however that the management likes the brushes cleaned every day and hung on the hooks provided for them. When I am cleaning the bathrooms this

233

is one of the things I must remember to do. Other things are airing bed clothes on the window sills, polishing the doors and the boards of the passages and the bannisters and changing sheets and pillow cases and towels. There is a Swiss girl doing the work with me, she doesn't speak any English. She is strong and quick and, since we can't speak, no time is wasted in conversation.

As it was meal time Irma and Hilde couldn't come down to the train, but the outside man was sent down to bring me up to the Berghof and Irma and Hilde were waiting on either side of the hall door to greet me. They had come along from the kitchen where they were preparing lunch. "One hundred plates of salad!" Irma said kissing me on both cheeks, Hilde did the same. "We are busy but we leave to come to see you arrive!" They had on clean white overalls and both wore their grey hair brushed smooth and combed tightly into buns at the back. They seem smaller than on the ship. Their brown polished shoes are the same.

A hundred guests in the vegetarian Gasthaus Berghof. Every day Irma and Hilde bend over the long scrubbed table making the plates of salad, arranging grated carrots, slices of cheese, quarters of tomatoes and spears of asparagus and sprinkling dates, prunes, nuts and olives on crisp, shining beds of lettuce or chopped cabbage. At one end of the table are bowls of sour cream and curds and hard boiled duck eggs. It is very light and clean in the kitchen, the fresh mountain air seems to be inside the house as well as outside. Irma and Hilde arrange the salads to look like flowers on the plates. Every day a different arrangement.

I wake early while it is still dark. When I am half asleep I hear the noise of an approaching car. In the quietness the car pauses on the bend in the track, the tyres turning slowly grip the gravel and there is a moment of hesitation before the car comes on down over the gravel. I can hardly bear the sound, it is here at the Berghof of course and not there at Laura's place. No headlamp comes up to this tiny room high in the eaves of this house and there are no dogs starting up, no

234

children crying and there's no Murphy to shout. I might hope for Laura's voice but it is not here.

In front of the Berghof is a wide gravel drive which encircles a white stone goddess seated in her water-lily fountain. A car turning slowly here sounds like a car on the track at Laura's.

After I told Laura about Irma's letter she said if I would take a little rest she had a few things she ought to do before the rain. She said she really hoped we would have the summer shower and she made me comfortable on the bed before going outside.

Later on I looked in her study and she had taken her gun, it was not in the corner by the desk. I lifted the folds of the curtain but it was not there. I never knew her to take the gun before. I looked everywhere for her but couldn't find her and I searched in all the wild and lonely places around the house.

At Laura's place I always woke up when she creaked about on the floorboards early in the morning. Often I turned over and went on sleeping after she had gone out.

"Come along Andrea, if we're to go to town today to order your clothes we must start in a few minutes. Come along dearest, wake up!" she said kissing me softly. "Wake up! I want to take you to town to the tailor, you have to be measured."

We had to leave before it was light and we drove with the sunrise behind us and saw the mist fraying between the trees in the jarrah forest. Laura said she loved the road, every rise or curve brought something fresh to see. She said the quiet red brown cattle standing in the paddocks in the early morning sunshine made her feel tranquil. Even the white fences and the rose gardens of the suburb just before we reached town seemed pleasant when I was in the car with her.

I sat up close beside Laura while she drove. I loved to sit close. She was so happy. She sang in the car. I wanted to be happy too. She disliked shopping she said, but this time it was different. She instructed the tailor so carefully about my riding clothes, she wanted to choose exactly the right cloth and then the right boots. And then later the buying of wine and the extravagant shopping for groceries. English cheeses and French cheeses, a special blend of coffee from four different kinds of beans, tins of soups and oysters and artichoke hearts, jars of preserved fruits and cranberries and mushrooms in sauces I'd never heard of. And everything was made into parcels, tied with string and put in boxes in an old fashioned way as if it was her father shopping. She is gracious in shops and the shop people leave what they are doing to ask her what they can get for her. She never forgets where her car keys are and she remembers what she wants to buy.

"I'm so happy!" she said. The sun was behind us on the way home, the sunlit golden countryside spread out on either side of the road seemed so peaceful. Dusk and then darkness. I leaned close against Laura and sometimes I felt her cheek against my hair.

Oh Laura. Dear Laura.

"Water is the last thing to get dark," she said. I must have been dozing there in the car beside her. "Water always shines with a last light, see over there," she said. "That dam, which is not mine, marks the boundary of my land," she went on. "My fence is there, can you see the dark post? That's the beginning of my fence on the other side of the water. Once we reach this fence we are almost there," she said. "That's the far end of my long paddock."

In the night the dam looked very big, the banks high and bare on one side, slippery and dangerous and black dead trees stood in the unrippled water.

"I don't like it much," I said.

"Neither do I," she said. "But since it isn't mine I don't mind it, and I'm always glad to see it!"

Every morning now it seems I wake up so cold and remembering things. And on my way down to the pantry where we sit, Irma and Hilde and the Swiss girl, for our rye bread and coffee I try not to think of Laura.

I try not to think of Laura and the grey dilapidated weatherboards of her house on that far away slope.

From almost every window here it is possible to look at mountains and beyond these mountains to more mountains. All the mountains are covered in snow. It is winter here. On one side of the house there is a steep ravine of dark trees and the house itself seems to hang over this ravine on a kind of platform, a mountain garden. There is a main building with long windows and balconies and then there are all sorts of summer houses and winter huts designed for the pleasure and convenience of the guests.

The place is busy all the year round, people come for so many reasons, the mountains, the snow, the air, the concerts, the company, the salads . . .

I have come here to work. It was Irma's idea. She had the idea on the ship, she told me about the place.

"My daughter has nice apartment in Vienna," she said. "Near ze Danube, you could visit there!" She thought I would get healthy at the place in the mountains where she lives and works. "Iss a holiday resort, always work to be had and later when your healse comes beck you go beck to your teaching. You think about it?" she asked me. But I was going to Christopher.

Irma wrote to me. She didn't know when she wrote that I would be with Laura, and she didn't know I would be having a baby. When her letter came to me at Laura's place, it was sent on by Christopher. I didn't tell Laura. I couldn't tell her about it or about my teaching job still being available if I wanted to go back. At that time I couldn't see it as ever being possible. There were so many things I didn't tell Laura when it would have been better to tell her.

"I understand," she said. When it concerned me, there was nothing she couldn't understand.

I am trying to live this new life, really trying. During the few days I have been here I keep wanting to cry. I try not to think of Laura and the different things she used to be doing at the different times of the day. I don't even know what time it is over there so what's the use of remembering the times of the day as they were.

"It's such a lovely way to wake up," Laura said. "It's so

sweet, Andrea, to wake up beside you," and then she said, "I'm glad I wake up first because I do so love to watch you open your eyes and see you smile when you realise where you are."

This is what it was like to be loved by Laura and to be lying close to her, safe and warm and soft, and to look up and see her eyes half closed watching me, amused, and so very tender. It's when I think of the things we said, the things we talked about and knew together I can't bear not having them any more and the long years of my life seem to stretch ahead, quite empty.

I know I must make an effort to live my life, to do my work. I must go to meals, go to bed, go to sleep, go to concerts and go out and meet people. I've even written all the things I must do on a piece of paper.

On that terrible day, in that intolerable heat and in the desolate quietness of that place I told Laura all about Irma's letter and I told her I wanted to go away. I told her I couldn't stand the loneliness. She listened, "I understand," she said. She said very little. She said she thought it was right for me to go. She wanted me to stay forever, she wanted to ask me to, she said so. She said there had been times when she had thought about my going and that she wouldn't be able to live if I wasn't with her. She said she knew she must be able to live without me. She agreed I should leave.

"If you're unhappy Andrea," she said, "your unhappiness is reason enough to leave." She didn't reproach me and she didn't tell me to try and be happy and she didn't reproach herself. It wasn't her fault I was unhappy and she didn't pretend to think it was. She said she could see it was not the way for me to live. She put me to bed to rest. The sun was suddenly hidden in clouds but the heat was still bad. I couldn't rest. Something rustled in the heap of old harness, perhaps it was a change in the wind because the outside door slammed by itself. I wondered where Laura was, what was she doing that had to be done before the rain? And then I found her gun was missing and I went everywhere looking for her. I suppose it was the cyclone or whatever they call it bringing

238

in the cloud, I felt there was no air and I was afraid because I couldn't find her. Laura's place is the most lonely place on the earth if she's not about.

It was very quiet there too on that Sunday after all our visitors had gone. It wasn't such a bad day after all, perhaps Laura really felt it more than I did. She had to take two white capsules and go straight to bed when it was over. All day she was such a good hostess; we heard her dropping forks in the kitchen.

"Oh Bugger!" her well-bred voice came through to the verandah, and then she dropped a plate. She was always spilling and dropping.

"Oh Bugger!"

"You're not operating now Laura," Rodney called out and she came from the kitchen, laden with food, and laughing.

I had the afternoon with Christopher and I managed not to tell him about the baby. He'll never know. Laura said it was better he should never know. I'll never see him again and I'll never see Laura again.

"Satan in confusion terror-struck departs" Rodney Glass sang as they crossed the yard and packed themselves into the cars and they drove up the track, one car after the other, three cars in the dust, all tooting their horns, one after the other and then all of them together. And all their voices calling out.

"Goodbye!" "Goodbye Laura! Goodbye Andrea!"

"Thank you and Goodbye."

"Goodbye. Goodbye."

Christopher was busy tucking up Mother and the Meringue Pie and Junior, he was so hidden in bags and rugs we never had to say goodbye to each other.

And then the silence. Even the dogs quietened down and Mrs. Murphy's piece of curtain fell into place. The children were nowhere to be seen.

"At last!" Laura said.

The dust cloud hovered long after the sound of the engines had disappeared.

"The magpies are protesting," Laura came towards me smiling. She held out her hand to me.

We were alone again and we went into the untidy house together.

"Do you think those people feel somehow, wrong, when they are with us," I asked Laura.

"How so wrong?" she replied. "Again, you use that strange unprofitable word."

I began to gather up tea cups and plates half expecting to hear the cars and the horns, but they were really gone.

"Well what I mean is, do we make them feel odd in any way?"

"I don't think so. Can you explain more?" She looked tired. I suppose we were both tired; Laura, in particular, had prepared a great deal. Before I was even out of bed she was in the kitchen, wearing only her shirt and her knee-boots, beating up eggs for the caramel custard.

"Oh it doesn't matter," I said, I didn't want to tell her she looked tired. "Shall I make you something?" I asked her. She smiled her kind smile. "Let's both make each other something."

"Let's have some coffee and brandy," she said, "let's leave the dishes, I'm hellishly tired. What a day! It's been quite a day for us both!" She slopped brandy into the cups and over the saucers, her hand was shaking.

"I must really use the measure or cut out the stuff altogether," she muttered. We sat on the verandah while the sun was cradled for the last few moments in the branches of the old dead tree on the other side of the valley.

"Go on!" she said. "Try and explain."

"Well it's like this. Christopher and I once went to a place, it was some time ago, a place beyond the dunes you know, not the ordinary beach. We were looking for a quiet place, we were looking for privacy d'you see? I've copied your way of speaking Laura, d'you hear me saying d'you see?

"I do Andrea," she smiled.

"We were looking for a place where we could be alone, it was very strange, quite horrible really and, until today, I had quite forgotten about it. We walked along by the sea quickly, we had had to make excuses to get away d'you understand. A little way off there was a man lying in the sun reading, and I thought how we would need to get beyond him and go back off the sands and hide ourselves in the dunes, and then I saw he was an old man, quite naked. He was like a great tired lion drooping. His huge nakedness amused us, the obvious tiredness of his body was so unlike what we were feeling. He took absolutely no notice of us and we laughed between ourselves. We didn't mind, there was no harm in someone sun-bathing naked. The usually deserted beach had other people; a little farther on there was another man lying on his side facing us. It was the white, very white skin of his loins with the dark patch of hair which startled me.

"He's naked too," I thought and I saw Christopher pretend not to notice. He even walked a bit into the sea pointing at something which wasn't there as if to try and make me look in another direction. A few young men were walking up the beach, they were well made, you know healthy, well-fed, wealthy looking as if they cared for their bodies. They wore smart expensive bathers and carried good towels. Further on more men lay sunbathing, it didn't matter really but suddenly we felt terribly uneasy. Suddenly we both wanted to leave the place quickly. We turned and started to walk back as fast as we could. I do remember this uneasiness it was so uncomfortable. A tall golden-haired young man came running, passing us, very lightly along the sand and about twenty little schoolboys were running behind him and he collected them round him on the sands. He must have been a teacher with his class but it wasn't quite so straightforward d'you see, because just above that part of the beach was the car park overlooking the sands and the sea. We walked up there and in every car there was a man sitting and all of them were looking intently down to the bronzed school master and his class. It was as if the little boys were being paraded for these men. It was really possible to feel a sort of excitement of desire and to feel excluded from it at the same time, and Christopher said that our own peculiar need seemed heightened by the awareness of other people's diversions. I was horrified. I'd never thought really that we were peculiar and never once had I considered what he might be thinking about us and it was soon after this, Laura, I began doing awful things, steaming open his letters, searching his pockets, trying to find out about his life, asking him where he'd been. Some days I didn't speak to him and other days I couldn't leave him alone and he began to have to lie to me. Oh Laura . . . I . . ."

"Andrea," she interrupted me quietly. "You're tired, don't go on talking and remembering, don't upset yourself. I understand completely. No, I don't think we make anyone feel odd or uncomfortable. I think it was the tension of seeking which made you both feel so uneasy on that beach. I am absolutely sure we didn't produce that feeling for our guests today. The women are too stupid. If Rodney and Michael feel anything on our behalf they might understand but might refuse to acknowledege it simply because they do understand. I think they all felt nothing today except themselves, the drive into the country and the acceptable social custom of food and drink." She held out her hand to me across the table.

"I can't explain everything, but Andrea, I do love you so much," she said in her low voice. "You mean so much to me! Come round this side, sit here beside me while the sun sets. Please come to me. Let's rest together, just for a little while. Please do come!"

I sat by her and she put her arm round me and held me close to her. She sighed deeply.

"You know Andrea," she said, "I'm afraid I'll have to go straight to bed. My head aches, I'm exhausted! I think I'm mixed up, as you call it, after this day. Too mixed up. I'm sorry!"

"Poor Dear Laura," I said, she did look tired. "Whatever did you think about Eva?" I asked in spite of myself, in spite of knowing she needed to rest. She smiled at me.

"I don't think I can answer that just at this minute, I

242

don't think I really know," she said, and gently she stroked my arm. "Here is a bit of a poem by William Blake,

> *The sun descending in the west*
> *The evening star does shine;*
> *The birds are silent in their nest*
> *And I must seek for mine.*
> *The moon, like a flower,*
> *In heaven's high bower,*
> *With silent delight*
> *Sits and smiles on the night.*

"Let's forget about visitors and people and the outside world", she said. "Let's forget about everything." A bit later she asked me to get her the capsules and a drink of water.

While I searched for Laura the sky was very dark and I thought I would choke in the heat. I was frightened because of the gun not being in its accustomed place. We had rushed headlong into the summer; Laura explained it to me how the season changed overnight, she tried to help me when I couldn't stand the heat. "It's not always as bad as this," she laughed at me. I couldn't find Laura, I tried to call her but my voice wouldn't come. In the little clearing by the top paddock the hot earth seemed to come up towards my face and, when I turned, the sky was darker and the brown slopes on the other side of the valley grew higher into the clouds as if they would come toppling and crash over Laura's place burying us forever. The earth was falling, thunder crashed and I ran, half stumbling, along the top paddock and then I saw her.

I never saw Laura do anything violent before. I saw Laura with her gun, she was behind Murphy's house in a wired off yard level with the back of the big barn. I saw Murphy, agitated on bent legs prancing sideways and Laura, at the edge of the barn, with her gun. I saw the strength and grace with which she took aim. And as Murphy, urging with his whole body, sent the ram, stupid with fear, running, Laura shot and killed the terrified animal. The shot startled the geese and the quiet valley was filled with their angry noise. Crows and magpies flew and swooped aimlessly, calling and crying under the thunder clouds. The ram lay in the dust twitching. Laura put down her gun and was on the dead creature at once with one knee pressed to its side. I saw her knife and Murphy's as they started to deal with the carcass. I couldn't stand the sight of it. The little girls were standing near the back door of their ugly house watching. If Mrs. Murphy had not been in hospital, she too would have hovered there. An eager angel of death.

I must have started to scream then. I don't remember, I think I ran screaming and I was still screaming when I reached the kitchen. Laura came in at once. She slapped my face with her blood-stained hand.

"Stop it Andrea!" she said "stop it at once!" And she put her gun behind the door and went out. I heard the water running into the basin while she washed herself.

The thunder was rumbling all round the valley and I followed Laura into the bedroom while she changed her clothes. "Oh Laura I thought you . . . ," I was wailing like a child. "O Laura I thought . . ."

"What did you think Andrea?" her voice was stern as if she was being stern with herself as well as with me.

"When I couldn't find the gun d'you see Laura, I thought you'd gone off to, well, to hurt yourself in some way. I was so afraid . . ."

Laura laughed, it seemed her voice was not really hers.

"It would be impossible to do anything to oneself with that gun," she said. "I suppose one could shoot one's own foot, but that would be such a nuisance." She·brushed her hair quickly and went to the window as if to move away from me.

"I'm sorry Laura."

"You've no need to be sorry Andrea," she said. "Look, here's the rain coming. Can you smell the sweet sharpness of it?" We stood side by side at the open window watching the rain come along the valley, long sweeps and pourings of rain. I stood close to Laura but she didn't put her arm about me and I couldn't ask her to. She seemed held within herself. Suddenly she said,

"I had to shoot the ram. It's awful really. Sometimes you have to do something you don't want to do, something you can hardly bring yourself to do." I listened to her. The rain was pouring now heavily on the roof and washing down over the verandahs so that the view was obliterated, it was like trying to see through thin waterfalls.

"Lovely rain," Laura said, I wished she would squeeze my arm or take me close to her but she didn't touch me. And again she didn't speak for some time and then she said, "The ram was very valuable. He cost a great deal, but that isn't the point. I couldn't do anything for him except shoot him. He was caught by the horn on the fencing wire, the other end of the long paddock. He must have been caught some time before Murphy found him, and by that time he'd gone crazy. They're very strong you know and they pull and push and damage themselves. He had a deep wound d'you see Andrea, it had gone too far and the maggots had eaten away too much but there's no point in going over it. I should have gone round the fences days ago! Never mind!"

"Don't be upset Laura," I said after a pause.

"No," she said. "There are times when there is nothing one can do and when one mustn't be upset!" I could tell from the tone of her voice that she was.

"I keep thinking of Murphy too," she said suddenly. "He couldn't get the ram off the fence, the two of us couldn't get him off, he pushed against it too hard, we had to cut the wires and that wasn't easy either. Poor Murphy," she paused, "poor Murphy," she said. "He keeps telling me what the doctors are doing for Mrs. Murphy as if there was something that could be done for her. One thing is certain, we can't shoot her however much she needs to be shot. Perhaps we shouldn't shoot a ram, I don't know," she seemed to be half talking to herself. We watched the rain. We were together standing there but there was something so withdrawn about Laura it was as if we both stood there alone. I wished she

245

would say something to comfort us and I thought how terrible I had been all through the hot days.

"It's a bit cooler," I said in a little voice. She didn't answer and I wondered if she had heard. "I'm sorry Laura," I tried again but she ignored me. She seemed to listen to the rain as if she was listening to music but she did not take me with her into the listening. She just stood there very pale and withdrawn and angry I thought. I felt the baby move and I wanted to sit down and cry again but I didn't dare to move.

The rain stopped as suddenly as it had started. "There's still some cloud," Laura said as if to herself. "Someone else will get that I suppose." She looked at me in a way I had never seen her look before.

"Laura . . . I . . ."

"Andrea, there's blood on your face, it's the ram's. I must have put it there. Go and wash your face." She spoke sharply.

I went blindly, tears coming quietly and quickly so that I couldn't see.

I ran some water in the shabby basin and peered at myself in the cracked mirror Laura has. My face shocked me, it didn't look like me all pale and sunken round the eyes, and I began to wash my face, bending over the basin.

"Let me help you," I felt her beside me. There is hardly any space in the little bathroom and her body was touching mine. "Andrea," she said so softly. "Let me . . ." she dried my face with the towel. The next moment she had her arms round me.

"I can't kill," she said, "and be myself immediately afterwards." She held me close.

"Everything's so hopeless!" I said.

"No it isn't, you're not yourself after the heat and you had a fright," she said. "I made a mistake too," she tightened her arms and gently kissed my hair. "I was about to make a terrible mistake," she said in her low voice. "A really terrible mistake!"

"How so Laura? What d'you mean?" she stopped my questions by kissing me, a deep tender long kiss.

"Oh Andrea," she stroked my hair, "I nearly was so very very stupid!" We went together into the untidy kitchen. "We'll clear up later," Laura said. "Come on, I'll take you for a little drive in the forest, you'll feel better now that it's been raining."

Laura went down to record the rainfall. The magpies were everywhere laughing, crying and calling, caressing the afternoon. Laura said they liked the rain too.

It was damp and cool between the dripping trees, everything sparkled with drops of water and there was the sharp fragrance of the wet leaves and the wet earth. Laura said it reminded her of the smell of an anaesthetic.

We were very close, it's remembering that closesness makes me want to cry now. We talked about my coming here she said it was better so, better that I get right away to a life of my own only she didn't say it quite in those words. She said she knew I had to go away and to make it, as she thought, easier she tried to discipline herself, she tried to stop loving me. "But it was so silly of me," she said. "I couldn't do it! I do love you so much Andrea," her kind eyes were full of tears. "So I'll go on loving you right up to the time you leave and afterwards. It does seem so pointless to try to do anything else. It simply isn't possible d'you see Andrea. I was making a mistake to try not to love you."

"Dear Laura, I'm so grateful . . ."

"I'm the grateful one, remember," she laughed. "Don't let's get that confused!"

And she talked a bit about our lives.

"Once there was a German poet, you'll have to brush up your German!" she said. "He said something like this: 'if I can make a fruitful land between rock and stream or if I can find, an orchard between rock and stream'; the idea appeals to me immensely. We can both be doing that wherever we are." And then she reversed the car the whole way along the track. "The sand's too soft," she said. "We'll get bogged if we go on, and there's no room to turn." She sat so easily in the car, one hand

247

on the wheel and one arm along behind me as she took the car slowly back.

I saw the strong muscles of her neck as she turned her head and, because her shirt was not properly buttoned, I saw the curve of her breast and I longed to ask her to stop the car so that I could lie down with my head on that breast and cry away my life with her to comfort me.

"We'll both need courage," Laura said just then and she smiled at me as the car groaned and jolted all the way back.

Laura did everything for me. She planned my journey and arranged my air ticket, she did the whole thing by letter with the travel agent. She wrote to a clinic in Zürich where she had spent a study year once and from the Director there she got the name of an obstetrician in Vienna. That's so like Laura, only the best will do for her. She made me promise to see this doctor as soon as I arrived.

"I'm not anxious d'you see Andrea," she said. "I'm just wise!"

I left without seeing Mother or Christopher. I wrote a note to Christopher from Rome to tell him I'd gone. He lets people think he's got a crazy sister. "My mad sister . . ." he says, perhaps that's the easiest way for him. Meringue Pie thinks I'm mad or pretends to, I don't think she's capable of thinking. She used to come top in elocution at school. Her name was always on the programme on Speech Night. Recitation: Margaret Fort.

One year they made a mistake spelling her name — "Blow the Winds Southerly", Recitation: Margaret Fart — and Onion Breath was furious. Meringue Pie was her favourite pupil for the whole time we were there.

Oh God Christopher! But it's better this way. I keep telling myself it's better like this. Laura says it is. A clean break they would call it in a magazine correspondence column. But has anyone ever written to ask about something so very indelicate and improper as my problem.

Of course Irma doesn't know all this. But this morning she stopped by me in the kitchen and said, "If one needs to cry is better to cry," just like that. It's as if she understands things, perhaps it showed that I'd been crying in the night.

It's when I'm awake in the night I long for Laura so much. It's because I'd got used to having her sleep beside me, she always put her arm over me and I slept beneath its weight. And in the morning, when she'd gone, there was always the hollow in the pillow where her head had been all night. Sometimes I moved over to her pillow and went to sleep again in her place in the bed. This bed here is long and narrow, and it's cold.

Laura could make living so full of love and care, it didn't matter what she did. Sometimes I went with her when she carried pails of oats across to the sheep and the calves. There were not many animals but their crying came along the quiet valley at dusk and they jostled against the fence as she gave them their feed.

"They do love you Laura," I couldn't help laughing.

"Oh," she laughed too. "It's the other way about. I'm the one who loves! It's the food they're loving."

Whatever she did for me she did with love, even the internal examination which she thought she should do was gentle and slow like the tender preludes to our love-making.

"Everything seems absolutely normal," she announced. "Every bit of you seems well positioned. Very good!" she said and covered me over with the sheet.

"Were you like you are with me with all your patients?" I asked her. She stood by the bed looking down at me, smiling.

"What do you think," she asked laughing. She laughed such a lot then, it was just before the really hot weather came, we had talked things over and I'd decided to stop with her and have the baby and we'd work the farm together. But that was before I broke up in the heat; the heat and the advancing pregnancy were all too much.

"Now just what do you think!" she laughed and then she said, "sometimes d'you know, it did happen that a woman, perhaps a very lonely woman, took the examination as a caress. When I felt this I was touched, d'you know, Esmé, Dr. Gollanberg, had quite a bit about this in her writing. It's not unknown."

Laura laughed at the calves when they raised their heads and looked at us.

"Dear little faces and such round ears!" she said. And they stared at her with oats stuck all round their black mouths like children with jam and breadcrumbs on their cheeks.

Irma talks all the time when we have our meal time. She does it to help me. She tells things about her own life when she was a young woman. Years ago in the park of Schönbrunn, in the days when it was the summer residence of the Emperor, people were allowed to walk there and enjoy the flowers and the fountains and the cool shade but were not allowed to take perambulators. "No baby waggons," Irma says in her quaint English. "Und I wanted so much to be in the beautiful place, so I carry my big fat baby in my arms, und when I came home I thought my arms would break. Ach! He was so heavy!"

Rosemarie the Swiss girl has a little daughter I discover. She is being cared for by the nuns in the convent school down in the valley. Shyly she showed me some pink knitting; she knits all the time when we sit down for a meal or in the evenings when we have finished the work. I nodded and smiled at the knitting, it looked like a small vest for a doll, she pushed it towards me, smiling and nodding too.

"Iss for you," Irma explained. "Iss somsing for readiness, for your little one."

"Oh," I said, and Irma said

"I will say Danke to her for you."

"Thank you," I said. Irma spoke to Rosemarie who looked pleased at whatever it was Irma was saying. Suddenly I felt too tired to look pleasant any more.

"Let us make small walk," Irma said to me. "Before we make the kitchen."

We walked slowly round the goddess, our feet crunching very lightly on the clean thin snow on the gravel. Music came gently from the long windows to the left of us. The phrases stopped and were repeated and then hesitating shy slow notes followed, another phrase followed the first one and then another. Someone was practising the cello, my eyes filled with tears.

However can I bear to listen to the cello ever again. However can I listen to any music. The taste of tears is really bitter, and I thought that the water at Laura's place was bitter!

"Tonight is the quartet," Irma comforted. "They come up from Vienna. Loffly musik. You will like very much. Nice place," she said. "Nice peoples come. Rosemarie is engaged now since six months, such a pleasant younk man, he is comink next week again mit others, this musik festival just now bring very nice peoples you will see! Very nice young men and vimmin too. Nice!"

We continued to walk. Irma quietly talking to me said "Iss gut to have children, it does not always seem so at first but later iss gut. If I hadn't sons," she said, "I would never see Stromboli erupt! I would never make trip all round ze vorlt. If I hadn't my daughter why should I even make small journey to Vienna. I go to see her of course, so I go. It is because to see my children I make journeys. Iss gut to make visits," she waited a moment and then she said, "You also will make trip. You will go beck one day."

I shook my head and turned away because of the tears.

"We shall see," Irma said. "Und now we mosst go indoors to make the kitchen und later we make quartet!"

Laura said, "Oh Andrea I wish I didn't love you so much. I don't want you to go. I can't give you up," and then she asked me to forgive her for saying things which shouldn't be said. "At least Andrea," she said, "you'll let me take you to the airport."

"But you can't drive all that way," I said. "And all the way back alone! It'll be an all-night drive, Laura, alone, you can't do it. I won't hear of it!"

"You forget," she said, "I am used to being alone, before you came I was always alone. I want to take you to the airport so that we can be together here for as long as possible, till the last moment. I couldn't bear an unfriendly strange hotel for the last night and I won't bear the thought of you being alone in a hotel before you leave. So please, Andrea, let me drive you. Please."

On the last evening we were ready to leave and Laura told me to sit down a minute in the kitchen as she had something to say. My packed case was by the door and Laura had thrown two coats over the back of a chair. She thought it might be cold in the night at the airport. She always has to keep her back and shoulders warm. "Sometimes the east wind is so wretchedly cold especially after a hot day," she said, "my back's cold already!" she gave a shiver.

We looked like strangers dressed in clothes for the other world away from Laura's place. And then she said,

"Andrea, dearest, it's hard for me to say this, but we must be quite determined. For me it's the hardest thing I've ever had to do, giving you up, you know this don't you."

I said, "Yes Laura I know," and I couldn't look at her. I knew her eyes would be full of tears, I knew she was crying inside, somewhere deep inside, and there were no tears in my eyes then. I didn't weep then, I was preparing for a long journey and had, in every sense, already set out on it.

"I've been so happy here with you," she said.

"We've both been happy," I said.

"Dear Andrea, there must be no letters, not even thinking," she said and her voice shook. "We must go on with our lives in spite of what we feel now. I must explain straight out it's not just that this shut away life in this very isolated place is entirely unsatisfactory for you, it's more than that."

"What d'you mean Laura?" I suddenly felt afraid.

"I shan't come after you," she said, "The happiness we had together couldn't go on. I want it to end before there is a trap of unhappiness and no means of escape. D'you understand? Please try and understand what I'm saying."

252

She sat in her well-made clothes on one of the painted chairs, her left hand with the watch showing on her strong wrist was on the table. I thought she was going to reach out to take my hand but she didn't.

"You mean, if you, that is . . . you might, if you . . ." I paused, what she was thinking of was too awful for me to say. She hadn't slept and there were dark shadows below her eyes. Something like the knowledge of a quick deep pain seemed to cross from her brow to her cheek, a sensitive resemblance to the portrait of her favourite poet, Schiller.

"Go on," she said. "I think you know what I mean."

"You mean if it happens, well if it happens as it has for, well, like Eva," I managed to say. She nodded.

"Yes," she said quietly, "or something similar; there are other things too you know. Oh Andrea," she said. "I could not bear anything like that for us. I want you to leave. I want you to go now as we have arranged. Perhaps old age will come to me graciously, I prefer it with grace, but there is no choice. One simply cannot choose and perhaps my old age will be graceless and undignified . . ."

"But Laura!" I interrupted her. "That isn't my reason for going!"

"I know it isn't," she said. "But it's mine for wanting you to go. I won't get pompous about all the years and all the life you have before you," and she laughed. "I'll have to present you with Esmé Gollanberg's book, *Pinnacles and Plateaus, the sexual needs and attainments of women from thirty to forty,*" she smiled. "I mustn't tease you, perhaps I'm trying to make it easier," she said, "but saying things like that doesn't help!" She gave a little laugh. "Now let's talk about something else."

"Laura I won't go. I want to stay." I said. "We'll bring up the baby here as you suggested, we'll work the farm together like you said we would. I'm not going. I'm not leaving you. I won't. I've behaved badly Laura, I'm sorry."

"Andrea, that's enough!" she said. "We both have

reasons, very good reasons and we're going to stick to them." And then she said,

"Now there's one more thing. How are you for money?"

"Oh Laura, how can you ask . . ."

"Well it's a very real question. No-one can live or die for that matter without it. After all we know about each other and after all we've said how can it matter that I ask you this," she spoke in her old gentle way. She is always so well mannered in any kind of situation.

"I won't take money from you, if that's what you mean."

"Why not? It's such a small thing compared with the immense thing in our lives."

"No. Absolutely No!"

"I tell you what then, I'd like to have the Palomino. Will you sell her?"

"But she's yours!"

"Oh no, she was a present to you. I'd like to have her. Will you let me buy. Please Andrea?"

"Oh Laura, how could I."

"Please I really mean it. I could keep her till . . ."

"Laura! I'm not coming back, you remember."

"Yes yes I do remember, of course I do. We must remember what we said and we really do mean what we said."

"Yes that's right."

It's terrible thinking of that conversation now when I want her so much. All the time now I'm wishing I had been different that last evening when I was with her. I know now I could have been different. But all I thought of then was that I was about to get away from that place which had become so intolerable. Looking back as I am doing all the time I see it wasn't the place at all, it was me; it shouldn't have been so impossible to stand the loneliness and the heat. Laura often left her work to come to me, to spend time with me. Often she came in and washed herself and sat resting on the verandah, her long legs crossed, and her hands describing while she spoke. She sat with me talking and laughing, telling me things, arguing and discussing when she really needed to get things done on her land. On that last night I wasn't even tearful, not even sad about going away, I think I was somehow without feeling.

"Well then," Laura urged. "Please sell me the Dove. Look! I'll write a cheque now. Please let me I'd like to. You can change it somewhere on the way. Rome perhaps."

I put the cheque in my bag. She insisted. I feel I'll never use her money. I nearly refused it, nearly refused to take it but I'm glad I did take it because if I'd hurt her then it would be worse to think about that extra hurt now.

It's all this and the sadness of thinking of the long drive starting before sunset and going on into the night, empty in my mind, instead of being close to Laura as I could have been. And at the airport in the last few minutes, I could have looked into her eyes, I know she was looking at me, but I didn't look up, and then quite suddenly we were not together any more. I was on my long journey and she would already have been driving back the long way we had come. Each one of us alone.

Irma tells me things all the time.

Irma was in a strange country, a refugee because of the war, she told me. Because of the war she had to leave with her youngest child without knowing where her husband and older children were. She thought she would never bear it. And in a strange kitchen she had to wash and dry cups and jugs and things, and with every cup she hung up she said the names of her husband and of her children over and over again, thinking about them all the time and, when her tears came, she felt comforted.

"I have written to your friend the gnädige Frau Doktor," Irma says and she gives me the card to post. "Put on your own wishes and your name by all means," Irma says. "Then she has somsing from us bose!" But of course I can't write my name on the card to Laura.

"Dear Andrea," Laura said. "There must be no letters, not even thinking." That's what she said.

It is for her sake as well as mine.

"Don't forget time," Laura called to Peter Glass in her kitchen. "Time is such an important thing in the healing process, always remember this, nothing heals in a moment."

I wonder if Laura will heal and if I will and, if we do, how long will it take.

Irma's family are all grown up and going about their lives, she tells me about them. She has been working in the Gasthaus Berghof with her friend, Hilde, for years. She is happy with her life.

"The menechment is josst right for me und I am right for zem!" her teeth show their flashes of gold filling in her wide smile. "In time one finds what is josst right."

"Tonight is quartet," Irma says after our evening meal. "With cello! Every day so many good things und nice peoples for us. Tonight we shall sit und enjoy! In every Beethoven quartet there is a little dance und there is how do you call it, a cradle song." She takes my arm. "Come," she says "Let us go."

AN UNWRITTEN LETTER

Dearest, it's another Sunday. It's not the immediate thing one misses but something from before . . .

It's the time for the acacias, remember the sweet fragrance promising the flowers just about the time when you came? Every year I forget about the acacias till they come. It's the way of the seasons. The four seasons are like the four instruments in the quartet passing on their phrases of the music. The seasons pass on their fragrance. Sometimes the change is hardly enough to be noticed. The warm sweet fragrance of the flowers of the loquats (remember the tree just outside our bedroom window?) is a prelude to the sweetness of the flowering of the acacias across the valley. These massive trees are very fine this year and the air is heavy with their scent. I keep thinking of the time I dried your face.

Drying your little face, wiping it gently with the towel is like the soft reasoning notes of the second movement of a Mozart piano concerto. It is strange that remembering the action of drying your face, gently moving the towel over your forehead, your eyes, your nose and your mouth can take up so many hours of thought. So much tender thought.

As I said when you left I shan't come after you and there will be no letters. I can't stop myself from thinking even though I said there must be no thinking. I shall be writing this letter forever. I am writing it all the time but it will always be an unwritten letter. There must be no letters I said because neither of us could bear ultimately to send and receive letters which had no meaning. Neither of us could stand the impossibility of forcing letters.

One day when I went to Queens Meadow to collect my journals and newspapers there was a postcard from Irma at the post office. It's the second one I've had from her. Carefully she had written in her blue ink,

"If not happens what we want
Then will happen something better."

There was nothing about you, except what is written in Irma's two lines, perhaps this is the best for me to know of you.

And what is there about Murphy and Murphy's way. He is living somewhere up the back just off the track. He comes down with an old pail to get water. Once his own dogs jumped at him and tore his shirt under the arm, they would have bitten him but they just got the shirt. It was already torn, they just made it worse he told me. He and the children sleep on the ground, he keeps the two pigs in the car together with his good mattress he is trying to save. He is still trying to get his little boy back from the welfare people. Another six years he says the boy will be some use around the place. I think I am telling you the same things over again. Perhaps I have not explained that the work on the new house for the Murphys is held up over a drainage problem. What have I told you about Murphy? He is a good man you know. He is better than I could ever be. He really loved Mrs. Murphy. She died very soon after you had gone. I expect you realised every time she had to go to the hospital I hardly expected her to come back. But she had a tremendous hold on life, perhaps it was her curiosity, her wanting to know everything about people which kept her alive.

She was a terrible woman. It seemed to me she was evil but Murphy loved her. He was able to love her, and when she died, he sobbed by the fence. His thin face was all red and swollen and his eyes looked as if they had turned to water with his night of weeping. He wasn't going to be able to bear his loneliness he said and the harsh voices of the crows down the long paddock seemed to cry loneliness into the still sad morning.

"There is nothing so wonderful as having a woman turn to you in the night, of her own wish, because she wants you," he said to me. He said that about her. When he said it I knew what he meant. I thought about you, about our little ceremony with the belt and your little invitation and my eyes filled with tears for you and for me, not for Mrs. Murphy. Murphy knows the same things. Perhaps he too had little ceremonies. With all his feckless ways he knows and feels as we did.

Murphy knows things like the coming of an early wet winter after the full blossoming of the honey trees. And it was Murphy who told me to throw the mattock on the fire when the handle broke, I never thought of burning out the splintered wood and would have worked on it for days on my own.

"Take a sheep," I sometimes said to Murphy. "A good one for meat I mean." We have this strange arrangement, I am supposed to pay him a wage and supply him with meat, he is supposed to pay rent and work for me for his wage and meat. The whole thing fell through however, straight away at the beginning, it never worked.

Once when I told him to take a sheep he said, "You can get seven years for stealing and killing a sheep," and with a sort of half smile he said, "by rights I should be put away for life."

He often says things. Just after you had gone he reminded me of the sweetness of love as I knew it with you. It's strange that it was his love for Mrs. Murphy which reminded.

Like me he has to bear his loneliness.

I am safe on my land, I have to believe you are safe where you are. Neither of us need to wander in strange places which have no meaning for us. We need not rest under strangers' trees or stare into hostile gardens and, in our hearts, we need not walk and work alone.

This year my cash crop is broad beans. I am working my land as before. Until the boundary there is no feed. Once through my fence the country is in good heart. It is stocked, within reason of course which has ever been my policy, about two sheep to every acre. Simply, I call the foal Palomino. Like you his colouring is Palomino. I call him Palomino. I have no choice.